the THIRD edition

New Headway

Pre-Intermediate
Student's Book

John and Liz Soars

with Sylvia Wheeldon

OXFORD
UNIVERSITY PRESS

CONTENTS

LANGUAGE INPUT

SKILLS DEVELOPMENT

READING	LISTENING	SPEAKING	WRITING
'Blind Date' – a magazine article about the search for the perfect partner p10	'Best friends' – four people talk about their closest friends p9	Exchanging information – Dr Mary Steiner p8 Discussion – best friends p9 Discussion – blind dates p11	Describing friends – Correcting common mistakes p102
'Tales of two cities' – two people talk about their two homes in different countries (jigsaw) p18	'A 24/7 society' – a radio programme about night workers p20	Exchanging information – people's lifestyles p16 Describing your favourite room p17 Discussion – living abroad p18 Discussion – working at night p20	An email – Linking words *but, although, however, so, because* p103
'The name's Bond, James Bond' – an extract from *The Man With The Golden Gun* p26	A drama based on an extract from *The Man With The Golden Gun* p26	Telling stories *fortunately/unfortunately* p25 Exchanging information – a teenager goes on a spending spree p25	Telling a story – Position of adverbs and adjectives p104
'Markets around the world' – Bangkok, Provence, and Marrakech (jigsaw) p34	'I bought it on eBay!' – three people talk about things they have bought on eBay p33 Conversations in different kinds of shops p36	Information exchange – find the differences p32 Discussion – talking about markets p34 Group work – shopping in your town p36	A postcard – Synonyms in writing p106
'Brat camp' – where parents send their out-of-control teenagers p42	A song – *The voice within* p41	Roleplay – What are you doing tonight? p41 Talking about problems and advice p41 Discussion – teenagers and parents p42 Talking about books, films and TV programmes p44	Filling in a form p107
'London, the world in one city' – Is London the most cosmopolitan city in the world? (jigsaw) p50	'The best things in life are free' – five people talk about things they love that don't cost anything p49	Comparing things *Skiing is more exciting than sitting on the beach.* p48 Talk for one minute – my favourite free thing p49 Discussion – immigrants in your town p50	Describing a place – My home town: relative pronouns *who/that/which/where* p108

3

LANGUAGE INPUT

SKILLS DEVELOPMENT

1 Getting to know you

Tenses • Questions • Using a bilingual dictionary • Social expressions 1

STARTER

1 Match the questions and answers.

Where were you born?	A year ago.
What do you do?	Three times a week.
Are you married?	In Mexico.
Why are you learning English?	Because I need it for my job.
When did you start learning English?	I'm a teacher.
How often do you have English classes?	No, I'm single.

2 Ask and answer the questions with a partner.

TWO STUDENTS
Tenses and questions

1 **T 1.1** Look at the pictures. Who are the two people?
Read and listen to Marija. Complete the text, using the
verbs in the box.

'm enjoying	'm going to work	live	lasts
'm studying	~~come~~	speak	spoke	went

Hello! My name's Marija Kuzma and I (1) ___come___
from Zagreb, the capital city of Croatia. I'm 20, and I
(2) _____ medicine at the University of Zagreb.
The course (3) _____ six years, and it's all in
English! It's hard work, but I (4) _____ it a lot.

I (5) _____ at home with my mother, father, and
grandmother. I can speak three foreign languages –
English, French, and Italian. I (6) _____
Italian because my grandmother's from Italy,
and she always (7) _____ to me in
Italian when I was very young. I speak
English because I (8) _____ to an
English-speaking high school.

After I graduate, I (9) _____ for
Médecins sans Frontières in West Africa,
because I want to travel and help
people.

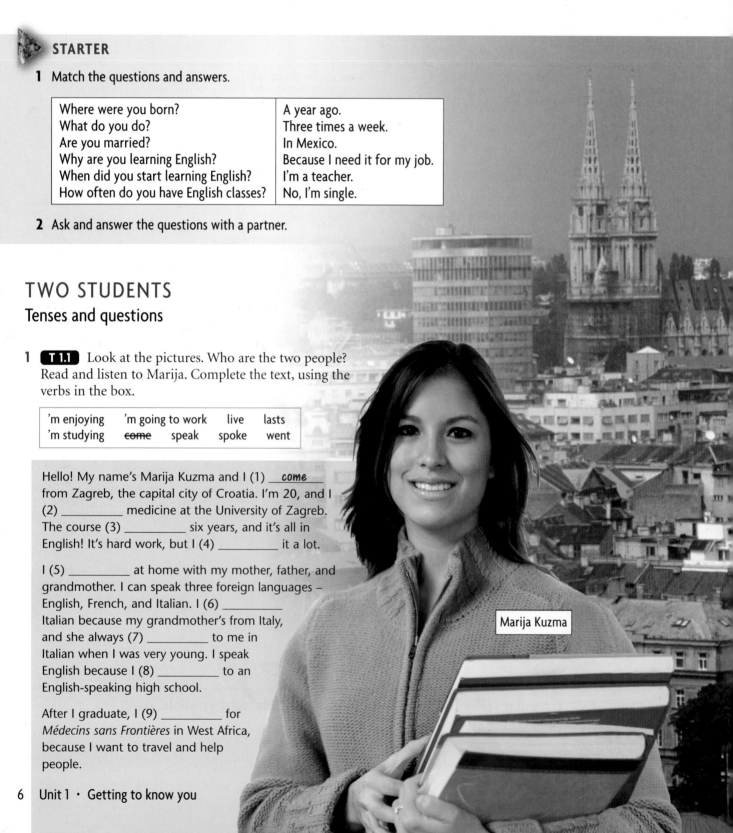

Marija Kuzma

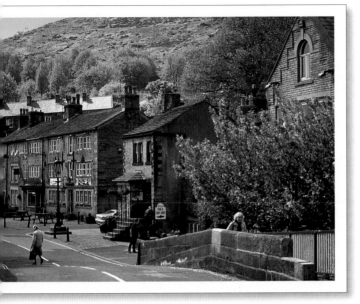

2 Look at the photo of Jim. Complete the questions about him.

1 _Where does he_ come from?
2 _whar do you_ live?
3 _who do_ live with?
4 _____ do before he retired?
5 When _do you_ leave school?
6 What _____ studying?
7 How many children _____ have?
8 What _____ do next year?

T 1.2 Listen to Jim, and answer the questions. Ask and answer them with a partner.

3 Complete the questions to Jim.

1 'Do ___you have___ a job?'
  'No, I don't. I'm retired. I'm a student now.'
2 'Which university _____ to?'
  'I don't go to university. I study at home.'
3 '_____ the course?'
  'Yes, I am. It's wonderful.'
4 'What _____ at the moment?'
  'I'm writing an essay about *Don Quixote*.'
5 'Why_____ leave school at 15?'
  'Because my family was poor. We needed the money.'
6 '_____ to visit next year?'
  'My son and his wife. They live in Spain now.'

T 1.3 Listen and check.

Jim Allen

GRAMMAR SPOT

1 Find examples of present, past, and future tenses in the tapescripts about Marija and Jim on p116.

2 What are the tenses in these two sentences? What is the difference between them?
  She lives with her parents.
  She's living with an English family for a month.

3 Match the question words and answers.

What . . . ?	Because I wanted to.
Who . . . ?	Last night.
Where . . . ?	$5.
When . . . ?	A sandwich.
Why . . . ?	By bus.
How many . . . ?	In New York.
How much . . . ?	Jack.
How . . . ?	The black one.
Whose . . . ?	It's mine.
Which . . . ?	Four.

▶▶ **Grammar Reference 1.1, 1.2 and 1.3 p127**

PRACTICE

Talking about you

1 Ask and answer the questions in small groups.

- Where … live?
- Who … live with?
- What … like doing at the weekend?
- What … do last weekend?

> Where do you live?

> How many languages … speak?

> How … you come to school this morning?

Make more questions. Use some of the question words in the Grammar Spot on p7. Ask your teacher some of the questions.

2 Each of the questions has *one* word missing. Write it in.

1 Do you like listening to/music?
2 What sort of music you like?
3 Do you often jeans?
4 What your teacher wearing today?
5 Where you go on your last holiday?
6 What did you yesterday evening?
7 What you doing this evening?
8 What are you going do after this course?

T 1.4 Listen and check. Ask and answer the questions with a partner.

3 Write a paragraph about you. Use the text about Marija on p6 to help you.

Check it

4 Choose the correct verb form.

1 Marija *comes / is coming* from Zagreb.
2 Jim *speaks / is speaking* Spanish and English.
3 Today he *wears / is wearing* jeans and a shirt.
4 *Are you liking / Do you like* black coffee?
5 Last year I *went / go* on holiday to Florida.
6 Next year my sister *studies / is going to study* at university.

Exchanging information

5 Look at the picture of Dr Mary Steiner. She's a radio agony aunt. What do radio agony aunts do? Who phones them? Why?

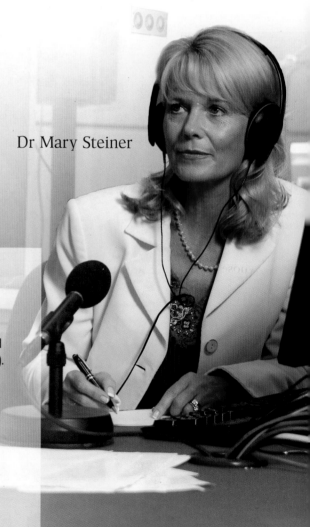

Dr Mary Steiner

6 Work with a partner. You have different information about Dr Mary Steiner. Take it in turns to ask and answer questions.

Student A

Look at the information on p143.

Dr Mary Steiner lives in … (*Where?*). She's married and has twin sons.

Student B

Look at the information on p146.

Dr Mary Steiner lives in Santa Barbara, California. She's married and has … (*How many children?*).

> Where does Mary Steiner live?

> In Santa Barbara, California.

> How many children does she have?

> She has twin sons.

LISTENING AND SPEAKING
Best friends

1 Discuss the questions in pairs.
- How many good friends do you have?
- Do you have a best friend?
- Why is he/she your best friend?

2 Look at the photos. You are going to hear Michael, Dominic, Brianna, and Shona talk about their best friends.
T 1.5 Listen and complete the chart.

Best friend	Whose friend?	When did they meet?	Why are they friends?
Kirsty			
Sammy			
Dave and Azam			
Caleb			

Michael

Dominic

3 Work with a partner. Answer the questions.
1 Which friends talk to each other about their problems?
2 Which friends share the same hobby? What is it?
3 Which friends only see each other once a year?
4 Which friends go to school?
5 Whose friend likes Indian cooking?
6 Whose friend has a dog called King?
7 Whose friend is tall?
8 Whose friend is like a brother?

T 1.5 Listen again. Check your answers.

Language work

4 Match the verbs with the words or phrase.

become	the Internet
play	emails
send	friends
give	on the phone
talk	football
have	together
grow up	parties
go on	advice

Sony Ericsson

Brianna

Shona

▶▶▶ **WRITING** Describing friends *p102*

READING AND SPEAKING
A blind date

1 What's your star sign? Find out all the star signs in the class. Which is the most common? Do you think it's interesting or necessary to know the star sign of your boyfriend/girlfriend?

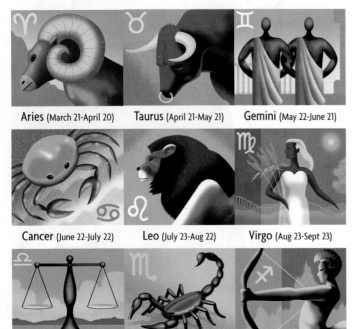

Aries (March 21-April 20) Taurus (April 21-May 21) Gemini (May 22-June 21)

Cancer (June 22-July 22) Leo (July 23-Aug 22) Virgo (Aug 23-Sept 23)

Libra (Sept 24-Oct 23) Scorpio (Oct 24-Nov 22) Sagittarius (Nov 23-Dec 22)

 Capricorn (Dec 23-Jan 20) Aquarius (Jan 20-Feb 19) Pisces (Feb 20-March 20)

2 Look at the photos and headings in the newspaper article. What is a blind date? What does the *Evening Star* do? Who are the people? What are their star signs?

3 Work with a partner. Read about Matt and answer the questions.
1 What is his job? Does he enjoy it? How do you know?
2 What did he do after university?
3 Why does he like being back in London?
4 Where does he go in summer? Why?
5 What does he like doing there?
6 What does he do in London at weekends?
7 Who is his perfect partner? What is most important?

4 Read the information about the three girls carefully. Who do you think Matt will choose? Why? Discuss your ideas with your partner and then the class.

Blind Date

Who is looking for the perfect partner this week?

MATT 29, a climate change scientist from Balham, South London
Star sign: CAPRICORN

I travel a lot in my job. I go to meetings and conferences all over the world. It's great for me, because I studied oceanography and environmental science at university. After university I spent a lot of time at sea on scientific research ships. Now I'm back in London, it's much better for my social life. I have a lot of friends.

But I miss the sea, so, in summer, when I want to relax, I like going to the coast, and sometimes I spend the weekend camping with friends, having barbecues and diving or surfing. It's great to get away from the city and go to a different world.

I also enjoy weekends in London. I like meeting friends, having a few beers, going to a football match. I'm an Arsenal fan. I sometimes go clubbing but not very often, and I love Indian food. I go to an Indian restaurant at least once a week.

Who is his perfect partner?
My perfect partner is outgoing, funny, and good to talk to. She dresses nicely, but isn't too worried about fashion. Someone who enjoys having a good time in the city but also likes travelling, sports, and country life. This is very important to me.

Every week the EVENING STAR helps a single person choose the perfect partner and have a date in an expensive restaurant. The couple then tell the STAR what happened.

Who do you think Matt will pick from these three lovely girls?

MIRANDA, 29
Star sign: SCORPIO

Lives: Camden Town, North London

Job: A lawyer, loves her job, but it's hard work so she needs to relax.

Interests: Dancing, going to clubs, pubs, and the cinema. Meeting friends to exchange news. ('I have lots of friends.') Visiting art galleries sometimes.

Hates: Men who are crazy about football.

Clothes: Loves designer clothes. 'I spend too much money on clothes.'

Food: Italian, French, and a McDonald's 'but only after a night out clubbing!'

Love life: Lots of boyfriends. Last relationship ended a few weeks ago.

Perfect partner: Good-looking, good fun and good to talk to.

BETH, 25
Star sign: PISCES

Lives: Clapham, South London

Job: Bookstore manager, 'I love working with books.'

Interests: Reading, the theatre, art galleries, cycling ('I cycle to work'), and walking. 'Sometimes I really need to get out of London and walk in the country.'

Hates: 'I can't think of anything.'

Clothes: Comfortable. 'I like to look nice but I don't think too much about clothes.'

Food: Vegetarian. Loves Indian food because 'there are so many delicious 'veggie' dishes'.

Love life: One long relationship, ended six months ago.

Perfect partner: Someone who's kind and good to talk to, who likes both town and country life.

HOLLY, 30
Star sign: CAPRICORN

Lives: Canary Wharf, by the River Thames

Job: Fashion designer. 'I started studying art history, but changed to fashion design.'

Interests: Travelling, skiing ('I'm learning to snowboard now'), going out with friends to restaurants, bars, and clubs.

Hates: People who smoke.

Clothes: 'Of course, I love clothes. I always try to look good, but I like to be casual and comfortable sometimes.'

Food: Loves all food. 'It's a problem. I just love going out to restaurants, all kinds.'

Love life: Two long relationships. One just finished.

Perfect partner: Good-looking and good fun. Someone who likes sports, travel, and adventure.

Listening

5 **T 1.6** Listen to Matt. Who did he choose? Why? What happened on the date? Are they going to meet again?

6 **T 1.7** Listen to the girl he chose. What impression do you get of the couple? What kind of people are they? Do you think they will stay together? Why?

Language work

A friend arranges a blind date for you. Write questions to ask your friend about your date. Use all of these question words. Compare questions with another student.

Who ...?   What ...?   Why ...?   When ...?   Where ...?   How ...?

What do you think?

- Are blind dates a good idea? Why? Why not?
- Why do people go on blind dates?
- Do you know anyone who has been on a blind date? Was it successful?
- Would you like to take part in a newspaper blind date like this one?

VOCABULARY AND PRONUNCIATION
Using a bilingual dictionary

1 Look at the entry from an English~Spanish dictionary.

the pronunciation in phonetic symbols

the translation

the word used in an example sentence.

the part of speech:
n = noun
v = verb

book /bʊk/ **1** *n* libro: *I'm reading a book by Cervantes at the moment.* (*notebook*) cuaderno; (*of cheques, tickets*) talonario **2** *v* (*seat, room*) reservar: *I booked a table at the restaurant for four people.*
booking office /'bʊkɪŋ ˌɒfɪs/ *n* taquilla
bookseller /'bʊkselə(r)/ *n* librero
bookshelf /'bʊkʃelf/ *n, pl* ~**shelves** /~ʃelvz/ estante

Information in brackets (...) helps you to find the right translation.

Other words made with **book** (compounds) are in separate entries.

2 What part of speech are these words? Write *n* (noun), *v* (verb), *a* (adjective), *adv* (adverb), *prep* (preposition), or *pt* (past tense).

com'puter ___n___	'wonderful _____	on _____	'quickly _____
poor _____	in _____	came _____	went _____
speak _____	'usually _____	en'joy _____	'factory _____

3 These words have more than one meaning. Write two sentences that show different meanings. Use a dictionary.

book	I'm reading a good book.	I booked my flight online.
kind		
mean		
flat		
can		
play		
train		
ring		

T 1.8 Listen and compare.

4 Here are some of the words from exercises 2 and 3 in phonetic symbols. Read them aloud, then write them.

▶▶ **Phonetic symbols *p159***

1 /'wʌndəfl/ _____
2 /kəm'pju:tə(r)/ _____
3 /flæt/ _____
4 /spi:k/ _____
5 /keɪm/ _____
6 /mi:n/ _____
7 /rɪŋ/ _____
8 /treɪn/ _____
9 /'kwɪkli/ _____
10 /'fæktri/ _____

5 What are the everyday objects in the pictures? Look around the room you are in. Find five things you don't know the words for in English. Look them up in a dictionary and check the pronunciation.

EVERYDAY ENGLISH
Social expressions 1

1 In everyday situations we use a lot of social expressions.

> Hi, Anna. How are you?

> I'm fine, thanks. How are you?

T 1.9 Listen and repeat. Which words are stressed?

Music *of* English – stress and intonation 🎵🎵

Every language has its own 'music' (stress and intonation).

1 Sentence stress

T 1.10 Listen and practise.

Thank you very much indeed.
I'm sorry. I can't come tonight.
Can you help me with this exercise?

2 Intonation English goes higher and lower than many other languages. **T 1.11** Listen and practise.

Good morning!   *Excuse me!*   *Can I help you?*

---

2 Look at the photos. What do you think the people are saying?

3 Match an expression in **A** with one in **B**. Which expressions go with the photos? Which are more formal?

A	B
1 Good morning!	a Bye! See you later.
2 See you tomorrow!	b Of course I can. No problem.
3 How do you do?	c Never mind. Perhaps another time.
4 Thank you very much indeed.	d Thanks! Same to you.
5 Excuse me!	e Good morning! Lovely day again.
6 I'm sorry. I can't come tonight.	f Yeah! About nine, in the coffee bar.
7 Can you help me with this exercise?	g It doesn't matter. You're here now.
8 Can I help you?	h Not at all. Don't mention it.
9 Bye!	i No, thank you. I'm just looking.
10 Bye! Have a good weekend!	j How do you do? Pleased to meet you.
11 Sorry I'm late.	k Cheers!
12 Cheers!	l Yes. Can I help you?

T 1.12 Listen and check. Pay attention to the stress and intonation. Practise saying the expressions and responses with a partner.

4 Test your partner. Say an expression from **A** in exercise 3. Can your partner give the correct response from **B**?

5 With your partner, write two short conversations that include some of the social expressions. Mark the stressed words. Act your conversations to the class.

13

2 The way we live

Present tenses • *have/have got* • Collocation – daily life • Making conversation 1

STARTER

What's your morning routine?

Complete these sentences about you.
Then compare with a partner.

I always …   I usually …
I often …   I don't … very often.
Sometimes I …   I never …

TWO DIFFERENT LIVES
Present tenses and *have/have got*

1 Look at the pictures. Who are the people? Where are they?

2 Read the paragraphs and match them with the correct person.
Write the letters *a-h* in the boxes for Anne-Marie and Lien.

T 2.1 Listen and check.

Anne-Marie Boucher has a small family hotel with her husband, Pascal, near Quebec City, Canada.

1 ☐   2 ☐   3 ☐   4 ☐

Now

a She lives in a room with 14 other women in the factory dormitory, seven hundred miles from her family. The factory where she works employs 15,000 workers, nearly all of them women in their twenties.

b It's situated on the coast outside the town and near two national parks. She says, 'Our hotel has got wonderful views of the St Lawrence River and the Isle of Orleans.'

c She works from 8 a.m. to 7 p.m. She has just an hour for lunch. She says, 'I work five and a half days a week, but I usually do overtime in summer. It's very tiring. When I'm not working or studying, I sleep.'

d Her monthly wage is about $65, enough to send a little back home to her family, and to pay for computer classes and English classes in town. She says, 'I haven't got any money left to buy things for me.'

3 Answer the questions.

1 What are their jobs?
2 What's good about their jobs? What's not so good?
3 Who has the better job?
4 What languages do they speak?
5 What are they doing now?
6 What do they want to do?

GRAMMAR SPOT

1 Which two tenses are used in the texts?
  Give examples of both.

2 Look at the sentences. Which refers to *all time*?
  Which refers to *now*?

  He works in a bank.
  He's working hard for his exams.

  She has a hotel.
  She's having a computer lesson.

3 Underline *have* and *have got* in the texts.
  Find negatives.
  Is *have got* more formal or informal?

▶▶▶ **Grammar Reference 2.1–2.4 p128**

---

4 Read Lien's and Anne-Marie's answers. Complete the questions with *you*.

1 'Do _____ job, Lien?'
  'No, I don't like it much. My hands hurt all the time.'

2 'What _____ at the moment?'
  'I'm having a computer lesson.'

3 '_____ any brothers or sisters?'
  'I've got a brother. He lives with my parents in Hunan province.'

4 'Where _____ , Anne Marie?'
  'Well, we don't usually go on holiday, so we're lucky to live in this beautiful place.'

5 'Why _____ the dogs so hard at the moment?'
  'Because I want to race in a competition next year.'

6 'How many _____?'
  'I've got twelve! They don't live in the hotel, of course.'

T 2.2 Listen and check.

Lien Xiaohong is 22. She lives and works in a toy factory in Guangdong province, China.

1 ☐ 2 ☐ 3 ☐ 4 ☐

e She has visitors from all over the world. She says, 'We speak French, English, and a little Italian, which is very useful! Our guests keep us busy both summer and winter, so we've always got lots to do.'

f They don't have much free time. 'But I like it that way,' she says. 'And I love meeting new guests.' In winter it's very cold, –10°C. Their guests go skiing or snowmobiling in Mont Sainte-Anne Park.

g It's the evening now, and she is having a computer lesson in a private school. 'There are two skills that are essential these days,' she says. 'English and computers. One day I want to be my own boss.'

h It's January now, and she is enjoying her favourite sport, dog-sledding. She's got twelve dogs, and she's racing them across the snow. She says, 'I'm working the dogs very hard at the moment. Next year I want to race in a dogsled competition. It's really exciting.'

Now

PRACTICE

Talking about you

1 Look at the forms of *have* and *have got* in the question, negative, and short answer.

> Do you have a car?
> Yes, I do.   No, I don't.
> Have you got a car?
> Yes, I have.   No, I haven't.
> I don't have a car.   I haven't got a car.

T 2.3 Listen and repeat.

2 Ask and answer about the things with a partner, using *have* or *have got*.

- a computer
- a DVD player
- a camera
- a credit card
- an iPod
- a mobile phone
- a bicycle
- any pets
- any brothers and sisters
- your parents/a holiday home
- your teacher/a car

Exchanging information

3 **T 2.4** Look at the photo of Miguel. Listen to the interview with him and complete the chart.

Name and age	Miguel, 21
Town and country	
Family	
Occupation	
Free time/holiday	
Present activity	

4 Look at the photos of Chantal, and Mario and Rita. Work with a partner. Take it in turns to ask and answer questions to complete your chart.

Student A Look at p144.
           Ask about Chantal.
Student B Look at p147.
           Ask about Mario and Rita.

T 2.5 Listen and compare.

> Where does Chantal come from?
> Marseilles, in France.

> Where do Mario and Rita come from?
> Siena, in Italy.

Check it

5 Tick (✓) the correct sentence.

1. ☐ Where you go on holiday?
   ☐ Where do you go on holiday?

2. ☐ Do you have any children?
   ☐ Do you have got any children?

3. I'm Hans.
   ☐ I'm coming from Germany.
   ☐ I come from Germany.

4. This is a great party!
   ☐ Everyone is dancing.
   ☐ Everyone dances.

5. ☐ I don't have a mobile.
   ☐ I no have a mobile.

6. Jack's a policeman,
   ☐ but he doesn't wear a uniform.
   ☐ but he no wear a uniform.

7. 'Where is José?'
   ☐ 'He's sitting by the window.'
   ☐ 'He sits by the window.'

8. ☐ I'm liking black coffee.
   ☐ I like black coffee.

VOCABULARY AND SPEAKING
Daily life

1 Work with a partner. Match the verbs and nouns.

have	the news on TV
wash	your friends
watch	your hair
text	breakfast

have	an email
clear up	the mess
do	a shower
send	the washing-up

make	to music
relax	your homework
listen	a cup of coffee
do	in front of the TV

cook	magazines
go	a meal
put on	make-up
read	to the toilet

T 2.6 Listen, check, and repeat.

2 Where do *you* usually do the activities in exercise 1? Write them in the chart.

Kitchen	Bathroom	Living room	Bedroom

Discuss with your partner. Then use some of the verbs and nouns in exercise 1 to tell your partner about your daily life.

3 Complete these sentences with the correct words.

1 I never _____ breakfast on weekdays, only at weekends.
2 I have a hot _____ every morning and every evening.
3 My sister washes her _____ at least four times a week.
4 She didn't have time to _____ any make-up this morning.
5 My brother never reads books or newspapers, he only reads music _____ .
6 I don't often do the _____ because we've got a dishwasher.
7 I'm going to _____ a cup of coffee. Does anybody want one?
8 My dad always _____ the ten o'clock news on TV.
9 My mum says I text my _____ too much.
10 *You* made this mess, so *you* _____ it up!
11 Can I _____ an email from your computer?
12 How can you listen to _____ while you're working?
13 I'm always so tired after work, I just want to _____ in front of the TV.
14 I cooked a _____ for ten people last night.
15 I didn't forget to _____ my homework, I forgot to *bring* it.
16 Can you wait a minute? I need to _____ to the toilet.

T 2.7 Listen, check, and practise the sentences.

4 What is your favourite room? Why do you like it? What do you do in that room? Write some notes about it.

My bedroom – I've got lots of posters on the walls. I listen to music and do my homework. I watch TV with my friends ...

5 Describe your favourite room to a partner and say what you do there. Don't say which room it is. Can your partner guess?

▶▶ **WRITING** An email *p103*

1 Discuss the questions.

1 Do you know anyone who has lived or is living in another country? What did/do they think of it?

2 Do you know anyone who travels a lot? Is it for work? Where do they go? How long are they away?

2 Read the title and introduction to the magazine article. Why is it easier for people to have different lives these days?

3 Work in two groups.

Group A Read about Claire Turner.
Group B Read about Joss Langford.

Answer the questions.

1 Which two countries does she/he live and work in?

2 What does she/he do?

3 How often does she/he travel? How does she/he travel?

4 What kind of house does she/he have in each country?

5 What kind of lifestyle does her/his partner have?

6 How does she/he live differently in each country?

7 Is there anything she/he misses or doesn't like?

8 What does she/he say about language?

4 Find a partner from the other group. Tell each other about your person, using your answers to exercise 3 to help you.

5 Answer the questions with your partner.

1 What things do Claire and Joss have in common?

2 Who travels more?

3 Who enjoys their lifestyle more? Why?

What do you think?

- Whose lifestyle would you prefer, Claire's or Joss's?
- What do you like best about living in your country? What would you miss if you lived abroad?
- Which other country would you like to work in?

Tales of two cities

Most of us have just one home, one job, one lifestyle. But in the 21st century, cheap travel and communication technology have made the world smaller and smaller, so that we can work and live almost anywhere. More and more people have two places they call 'home'. **Claire Turner** and **Joss Langford** talk about their two different lives.

Cambridge – Nuremburg
Joss Langford, 29, snowboard designer

'In Germany, I feel European. In England, I feel English,' says Joss. Every two weeks, Joss leaves his farmhouse home near Cambridge for another farmhouse near Nuremberg. 'Both places are really flat,' says Joss.

It's a strange choice of landscape for a snowboard designer. 'I design in England, build in Germany, then drive to Switzerland to test the boards.' The distance between my homes in England and Germany is almost 1,000km door-to-door. He knows this because he sometimes drives. It makes a nice change from flying. Joss flew 100 times last year. He doesn't mind all the air travel, but there are disadvantages. 'It's exhausting, and I've always got a cold', he says. 'People think it's glamorous, but I don't fly first class.'

In each country he has a social life and a local pub. Although Joss speaks German, people in Nuremberg always want to practise their English. In Cambridge, he lives with his partner, Kate. She travels a lot in in her job, too. 'I call her before bedtime. Sometimes our planes cross in the skies.'

In Nuremberg, he rents a room with his colleague. 'There, I eat more meat and drink more beer. I watch TV because I don't have one at home. I know all the German celebs! I'm not lonely. I have a second home, not a hotel room. I have a German life in Germany, and an English life in England.'

Manchester – New York
Claire Turner, 33, gallery owner

Claire holds up her hands to show her nails. 'Don't they look awful!' she cries. 'I so miss New York manicures.' That's not all Claire misses about her other life in the USA. For two years she has divided her life between her home town, Manchester, in the north of England, and Brooklyn, New York. She has an art gallery – and a home – in both places. She flies once a month, and spends about a month at a time in each.

'I dress differently in New York: pearls, contact lenses, no jeans, and I wear my hair up. Americans love the English accent, so I feel I should act the part.' After work in New York, she may sip a glass of wine or fruit juice in a trendy bar, but after work in Manchester she goes to the local pub for a pint of beer. Her two homes are similar, though. 'In Brooklyn, I share a rooftop flat with an artist. I can actually see the sky!' She can see the same stars from her city-centre loft in Manchester.

Claire loves her transatlantic lifestyle. Her husband travels a lot in his job, too. They met in Manchester and married in New York. 'We're not always in the same country, but our lives are going in the same direction!'

LISTENING AND SPEAKING
A 24/7 society

Nighthawks, Edward Hopper, 1942

1 Look at the famous painting. Discuss the questions in groups.

1 Who painted it? What is it called?
2 What time of day is it?
3 Where are the people? Who are they?

2 Work with a partner. What is a 24/7 society? Which jobs need people to work at night? Make a list.

3 **T 2.8** Listen to a radio programme about four night workers: Jerry, Jackie, Doreen, and Dan. Complete the chart. Listen again and check your answers.

	Place of work	Hours	Why working nights?	Problems
Jerry				
Jackie				
Doreen				
Dan				

Jerry

Jackie

What do you think?

Discuss these questions.

• Who has the best job? Who has the worst job?
• Do you know anybody that works at night? What do they do? What do they think about it?
• Could you work at night? Why?/Why not?

Doreen

Dan

EVERYDAY ENGLISH
Making conversation 1

1 **T 2.9** Listen to two conversations. Nicole and Marco are foreign students in Britain. Their teachers, James and Catherine, are trying to be friendly. Which conversation is more successful? Why?

James & Nicole

Marco & Catherine

Music of English – highs and lows ♫♪

Highs and lows
A flat intonation makes you sound bored. To show you're interested, your voice needs highs and lows.

1 **T 2.10** Listen and compare Nicole and Marco's answers.

N Paris. I come from Paris.

M I come from 'Roma', or as you say

in English, Rome.

2 **T 2.11** Listen and repeat.

M And you, Catherine, where do you come from?

C I'm from Dublin, in Ireland.

M Oh, I'd love to visit Ireland one day.

C You must. It's really beautiful.

---

2 Obviously, it is impossible to tell someone how to have a conversation, but here are some things that help.

- Ask questions.
- Don't just answer *yes* or *no*.
- Try to add a comment of your own.
- Don't let the conversation stop.
- Show that you're interested, both with words and voice.

Find examples of these in Catherine and Marco's conversation on p117.

3 Work with a partner. Practise Catherine and Marco's conversation on p117.

4 Match a line in **A** with a reply in **B** and a further comment in **C**.

A	B	C
1 What lovely weather we're having!	I'm enjoying it a lot.	Was it a good game?
2 What terrible weather!	Yes, no problems.	That's really kind of you.
3 How are you today?	I'm very well, thanks.	We all went to that new night club in King Street.
4 Did you have a nice evening?	No, I missed it.	The plane was a bit late, but it didn't matter.
5 How do you find living in Chicago?	Thank you. I'm glad you like it.	I just hope this rain stops soon.
6 Did you have a good journey?	Thank you very much.	I got it in the sale for only £40.
7 Did you watch the football yesterday?	Yes. Excellent, thanks.	How about you?
8 What a lovely jacket you're wearing!	Yes, wonderful, isn't it?	It was a bit strange at first, but I love it now.
9 If you have any problems, just ask me.	I know. Really awful, isn't it?	Just like summer!

T 2.12 Listen and check. Practise the conversations with a partner.

5 Think of three questions to ask your partner about each of these subjects.

- before class today
- something he/she is wearing
- learning English

Have conversations. Try to sound interested and keep the conversation going.

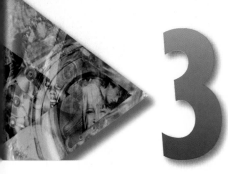

3 What happened next?

Past tenses • Adverbs • Time expressions

Here are the past tense forms of some irregular verbs. Write the infinitives.

1	_be_ was	7	_____	did
2	_____ were	8	_____	got
3	_____ went	9	_____	had
4	_____ saw	10	_____	made
5	_____ thought	11	_____	came
6	_____ put	12	_____	said

WHAT A MYSTERY!
Past Simple

1 Read the beginning of the newspaper article. Who do you think is the 'dark figure'? Why did he open the other doors? Why did he go to the kitchen? Where do you think the story is taking place?

2 **T 3.1** Read and listen to the rest of the article. What are the answers to the questions in exercise 1?

Who let the dogs out? Woof! Woof!

It was night. A dark figure carefully unlocked the door and went out. He looked around. Was there anybody there? No, all was quiet. He ran quickly to some other doors and opened them. Then he went straight to the kitchen ...

Last month, strange things began to happen at London's Battersea Dogs' Home. Every morning when the staff arrived, they saw that a lot of the dogs were out of their cages. It was a mystery. 'It happened so many times,' said Amy Watson, one of the staff. 'We even thought that perhaps it was the ghost of Mary Tealby.' They say that Mary Tealby, who started the Home in 1860, comes back at night to haunt it. So they put cameras in all the cages and filmed what happened.

Next day the staff watched the film. They were amazed at what they saw. Red, a four-year-old lurcher*, used his teeth to open the door of his cage. Then he did the same for his friends in the next cages. All the dogs got out and had a great time. Amy told us, 'They ate lots of food, had lots of fun and games, and made lots of mess!'

Reporters from Japan, Germany, and America came to film Red, and 400 people phoned because they wanted to give him a home. Red's a famous film star now. 'He's a real celebrity!' said Amy.

*A type of dog

3 What are the past forms of the verbs from the article? Which are regular? Which are irregular?

look	_____	start	_____
run	_____	watch	_____
open	_____	use	_____
begin	_____	tell	_____
arrive	_____	eat	_____

4 **T 3.2** You will hear six incorrect sentences about the story. Correct them using negative sentences. Then listen and repeat.

It happened every morning.

> It didn't happen every morning. It happened every night!

5 Complete the questions.

1 What ___did Red do___?
   He opened all the cage doors.
2 Why _____ the doors?
   Because he wanted to go to the kitchen.
3 How often _____ ?
   Many times.
4 Who _____ Amy _____ it was?
   The ghost of Mary Tealby.
5 What _____ they _____ in the cages?
   Cameras.
6 How _____ the doors?
   With his teeth.
7 _____ a good time?
   Yes, they did. They had a great time.
8 Why _____ phone the dogs' home?
   Because they wanted to give Red a home.

T 3.3 Listen and check. Ask and answer the questions with a partner.

Please make sure my kennel door is always locked – I can open them!

GRAMMAR SPOT

1 What tense are nearly all the verbs in the article? How do we form the question and negative?

Spelling

2 Write the Past Simple of the regular verbs.

a	look	_____	c	arrive	_____
	play	_____		use	_____
	want	_____		decide	_____
b	try	_____	d	stop	_____
	study	_____		plan	_____

- How is the regular past tense formed?
- How is the past tense formed when the verb ends in a consonant + *y* ?
- When do we double the final consonant?

Pronunciation

3 **T 3.4** Listen to the verbs in exercise 2. What is the pronunciation of *-ed* ? Is it /t/, /d/, or /ɪd/? Make three lists.

look**ed** /t/   play**ed** /d/   want**ed** /ɪd/

T 3.5 Listen, check, and repeat.

▶▶ **Grammar References 3.1 p129**

▶▶ **Irregular verbs p158.**

PRACTICE

Making connections

1 Match the verb phrases. Make sentences using both verbs in the past. Join the sentences with *so*, *because*, *and*, or *but*.

The phone rang, so I answered it.

1	phone ring	mend it
2	feel ill	pass it
3	make a sandwich	wash my hair (2)
4	have a shower	nobody laugh
5	lose my passport	be hungry
6	call the police	go to bed (1)
7	printer break	say sorry
8	forget her birthday	find it later
9	take my driving test	answer it
10	tell a joke	hear a strange noise

T 3.6 Listen and compare your answers.

Talking about you

2 Ask and answer these questions with a partner.

What did you do ... ?
- last night
- on your last birthday
- on your last holiday
- last weekend
- last New Year's Eve

Ask for more information, using the Past Simple.

Who ...?   Why ...?   Where ...?   How ...?   How many ...?

PARTNERS IN CRIME
Past Simple and Continuous

1 Check the meaning of these verbs. What are the past forms? Which two are regular?

fill	steal	hide	throw	spend
destroy	take	cut	think	

2 Look at the photos and read the newspaper story. Complete 1–9 in the story with the past forms of the verbs in exercise 1.

3 Answer the questions.
- What did Stephane Breitweiser steal?
- Was his mother also a thief?
- Why did she go to prison?

4 Put these lines into the story (…).
a where he **was living** with his mother
b while he **was working** as a lorry driver
c just as they **were closing**
d while they **were having** supper
e because he **was wearing** a security guard's uniform

T 3.7 Listen and check.

GRAMMAR SPOT

1 What tense are the verb forms in exercise 4?

2 How do you form the question and negative of this sentence?

   He was working.

3 Look at these sentences. What are the differences?

   When they arrived, she made coffee.
   When they arrived, she was making coffee.

Pronunciation

T 3.8 Listen and repeat.

He was /wəz/ working.
Where was /wəz/ he living?
They were /wə/ having supper.
What were /wə/ they doing?

▶▶ **Grammar Reference 3.2 and 3.3 p129**

---

5 Take it in turns to read aloud parts of the story of Stephane and his mother.

The thief, his mother, and $2 billion

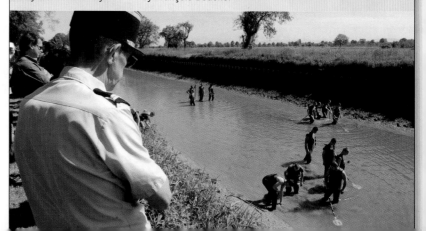

Breitweiser leaving court

STEPHANE BREITWEISER, 33, from Alsace, in France, is the greatest art thief in Europe. For over six years, (…), he (1)_____ 239 paintings from museums in France, Austria, and Denmark. He went into the museums (…) and (2)_____ the paintings under his coat. Nobody looked at him (…).

Back in his apartment, (…), he (3)_____ his bedroom with priceless works of art. His mother, Mireille, 53, (4)_____ all the paintings were copies. One day (…), the police arrived, and they (5)_____ Stephane to the police station. Mireille was so angry with her son that she went to his room, took some paintings from the walls, and (6)_____ them into small pieces. Others she took and (7) _____ into the canal. Altogether, she (8) _____ art worth two billion dollars!

Both mother and son (9)_____ many years in prison.

Madeleine d'Ecosse by Corneille de Lyon

Berger endormi (The Sleeping Shepherd) by François Boucher

PRACTICE

Discussing grammar

1 Choose the correct verb form.

1 I *saw / was seeing* a good programme on TV last night.
2 While I *shopped / was shopping* this morning, I *lost / was losing* my wallet. I don't know how.
3 Last week the police *stopped / were stopping* Alan because he *drove / was driving* at over eighty miles an hour.
4 'How *did you break / were you breaking* your leg?'
'I *skied / was skiing* and I *hit / was hitting* a tree.'
5 When I *arrived / was arriving* at the party, everyone *had / was having* a good time.
6 *Did you have / Were you having* a good time last night?

2 Complete the sentences with the verbs in the Past Simple or Past Continuous.

1 While I _was going_ (go) to work this morning, I _met_ (meet) an old friend.
2 I _didn't want_ (not want) to get up this morning. It _was raining_ (rain) and it was cold, and my bed was so warm.
3 The phone _rung_ (ring) just as I _was leaving_ (leave) the office.
4 When I _picked_ (pick) up the phone, there was no-one there.
5 I _said_ (say) hello to the children, but they didn't say anything because they _were watching_ (watch) television.

fortunately/unfortunately

3 Continue this story around the class.

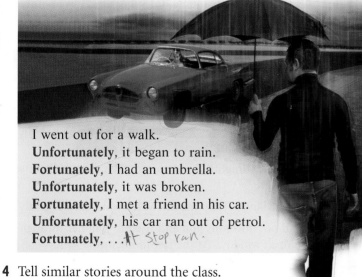

I went out for a walk.
Unfortunately, it began to rain.
Fortunately, I had an umbrella.
Unfortunately, it was broken.
Fortunately, I met a friend in his car.
Unfortunately, his car ran out of petrol.
Fortunately, ... It stop ran.

4 Tell similar stories around the class. Begin with these sentences.

- I went for a walk in the park on Sunday.
- It was my birthday last week.
- We went out for a meal last Saturday.
- There was a really good film on TV last night.

Exchanging information

5 Read the headline and look at the photo. What did Hugo buy? What is a *spending spree*?

Teenager goes on spending spree with father's credit card

BIG SPENDER: Hugo Fenton-Jones

6 Work with a partner. You have different information. Take it in turns to ask and answer questions. Don't look at your partner's story.

Student A	Student B
Look at the newspaper story on p143.	Look at the newspaper story on p146.
Teenager Hugo Fenton-Jones stole ... (*What?*) while his father was working in the garden.	Teenager Hugo Fenton-Jones stole his father's credit card while his father was working ... (*Where?*).

What did Hugo steal?

He stole his father's credit card.

Where was his father working?

He was working in the garden.

LISTENING AND READING

The name's Bond, James Bond

1 Who is James Bond? Write down three things you know about him and share your ideas with the class.

2 Look at the posters from some of the James Bond films. Have you seen any of them? Do you know any more James Bond films?

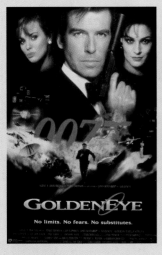

3 You are going to listen to an extract from *The Man with the Golden Gun.* Cover the story and look at pictures 1–8. What do you think is happening?

4 **T 3.9** Listen and answer the questions.

1 Name the people in the pictures. Where are they?
2 How did Mary Goodnight get into the room?
3 Why did she come to find James Bond?
4 Where did they go to talk?
5 What did Scaramanga say? What did he do?

5 Read the story. Find the lines in the text which go with each picture.

The Man with the Golden Gun

① JAMES BOND got back to his hotel room at midnight. The windows were closed and the air-conditioning was on. Bond switched it off and opened the windows. His heart was still thumping in his chest. He breathed in the air with relief, then he had a shower and went to bed.

At 3.30 he was dreaming, not very peacefully, of three black-coated men with red eyes and angry white teeth.
② Suddenly, he woke up. He listened. There was a noise. It was coming from the window. Someone was moving behind the curtain. James Bond took his gun from under his pillow, got quietly out of bed, and crept slowly along the wall towards the window. Someone was breathing heavily behind the curtain. Bond pulled it back with one quick movement. Golden hair shone in the moonlight.

'Mary Goodnight!' Bond cursed. 'What the hell are you doing here?'

'Quick, James! Help me in!' Mary whispered urgently.

⑤ Bond put down his gun and tried to pull her through the open window. At the last moment the window banged shut with a noise like a gunshot. Bond cursed again.

Mary Goodnight whispered, 'I'm terribly sorry, James!'

'Sh! Sh!' said Bond. He quickly led her across the room to the bathroom. First he turned on the light, then the shower. They sat down together on the side of the bath.

Bond asked again. 'What the hell are you doing here? What's the matter?'

'James, I was so worried. A 'Most Immediate' message came from HQ this evening. A top KGB man, using the name Hendriks, is staying in this hotel. He knows you're here. He's looking for you!'

'I know,' said Bond. 'Hendriks is here all right. So is a gunman called Scaramanga. Mary, did HQ say if they have a description of me?'

'No, they don't. They just have your name, Secret Agent James Bond.'

'Thanks, Mary. Now, I must get you out of here. Don't worry about me, just tell HQ that you gave me the message, OK?'

'OK, James.' Mary Goodnight stood up and looked into his eyes. 'Please take care, James.'

'Sure, sure.' Bond turned off the shower and opened the bathroom door. 'Now, come on!'

Suddenly a voice came from the darkness of the bedroom. 'This is not your lucky day, Mr Bond. Come here both of you and put your hands up!'

Scaramanga walked to the door and turned on the lights. His golden gun was pointing straight at James Bond.

6 Are these sentences true (✓) or false (✗)? Correct the false sentences.

1 James Bond felt happy to be back in his hotel room. ✓
2 Bond was dreaming about Mary Goodnight. ✗
3 A man with a gun woke Bond at 3.30 a.m. ✗
4 James was very pleased to see Mary Goodnight. ✗
5 Bond's gun went off while he was pulling Mary through the window. ✗
6 They talked while the shower was on. ✓
7 Bond knew that Hendriks was looking for him. ✓
8 James helped Mary get out of the hotel. ✗

What do you think?

7 Work in groups. Discuss these questions and try to work out the rest of the story.

1 Who is Scaramanga? Is he …
  … an assassin hired to kill James Bond? ✓
  … the leader of a terrorist group?
  … a poker player who lost his money to James Bond?

2 Who is Mary Goodnight? Is she …
  … James Bond's girlfriend?
  … in fact working for Scaramanga?
  … a secret agent like James Bond? ✓

3 What happens next in the story? Does Scaramanga …
  … kill Mary and James Bond?
  … capture Mary and James Bond?
  … capture Mary and take her to a secret island. ✓

4 What happens in the end?
  … James Bond escapes but Mary is killed.
  … Scaramanga is hurt but escapes with Mary.
  … James Bond saves the world and gets the girl. ✓

Read the story summary on page 149. Were your ideas right?

Language work

8 Write the past form of these verbs from the story. Which are irregular?

get	_got_	whisper	_____	breathe	_____
put	_____	wake up	_____	try	_____
take	_____	lead	_____	creep	_____
give	_____	shine	_____	stand up	_____

Telling the story

9 Tell the story to a partner in your own words. Use the pictures to help. Start:

James Bond got back to his hotel room at midnight. He was relieved to be back. He …

VOCABULARY AND SPEAKING
Adverbs

1 Many adverbs end in *-ly*. Match a verb in **A** with an adverb in **B**. They all come from the text about James Bond. Some have more than one possibility.

A		B	
① dream	④ creep	quietly ⑤	heavily ⑥
② wake up	⑤ get out of bed	peacefully ①	urgently ③
③ whisper	⑥ breathe	suddenly ②	slowly ④

2 There are also many adverbs that do not end in *-ly*. Find these examples in the text on p26–27.

back	still	here	again	first	together	just	straight

VOCABULARY SPOT

Position of adverbs

1 Adverbs do not usually go between a verb and its object.
*You speak English **well**.* (NOT ~~You speak well English.~~)
*I did my homework **quickly**.* (NOT ~~I did quickly my homework.~~)

2 Some adverbs can change position.
*It rained all day **yesterday**. / **Yesterday** it rained all day.*
*I woke up **suddenly**. / **Suddenly** I woke up.*

3 In which of these sentences can the adverb change position? Rewrite them.
1 *Tidy your room **first**. Then you can go out.*
2 *Can you **possibly** tell me the time?*
3 *We went for a walk. It started to rain **unfortunately**.*

---

3 Rewrite the sentences with the adverbs in brackets.
1 I was dreaming when a loud noise woke me up. (peacefully, suddenly)
2 My Grandma is 75 and she goes swimming. (nearly, still, regularly)
3 I unlocked the door and went into the night. (quietly, outside)
4 She whispered in his ear, 'Do you love me?' 'I do,' he replied. (softly, really, of course)
5 I was relaxing with a good book when someone knocked on the door. (just, really, loudly)
6 Break the eggs into a bowl and mix them with the flour. (first, then, together)
7 I got up and crept to the front door. (quickly, downstairs)
8 I work and I do my homework, but I don't get good marks. (hard, carefully, still)

T 3.10 Listen and check. Practise saying the sentences.

An adverb poem

4 **T 3.11** Work with a partner. Listen and then read the poem aloud, with feeling. Can you think of a title?

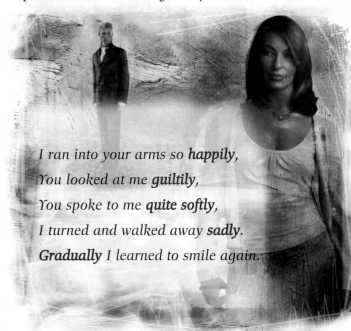

*I ran into your arms so **happily**,*
*You looked at me **guiltily**,*
*You spoke to me **quite softly**,*
*I turned and walked away **sadly**.*
***Gradually** I learned to smile **again**.*

5 Write a similar poem with your partner. You can choose the adverbs, or use these.

slowly	quietly	tragically	angrily	carefully
nervously	urgently	lovingly	suddenly	lazily

Read your poem to the class. Whose do you think is the best?

SHORT STORY

'Once upon a time, they lived happily ever after.'

▶▶ **WRITING** Telling a story *p104*

EVERYDAY ENGLISH
Time expressions

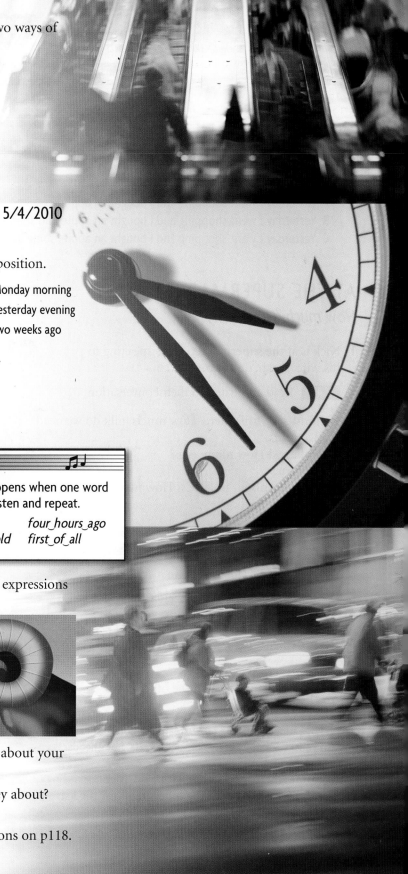

1 **T 3.12** Listen and read the conversation. What are the two ways of saying dates? Practise the conversation with a partner.

A Did you send Oliver a birthday card?
B I had no idea it was his birthday. When was it?
A On October the 11th.
B The 11th of October! That's a week ago. I'll phone him this evening and apologize.

2 Say the dates aloud in two ways.

June 2   August 31   July 4   May 1   September 17

7/1/1868   28/12/1901   14/2/1980   5/11/2002   5/4/2010

T 3.13 Listen and check.

3 Complete the time expressions with *at*, *on*, *in*, or no preposition.

_at_ six o'clock	_on_ Saturday	_in_ 1989	_on_ Monday morning
___ last night	_in_ April	_at_ the weekend	___ yesterday evening
_in_ the evening	_in_ summer	_on_ January 18	___ two weeks ago

Do you know *exactly* when you were born? Tell the class.

> I was born on Wednesday, the eighteenth of January 1989, at four o'clock in the morning.

Music *of* English – word linking   ♪♪

T 3.14 Words often link together when we speak. This happens when one word ends with a consonant and the next begins with a vowel. Listen and repeat.

this_evening   at_eleven_o'clock   last_autumn   four_hours_ago
this_afternoon   in_August   twenty-eight years_old   first_of_all

---

4 **T 3.15** Listen. Complete the conversation with the time expressions you hear. Which words are linked?

A What star sign are you?
B I'm Aries.
A Hey, so am I! When's your birthday?
B _1/04_ .
A I don't believe it! Same as me. Which year?
B _1990_ .
A That's amazing! We're like twins!

Listen again. Practise with your partner. Ask and answer about your birth signs and birthdays.

5 **T 3.16** Listen to three more conversations. What are they about? Write the time expressions you hear.

6 Work with a partner. Choose one of the three conversations on p118. Learn it by heart and act it out to the class.

▶▶ **Grammar Reference 3.4 p130**

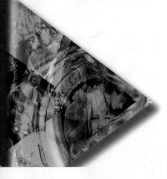

4 The market place

STARTER

Play the alphabet shopping game around the class.

A Yesterday I went shopping and I bought an **a**pple.
B Yesterday I went shopping and I bought an **a**pple and some **b**read.
C Yesterday I went shopping and I bought an **a**pple, some **b**read, and a **c**ar.

AT THE SUPERMARKET
How much/How many?

1 Nick is at the supermarket. He is speaking to his wife, Sarah, on his mobile.

> **T 4.1** Read and listen to their conversation.

N It just says 'milk' here. How **much** milk do we need?
S Two pints.
N And eggs? How **many** eggs?
S A dozen.
N And what about potatoes? How **many** potatoes?
S A kilo's enough.

GRAMMAR SPOT

Can we count milk (*one milk, two milks*)?
Can we count eggs (*one egg, two eggs*)?
When do we say *How much . . . ?*
When do we say *How many . . . ?*

▶▶ **Grammar Reference 4.1 p131**

2 Match the quantities with the other items on Nick's shopping list.

① a large tube	② just one brown loaf	③ a bottle of red
④ six rolls	⑤ four or five big ones	⑥ 200g of Cheddar

3 Continue the conversation with a partner.
Use the quantities with the other items on the list.

> The list says 'bread'. How much bread?
>> Just one ...

milk
eggs
potatoes
② bread
⑤ tomatoes

⑥ cheese
③ wine
① toothpaste
④ toilet paper

④ **T 4.2** Listen and complete the rest of the conversation.

N Is that everything?
S Let's have a look. We've got **some** _apples_, but there aren't **any** bananas. And we've got **some** _tea_, but there isn't **any** coffee.
N OK, bananas and coffee. What about orange juice? Is there **any** orange juice left?
S Let's see. There's **a little**, but not **much**.
N Orange juice, then. And vegetables? Have we got **many** vegetables?
S Well, we've got **some** broccoli and **a few** _carrots_, but there aren't **many** onions.
N Right, onions … _بصل_
S Oh, and don't forget – your nephews are coming tomorrow! We need something for them.
N OK, **lots of** crisps and _icream_. Anything else?
S I don't think so. But (for goodness sake,) _don't_ forget the nappies. Oh, and a big bunch of _____ for me!
flowers

GRAMMAR SPOT

1 Find eight count nouns (CNs) and five uncount nouns (UNs) in the conversation.

2 Put a tick (✓) or a cross (✗) in the columns.

We use …	with CNs	with UNs	in positive sentences	in questions	in negative sentences
some	✓	✓	✓	✓ (sometimes)	✗
any	✓	✓	✗	✓	✓
much	✗	✓	✗	✓	✓
many	✓	✗	✗	✓	✓
a lot/lots of	✓	✓	✓	✓	✓
a few	✓	✗	✓		
a little	✗	✓	✓		

3 Look at the forms of *something/ someone*, etc. Find three examples in the conversation in exercise 4.

some		thing
any	+	one/body
every		where

▶▶ **Grammar Reference 4.1 p131**

PRACTICE

Discussing grammar

1 Complete the sentences with *some* or *any*.

1 Have you got _any_ brothers or sisters?
2 We don't need _any_ olive oil.
3 Here are _some_ letters for you.
4 I need _some_ money.
5 Is there _any_ petrol in the car?

ة Many
ةر Much

2 Complete the sentences with *much* or *many*.

1 Have you got _much_ homework?
2 We don't need _many_ eggs. Just half a dozen.
3 Is there _much_ traffic in your town?
4 There aren't _many_ students in my class.
5 How _many_ people live in your house?

3 Complete the sentences with *a little*, *a few*, or *a lot of*.

1 I have _a few_ close friends. Two or three.
2 He has _a lot of_ money. He's a millionaire.
3 'Do you take sugar in coffee?' 'Just _a little_. Half a spoonful.'
4 'Have you got _a lot of_ CDs?' 'Hundreds.'
5 I'll be ready in _a few_ minutes.
6 I've learnt a lot of Spanish, but only _a little_ Russian.

Find the differences

4 Look at the picture. What things can you see?

5 Work with a partner. You have different pictures. Take it in turns to ask and answer questions to find the differences.

Student A	Student B
Look at the picture on p144.	Look at the picture on p147.

something/someone/somewhere

6 Complete the sentences with the correct word.

some any every no	+	thing one/body where

1 **A** Did you meet _any one_ nice at the party?
   B Yes. I met _some one_ who knows you!

2 **A** Ouch! There's _some thing_ in my eye!
   B Let me look. No, I can't see _any thing_.

3 **A** Let's go _some where_ hot for our holidays.
   B Yes, but we can't go _any where_ that's too expensive.

4 **A** I'm so unhappy. _no body_ loves me.
   B I know _some one_ who loves you. Me.

5 I've lost my glasses. I've looked _every where_, but I can't find them.

6 **A** Did you buy _any thing_ at the shops?
   B No, _no thing_. I didn't have any money.

7 I'm bored. I want _some thing_ interesting to read, or _some one_ interesting to talk to, or _some where_ interesting to go.

8 It was a great party. _every one_ loved it.

T 4.3 Listen and check.

THE AMAZING WORLD OF eBay
Articles

1 Is eBay popular in your country? What is eBay? What do people buy and sell on it? Do you or anyone you know use it? Tell the class.

2 Read about eBay. Answer the questions.
1 How much did the jet and the football cost?
2 How many people use eBay every day?
3 Who invented eBay?
4 When and why did he invent it?

The amazing world of …

Where can you buy a football kicked by David Beckham, or an old Learjet? On eBay, of course – the world's first global online marketplace. The football sold for £18,500, and someone paid $4.9 million for the jet! Every day on eBay, there are 34 million things for sale, and 125 million buyers and sellers. You can buy everything – stamps, jewellery, art, clothing, old cars, and anything strange and interesting. All you need is a computer and a little time.

Pierre Omidyar, a French-Iranian computer scientist, invented eBay in California in 1995. He wanted to create a website for everybody to buy and sell things, not just big businesses. He started the website as a hobby, but now it is the biggest business in the world!

PRACTICE

1 Complete the sentences with *a/an*, *the*, or nothing(-).

1 I bought __an__ unusual football on __/__ eBay. David Beckham kicked it in __the__ 2004 European Cup Final!

2 There was __an__ old Learjet for sale! __a__ famous film star paid __a__ lot of money for it.

3 __The__ film star who bought __the__ Learjet collects _____ aeroplanes.

4 eBay is __a__ very clever idea. It's __the__ biggest market in __the__ world.

5 I don't go out to __/__ work. I work at __/__ home on my computer.

6 I do all my shopping on __the__ Internet. What __a__ great way to shop!

I bought it on eBay!

2 **T 4.4** Listen to three people talking about what they bought on eBay. Complete the chart.

	Linda	Megan	Charlie
What did he/she buy?	cooker	shoes	car
How much did it cost?	£100	£2	£1000
Does he/she like using eBay?	yes	yes	Not now
Does he/she use eBay often?	yes	yes	yes but not for a while

Compare answers with a partner. Listen again and check.

Discussing grammar

3 Work with a partner. Find *one* mistake in each sentence.
1 He's postman, so he has breakfast at 4 a.m.
2 The love is more important than money.
3 I come to school by the bus.
4 I'm reading one good book at the moment.
5 'Where's Jack?' 'In a kitchen.'
6 I live in centre of town, near the hospital.
7 My parents bought the lovely house in the country.
8 I don't eat the bread because I don't like it.

4 Make two sentences, one with the definite article *the*, and one without, using the words in the box.

> ice-cream   money   chocolate   cats

> I think ice-cream is delicious!

> The ice-cream in this café is delicious.

Unit 4 · The market place   33

GRAMMAR SPOT

1 Find examples of the definite article (*the*) and the indefinite article (*a/an*) in the text.
2 Find examples of when there is no article.

▶▶ **Grammar Reference 4.2 p131**

READING AND SPEAKING
Markets around the world

1 Look at the pictures and discuss the questions.
1 What is the difference between a shopping centre and a market?
2 Do you ever go shopping in markets? Where?
3 Is there a market where you live? What can you buy there? Can you bargain for things?

2 Read the introduction to an article about three markets in very different parts of the world. Why are markets more interesting than shopping centres?

Markets around the world

Modern shopping centres, with their global brands and international designer names, look the same all over the world. So if you want to buy goods that are different, visit a market. There you can buy fine products made and grown locally.

3 Work in three groups.
Group A Read about Bangkok.
Group B Read about Provence.
Group C Read about Marrakech.

4 Answer the questions about your market.
1 Where exactly is the market?
2 What days and times is it open?
3 What food does it sell? Give some examples.
4 What other things does it sell?
5 What do you learn about the people who work there?
6 Describe the market. Find some adjectives.
7 What can you do after the market?
8 What do you learn about the town?

5 Find a partner from each of the other two groups. Use the photos to introduce your market. Then compare the three markets, using your answers in exercise 4.

What do you think?

Answer the questions with your group.

- Which of the markets would you like to visit most? Why?
- Have you visited a market in another country? If yes, describe it.
- Close your books and close your eyes. Imagine you are at the market you read about. Tell your partners what you can see.

▶▶ **WRITING** A postcard *p106*

The floating markets of Bangkok

Bangkok, the capital of Thailand, is a city of contrasts. The tall glass buildings look like any other modern city. But behind them is a place where life hasn't changed for over 100 years – the canals. Built in 1866 by the King of Thailand, these canals are home to many Thai people who still live and work there today. There are four floating markets around Bangkok, and the oldest and most popular is in the town of Damonen Saduak.

This market opens every day from 6.30 a.m. It's best to shop early and go by water taxi. After 9 a.m. the tourist buses arrive, and it's much too busy.

It's a colourful, noisy, fascinating place. Old ladies with huge hats sit in small boats, filled with tropical fruit and vegetables, fresh coconut juice and local food. Did you miss your breakfast? Then just call a seller for a bowl of hot soup. He'll get it from a cooker at the back of his boat!

But the boats don't just sell food. Would you like a traditional hat? A silk dress? A flowered shirt? Then just call and point. After the noise and excitement of the market, continue along the canal. Soon you'll see the wooden houses, orchards, and floating flowers of the canal villages. It's a lovely, peaceful way to finish your trip.

A perfect day in Provence

Every Sunday in a small town called Isle-sur-la-Sorgue in southern France there is a truly amazing market. Isle-sur-la-Sorgue is like Venice. The River Sorgue runs in and out of the old narrow streets and under the many bridges, and on market day every street and bridge is packed with stalls. From early morning, this sleepy little town becomes a noisy, busy place, with sellers calling to you in the singing accent of the south.

You can choose from an amazing selection of olives, hundreds of cheeses, and delicious roast chickens. But it is not just a food market. Antique sellers fill the pavements with beautiful old French furniture, and there are tables covered with antique lace and cloth. Flower sellers invite you to pick from their brightly coloured bunches of flowers. The air is filled with the smell of soaps, herbs, and lavender, all made and grown in Provence. Do you need a sun hat? Did you forget your beach towel? Your choices are endless.

Travellers fill their backpacks with delicious things for Sunday lunch: olive bread, tomatoes, ham, melon and, of course, a bottle of local rosé wine. At 1 o'clock everything closes, and everyone goes home. Then it's time to find a cool place next to the river for a perfect picnic on a perfect day in Provence.

The souks of Marrakech

Marrakech in Morocco looks like a Hollywood film set. It is a city of ancient, sand-coloured buildings and palm trees in the middle of the desert.

In the centre is the main square, Jemaa el Fna. Here you can see dancing snakes and drink Moroccan coffee. But behind the square is the real heart of the city. This is the souk (the Arab word for market). Hundreds of little shops and stalls are open from early morning till lunchtime, and again in the evening. The souk, with its narrow, busy streets, is divided into lots of smaller souks. There's the aromatic spice souk, the noisy meat souk, the colourful clothing souk, the gold and silver souk, and many more.

Finally, there's the carpet souk. Here, hundreds of handmade Moroccan rugs and carpets cover the pavements. No two rugs are the same. In Mr Youssaf's rug shop, he invites you to sit down among all the beautiful carpets. A silver teapot arrives with little glasses and Mr Youssaf talks about the different rugs, while his assistants roll them out one by one. Two hours later, after many glasses of traditional mint tea and lots of bargaining, you finally choose your rug and leave much poorer. Then it's time to return to the main square to watch the snakes and count your money.

VOCABULARY, LISTENING, AND SPEAKING
Shopping

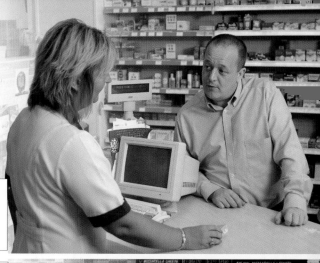

1 Look at the pictures. Where are the people? What can you buy or do in each place? Compare your ideas with the class.

2 Complete the table with the things in the box.

a T-shirt	an espresso	a parcel	tissues	envelopes
a tie	deodorant	aspirin	scales	shaving foam
a belt	a leather jacket	a doughnut	a book of stamps	
a toasted sandwich	a sparkling mineral water			

a chemist's	a café	a post office	a clothes shop
deodorant aspirin tissues shiving foam	toasted sandwich doughnut sparkling mineral water		a T-shirt tie belt leather jacket

T 4.5 Listen, check, and repeat. Mark the main stress on each word or phrase. Practise saying them.

3 **T 4.6** Listen to the four conversations. Answer the questions about each one.

1 Where is the conversation is taking place?
2 What does the customer want?
3 Can the shop assistant/cashier help?
4 What does the customer buy?

Music of English – sounding polite 🎵🎵

1 **T 4.7** Listen to two people asking for a coffee. Who sounds more polite? Practise the polite way of asking.

Good morning! Can I have a coffee?

2 **T 4.8** Listen and practise these polite requests.

Could I have some tissues as well, please?

I wonder if you could help me?

Can I try it on?

Shopping in your town

4 Do you often go shopping? What do you like going shopping for? What *don't* you like going shopping for?

5 Work in small groups. Make a list of the different shops in your area and what they sell. Talk about the different shops.

> There are two supermarkets.
> There aren't any ...

> There are a few good clothes shops.
> There aren't many ...

6 Which shops do you go to regularly? Which do you never go to? Why? Compare your lists and shopping habits with the class.

EVERYDAY ENGLISH

Prices

1 Look at the way we write and say prices. Practise saying them.

Written	Spoken
£1	a pound
50p	fifty p
£1.99	one pound ninety-nine
£16.40	sixteen pounds forty
$1	a dollar
50¢	fifty cents
$1.50	a dollar fifty
€1	a euro
€20	twenty euros

2 What's the exchange rate between sterling/US dollars and your currency?

There are about five … to the dollar.

In your country, how much is … ?

- a litre of petrol
- a pack of cigarettes
- a cappuccino
- a loaf of bread
- a pair of jeans
- a CD

3 **T 4.9** Listen to the conversations. What are they about? Write the numbers you hear.

Open extended hours 7 days a week
CHANGING the way you change money
Please keep your receipt
MTM Money Ltd   www.mtm.co.uk
- - - - - - - - - - - - - - - -
Date: 20/02/07   Time: 10:30   Cashier: 144
SELL NOTES
Product: DOLLAR ($)
Amount: 150.00
Rate: 1.8757
Commission: 2.00
Subtotal: 79.97

BUY NOTES
Product: POUND (£)
Amount: 79.97
Rate: –
Commission: 0.00
Subtotal: 79.97

Payment: Visa
Amount: $152.00
- - - - - - - - - - - - - - - -
Thank you for your custom

4 Complete the conversations below with the lines from the box.

How much is it?	Right, that's £2.40 change.
That's £24.50, please.	I am sorry. That's £7.40, then.
And can I cash a traveller's cheque for $100?	
That's £150, plus £2 commission.	
£8 for an adult, £4.50 for children under 12.	

1 A Hello. I'm looking for this month's edition of *Vogue*.
   B Over there. Middle shelf. Next to *Marie Claire* and *Cosmopolitan*.
   A Thanks. *how much is it?*
   B £2.60.
   A Here you are.
   B *Right that's £2.40 change*
   A Just a minute! I gave you a £10 note, not a £5 note.
   B *I am sorry. That's £7.40 then.*

2 A I'd like to change these dollars into sterling, please.
   B Right. How much is here?
   A $200.
   B *That's £150. plus £2 commission*
   A OK, thanks. *And can I cash traveller's cheque for $100?*
   B Certainly. Have you got your passport?
   A Yes, here it is.

3 A Hello. How much is it to get in?
   B *£8 for an adult, £4.50 for children under 12.*
   A OK. Two adults and three children, please.
   B Then it's cheaper if you have a family ticket. *That's £24.50. Please*
   A Thank you very much.

5 **T 4.10** Listen and check. Practise the conversations.

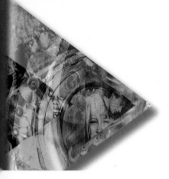

5 What do you want to do?

Verb patterns • Future forms • -ed/-ing adjectives • How are you feeling?

STARTER

Complete these sentences with ideas about you.

- One day I want to …
- Right now, I'd like to …
- I enjoy … because I like …
- On Sundays, I love …
- This weekend I'm going to …

HOPES AND AMBITIONS
Verb patterns

1 Match the people in the photo with their hopes and ambitions.

1 c I'd like to be a vet. I've got three pets – two rabbits and a kitten called Princess.
2 e I'm going to study hard and get really good grades in all my exams.
3 b I'm thinking of changing my job, because I'm tired of travelling all the time.
4 d I'm looking forward to going on a world cruise with my friend, Margaret.
5 e I'd love to be in a rock band. I want to play lead guitar.
6 a I hope to go back to college and train to be a primary school teacher.

T 5.1 Listen and check.

2 Listen again and complete the chart.

	Ambitions/Plans	Reasons
Ella	To be a Vet	She loves looking after her pets
Joe	He wants to be lead guitarist	He loves it and right all the songs.
Juliet	go to Uni	stading hard to get good grades
Hannah	to go back to college and train to be a primary school teacher.	she has work part time and she is enged.It
David	He wents to changing his Job and start his own businass.	He is tird of travelling.
Edie	she is going on a world cruise.	she engoes meeting new pcPole and seeing new places

3 Underline the examples of verb + infinitive and verb + -ing in exercise 1.

I'd like to be a vet … .

Look at the tapescript on p119. Find more examples.

b David, 46

a Hannah, 40

e Joe, 11

1 Complete the sentences with the words *go abroad*. Put the verb *go* in the correct form.

> I want *to go abroad*.
> I'd like . . .
> I'm looking forward to . . .
> I hope . . .
> I enjoy . . .
> I'm thinking of . . .
> I love . . .
> I'd love . . .

2 What's the difference between these sentences?

> *I like going to the cinema.*
> *I'd like to go to the cinema tonight.*

▶▶ **Grammar Reference 5.1 p132**
▶▶ **Verb patterns p158**

c Ella, 8
d Edie, 70
f Juliet, 16

PRACTICE

Discussing grammar

1 In these sentences, *one* or *two* verbs are correct, but *not* all three. Tick (✓) the correct verbs.

1 I _____ to live in a hot country.
   a ✓ *want*   b ☐ *enjoy*   c ✓ *'d like*

2 We _____ going to Italy for our holidays.
   a ☐ *are hoping*   b ☐ *'re thinking of*   c ✓ *like*

3 I _____ going shopping at the weekend.
   a ✓ *want*   b ✓ *like*   c ☐ *love*

4 I _____ to see you again soon.
   a ✓ *hope*   b ✓ *'d like*   c ☐ *'m looking forward*

5 Do you _____ learning English?
   a ✓ *want*   b ☐ *enjoy*   c ✓ *like*

6 We _____ having a few days off soon.
   a ✓ *'re thinking of*   b ☐ *'d love to*   c ✓ *'re looking forward to*

Make sentences with the other verbs.

I enjoy living in a hot country.

Making questions

2 Work with a partner and write **B**'s questions. Read the conversations aloud.

1 **A** I hope to go to university.
   B (What/want/study?) _____ ?

2 **A** One of my favourite hobbies is cooking.
   B (What/like/make?) _____ ?

3 **A** I get terrible headaches.
   B (When/start/get/them?) _____ ?

4 **A** We're planning our summer holidays at the moment.
   B (Where/think/go?) _____ ?

5 **A** I'm bored.
   B (What/like/do/tonight?) _____ ?

T 5.2 Listen and check. What are **A**'s answers? Practise the conversations again. Pay attention to stress and intonation.

Talking about you

3 Ask and answer the questions with a partner.

- Do you like learning English?
- Would you like to learn another foreign language?
- What are you thinking of doing on Saturday morning?
- What do you enjoy doing in the evenings?
- Do you want to get married one day?
- How many children do you hope to have?

FUTURE INTENTIONS

going to, will and Present Continuous for future

1 Match the photos and sentences.

1. ☐d They're going to buy a house.
2. ☐ I'll give you a lift to the station if you like.
3. ☐a She's going to travel round North America.
4. ☐ It's OK. I'll answer it.
5. ☐ Don't worry. I'll lend you some.
6. ☐ I'm going to stay in and watch the football on TV.

2 Use the sentences opposite to add one line **before** and one line **after** each sentence in exercise 1.

> *Why are Peter and Jane saving all their money?*
>
> 1 *They're going to buy a house.*
>
> *Really? Does that mean they're going to get married?*

3 ▭**T 5.3**▭ Listen and check. Practise the conversations with a partner.

before

I haven't got enough money.
What's Annie doing this summer?
The phone's ringing.
Oh no! I'm late. I'm going to miss my train.
What are you doing tonight?
~~Why are Peter and Jane saving all their money?~~

after

That's great. Can we go now? It leaves at five past.
Well if it's Susan, say I'm not in.
Thanks. I'll pay you back tomorrow. I won't forget. I promise.
Lucky her!
~~Really? Does that mean they're going to get married?~~
Oh, of course. Arsenal are playing Chelsea, aren't they?

GRAMMAR SPOT

1 All the sentences in exercise 1 express future intentions.
Which two future forms are used?
Which form means you've already decided?
Which form means you're deciding as you speak?

2 Notice the forms of *will*.

  I'll = short form   *I won't* = negative short form

3 The Present Continuous can express a future arrangement.

> What **are** you **doing** tonight?
> Arsenal **are playing** Chelsea tonight.

▶▶ **Grammar Reference 5.2 p132**

PRACTICE

Discussing grammar

1 Choose the correct verb form.

1 That bag looks heavy. *I'll carry / I'm going to carry* it for you.

2 I bought some warm boots because *I'll go / I'm going* skiing.

3 **A** Tony's back from holiday.
   B Is he? *I'll give / I'm going to give* him a ring.

4 **A** What *will you do/ are you doing* tonight?
   B *We'll see / We're going to see* a play at the theatre.

5 You can tell me your secret. *I won't tell / I'm not telling* anyone.

6 Congratulations! I hear *you'll get married / you're getting married*.

7 **A** I need to post these letters.
   B *I'll go / I'm going* shopping soon. *I'll post / I'm going to post* them for you.

8 **A** What *will we have / are we having* for lunch?
   B *I'm going to make / I make* a lasagne.

T 5.4 Listen and check.

2 **T 5.5** Close your books. Listen to the beginnings of the conversations from exercise 1. Complete them.

Check it

3 Correct the sentences.

1 'What you like to drink?' 'I have a coffee, please.'
2 Where are the changing rooms? I like try on these jeans.
3 I can't go out because a friend of mine will come to see me.
4 I'm looking forward to see you again soon.
5 I think to change my job soon.
6 Phone me tonight. I give you my phone number.
7 I see the doctor tomorrow about my back.

What are you doing tonight?

4 Work in pairs. You need to arrange a time to meet over the next few days. Talk together to find a time when you are both free.

Student A Look at your diary on p145.
Student B Look at your diary on p148.

> What are you doing on Monday afternoon?

> I'm playing tennis with Andy. Are you doing anything on Tuesday evening?

 **WRITING** Filling in a form **p107**

LISTENING AND SPEAKING
Song – *The voice within*

1 What are typical problems that young people have? Write down three and compare your ideas with a partner. Who can help with the problems? Is it always best to talk to other people?

2 **T 5.6** Close your books and listen to a song by Christina Aguilera, called *The voice within*. What do you think the problem is? Who is talking to who?

A parent to a child
A boyfriend to a girlfriend
A friend to a friend

3 Read the first verse and the chorus of the song.

The voice within

Young girl, don't cry.
I'll be right here when your world starts to fall.
Young girl, it's alright.
Your tears will dry, you'll soon be free to fly.

Chorus
When there's no one else, look inside yourself.
Like your oldest friend just trust the voice within
Then you'll find the strength that will guide your way.
If you will learn to begin to trust the voice within

Discuss the questions.

1 Do you think the person giving advice is older or younger? Why?
2 What does the person promise to do?
3 What is the advice in the chorus?
4 What does she mean by 'the voice within'?

4 **T 5.6** Look at the song on p150. Choose the best word in italics to complete the song. Listen again and compare.

Talking about you

• When do you ask others for advice? For what kind of problems? Who do you ask?
• When do you decide on your own?

READING AND SPEAKING
Brat camp

1 The teenage years can be difficult for both children and parents. Why, do you think? What can go wrong? Why do teenagers feel the need to rebel against their parents?

2 Work in small groups. Read the actions in the box. Decide which are *very bad*, and which are *not very bad* behaviour for a teenager. Complete the chart.

| telling lies   playing truant   arguing with adults   drinking alcohol |
| stealing   taking drugs   swearing   fighting and bullying   cheating in exams |

very bad	not very bad

3 Read the introduction and the first half of the article about Ned, Emily, and Jamie. Which of the activities in exercise 2 were they guilty of?

4 Answer the questions.
1 The brat camp is also called a 'behaviour camp' and a 'tough therapy camp'. Why?
2 Why are the parents so desperate? What do they hope will happen?
3 What does Ned's mother think is going to happen to him? Who does she blame?
4 Which of the teenagers …?
   • is selfish   • has a negative opinion of life   • sees hope in the future

5 Look at the pictures. What do you think happens at the camp?

6 Read the rest of the article. Did you guess what happens at the camp?

7 Answer the questions.
1 In what ways is life at the camp different for the teenagers? What can't they do?
2 What do they learn to do?
3 When can they go home?
4 What were the teenagers' first experiences of life in the camp?
5 How did life in the camp change them?
6 What are their hopes and ambitions now?

What do you think?
• Why do you think the teenagers have to give up the things from their old lives?
• Why is physical activity so important?
• Do you feel sorry for the teenagers? Or more sorry for the parents?
• Why do you think these teenagers had problems?

BRAT CAMP

What do you do with a teenager that swears at you, steals, lies, fights, drinks, takes drugs, and is completely out of control?

Desperate parents from all over the world are sending their difficult teenagers to behaviour camps in the Utah mountains, hoping that they will come back as the children they once knew and loved. Meet these three troubled teenagers. Will the tough therapy camp help them or will they return home the same rebellious brats?

Ten weeks. Three teenagers. One last chance.

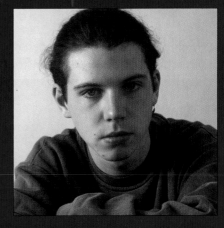

Ned, aged 16

Ned has always argued with his mother and no longer lives at home. 'I lie, steal, and cheat. I've got a drug problem,' he says. 'I hate everything.' His dad died when he was nine.

His mother says, 'He's going to end up in prison, and it'll be my fault.'

Emily, aged 15

Emily was a happy girl who did well at school. Now she plays truant all the time. Her behaviour changed at 13, when her mother remarried. She drinks a lot, stays out all night, and bullies her mother. 'It's my life and I can do what I want,' she says.

Jamie, aged 17

Jamie is a very intelligent boy, but five schools asked him to leave in just three years. His parents are divorced. 'I fight a lot,' he says. 'I'm going to end up in prison or seriously hurt if I don't go to this camp. I hope it helps.'

Far away from the outside world, the teenagers have to give up all the things from their old lives, including body piercings, cigarettes, music, mobile phones, and their fashionable clothes. There are a lot of rules to follow and physical activity is very important. They go on long hikes through the mountains, and sleep in tents at night. They learn to look after themselves and each other, and be responsible. They discuss their problems with the camp psychologist, who decides when they are ready to go home. The average time is ten weeks.

Ned felt very ill at first, as he couldn't take drugs any more. 'It was tough, but I feel better now. I don't feel depressed any more. I'm really looking forward to seeing my family. I'd love to live at home again,' he says.

Emily had to take out all of her 18 body piercings. She was shocked by camp life and cried all the time. 'I hated camp, but I've learnt that everything I do affects other people. I'm sorry I was so horrible to my mum. I hope I can go back to school. I want to be a nurse.'

At first Jamie had terrible problems following orders from the camp staff. But then he began to enjoy the outdoor life. He says, 'It was an incredible experience. I've got more self-control now. I'm going to join the army.'

VOCABULARY AND SPEAKING
-ed/-ing adjectives

1 Complete the sentences to describe these situations and experiences. Use an adjective from the box.

frightening	surprising	exhausting
relaxing	annoying	depressing

1 I heard footsteps in the middle of the night.
  'That's really ...'
2 The bus was full. I had to wait for the next one, so I was late for work.
  'That's so ...'
3 I saw Andy eating a burger! I thought he was vegetarian.
  'That's very ...'
4 I was lying on the beach in the sun all day yesterday.
  'How ...'
5 On my holiday it rained every day.
  'That's just so ...'
6 I ran my first full marathon on Sunday.
  'How ...'

T 5.7 Listen and check.

2 Imagine you were in the situations. How did you feel?

> I heard footsteps in the middle of the night.
> I was really frightened.

T 5.8 Listen and compare.

3 Complete the sentences. Use one of the adjectives.

shock-	
bor-	
excit-	**-ed**
confus-	**-ing**
disappoint-	
frighten-	
annoy-	
fascinat-	

1 **A** I watched a horror film on my own last night.
  B Were you _____ ?
2 **A** I spent four hours going round a museum.
  B Oh, no! Was it _____ ?
  A Actually, it was really _____ . I loved it.
3 **A** Did you see the way she behaved!
  B Yes, it was _____ . Don't invite her next time!
4 I had a second interview but I didn't get the job. I'm so _____ .
5 The teacher was _____ because all the students were late.
6 My daughter is very _____ because it's her birthday tomorrow.
7 I don't know how this camera works! The instructions are really _____ .

T 5.9 Listen and check.

4 What have you seen on television, DVD or at the cinema recently? What books have you read? What did you think of them? Tell the class.

> I read a spy story. It was very exciting.

> I saw a programme about DNA on TV last night. I was fascinated.

EVERYDAY ENGLISH
How are you feeling?

1 Look at the pictures. How are the people feeling?
Choose an adjective from the box.

angry   excited   worried   fed up   nervous   ill

2 All the lines in **A** answer the question *How are you feeling?*
Match a line in **A** with a line in **B**. Read them aloud with feeling.

A	B
1 I feel a bit nervous.	It's so wet and miserable.
2 I don't feel very well.	I'm going on holiday to Australia tomorrow!
3 I'm feeling a lot better, thanks.	We're in love!
4 I'm so angry!	I think I'm getting a cold.
5 I'm really excited!	My grandfather's going into hospital for tests.
6 I'm fed up with this weather.	I've got an exam today.
7 I'm a bit worried.	I don't think I have many friends.
8 We're really happy!	I got a parking ticket this morning. Sixty pounds!
9 I sometimes feel a bit lonely, actually.	Not quite back to normal, but nearly.

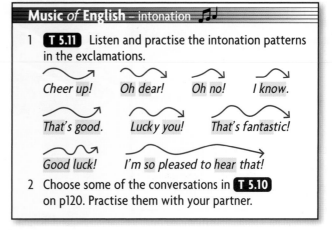

3 Choose a reply to the pairs of lines in exercise 2.

  a Cheer up! You've got me. I'm always here for you.
  b Oh dear! Why don't you go home to bed?
  c Oh no! Didn't you get one last week as well?
  d I know. We really need some sunshine, don't we?
  e That's good. I'm so pleased to hear that.
  f Lucky you! Have a good time!
  g That's fantastic! I'm so pleased for you both!
  h Good luck! Just do your best. That's all you can do.
  i I'm sorry to hear that! I'm sure he'll be all right.

T 5.10 Listen and check.

> **Music** *of* **English** – intonation 🎵
>
> **1** **T 5.11** Listen and practise the intonation patterns
> in the exclamations.
>
> *Cheer up!*   *Oh dear!*   *Oh no!*   *I know.*
>
> *That's good.*   *Lucky you!*   *That's fantastic!*
>
> *Good luck!*   *I'm so pleased to hear that!*
>
> **2** Choose some of the conversations in **T 5.10**
> on p120. Practise them with your partner.

4 Have conversations with a partner about these things:

  • a party   • a visit to the dentist   • winning £1000
  • a headache   • problems with parents   • the weather

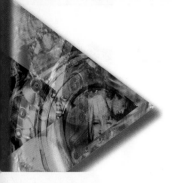

6 Places and things

STARTER

What is your favourite . . . ?

- town
- sport
- film
- food
- song
- building

Write your answers and compare with a partner.

MY FAVOURITE THINGS
What's it like?

1 Look at the photos of the singer Leroy and some of his favourite things? What are they?

2 Which of these adjectives do you think go with the pictures? Discuss with a partner.

sad	brilliant	beautiful	talented
spicy	shocking	funny	exciting
fantastic	delicious	amazing	

T 6.1 Listen to Leroy. Which adjectives does he use to describe his favourite things?

GRAMMAR SPOT

1 Match the questions and answers.

Do you like soul music?	*It's sad. / It's beautiful.*
What's soul music like?	*Yes, I do. / No, I don't.*

2 Which question in 1 means *Tell me about soul music*?

▶▶ **Grammar Reference 6.1 p134**

a

b

R&B singer Leroy

c
THE BEST OF
SOUL
The greatest soul hits of the last three decades

d
VINTAGE FUTURE CLASSICS EDITION WITH READING GUIDE
ALDOUS HUXLEY
BRAVE NEW WORLD

e

PRACTICE

What's London like?

1 Leroy is answering questions about his home town, London. Complete the questions with *is* or *are* and the correct words from the box.

> ~~London~~   the restaurants   the people
> the buildings   the night-life   the weather

1 **Q** What <u>'s London</u> _____ like?
  A Well, it's a really exciting city! There's so much going on all the time.

2 **Q** What _____ like?
  A It's OK, and not very cold in winter, but people don't come here for the sunshine!

3 **Q** What _____ like?
  A They're very interesting. They come from all over the world. London's a very cosmopolitan city.

4 **Q** What _____ like?
  A Fantastic! Lots of them are historical and famous, but there are some wonderful modern ones, too.

5 **Q** What _____ like?
  A They're great! You can find food from every country in the world.

6 **Q** What _____ like?
  A Oh, it's amazing! There are so many clubs and theatres, and, of course, the music scene is fantastic!

2 **T 6.2** Listen and check. Practise with a partner.

3 Ask and answer the same questions about the town or city you are in now.

GOOD, BETTER, BEST!
Comparatives and superlatives

Berlin   Tokyo   Detroit

1 Last year Leroy sang in these three cities. What do you know about them?

T 6.3 Read and listen to Leroy (**L**) and the interviewer (**I**). Complete the interview.

I Do you travel a lot, Leroy?

L Oh yeah. I sing all over the world. Last year I was in Berlin, Tokyo – oh, and of course, Detroit.

I And what are they _____ ?

L Well, they're all big, busy cities. Tokyo's the biggest and the _____ . It's _____ bigger _____ Berlin.

I And is it _____ interesting?

L Well, they're all interesting, but, in fact, for me the _____ interesting is Detroit.

I Really? Why?

L Well, in some ways, perhaps it isn't as interesting _____ the other two cities – it doesn't have historical buildings, or beautiful, old Japanese temples – but you see, Detroit is the birthplace of soul music and that's everything to me.

I I see. So Detroit's best for music. And what about food? Which is the _____ city for food?

L Ah, the food. For me there's no question, Tokyo definitely has the _____ delicious food – I just love Japanese food!

I I see. Is it even better _____ chicken satay?

L Ah, I don't know about that!

PRACTICE

2 Work with a partner. Compare some cities in your country.

Pronunciation

3 **T 6.4** Listen and repeat the sentences. Pay attention to the /ə/ sound.

/bɪgə ðən/
Tokyo's bigger than Berlin.

/əz bɪg əz/
Berlin isn't as big as Tokyo.

4 Practise these sentences with a partner.

Is Peter as old as you?

He's older than us, but younger than you.

Their teacher's funnier than ours.

Our lessons are more interesting than theirs.

T 6.5 Listen and check.

5 **T 6.6** Learn this poem by heart. Say it as a class.

**'Good, better, best.
Never, never rest
'til your good is better,
and your better best.'**

Test your general knowledge

1 Work in teams. Compare the things using the comparative and superlative forms of the adjectives.

> The ... is taller than the ..., but the ... is the tallest.

1	tall	Petronas Towers (Kuala Lumpur)
		Eiffel Tower (Paris)
		Empire State Building (New York)
2	small	Monaco Vatican City Andorra
3	big	Atlantic Ocean Arctic Ocean Pacific Ocean
4	fast	horse human elephant
5	expensive	Porsche Ferrari Rolls Royce
6	dangerous	lion shark hippopotamus

2 **T 6.7** Read your answers aloud. Listen and check. Which team has the most correct answers?

3 In your team, write one more general knowledge question comparing three things. Ask another team.

Talking about you

4 Work with a partner. Compare the things. Which do you like best?

Type of holiday	Type of film	Type of music
• skiing	• comedy	• jazz
• beach	• thriller	• rap
• sightseeing	• science fiction	• classical
• camping	• romance	• rock

Conversations

5 Work with a partner. Complete and then continue the conversations.

1 **A** I moved to a new flat last week.
  B Oh, really? What's it like?
  A Well, it's ___bigger___ than my old one but ___it isn't as modern, and___ …

2 **A** I hear Alice and Henry broke up.
  B Yeah. Alice's got a new boyfriend.
  A Oh, really? What's he like?
  B Well, he's _____ than Henry, and …

3 **A** We've got a new teacher.
  B Oh, really? What's she like?
  A Well, I think she's the _____ teacher we've ever had …

4 **A** Is that your new car?
  B Well, it's second-hand, but it's new to me.
  A What's it like?
  B Well, it's _____ than my old car, …

Choose a conversation. Learn it by heart. Act it to the class.

T 6.8 Listen and compare.

Check it

6 Correct these sentences.
1 He's more older than he looks.
2 Jessica's as tall than her mother.
3 **A** What does New York like?
  B It's really exciting!
4 London is more expensive that Paris.
5 The University of Oxford is one of oldest universities in Europe.
6 He isn't as intelligent than his sister.
7 This is more hard than I expected.
8 Who is the most rich man in the world?
9 Everything is more cheap in my country.
10 Rome was hotter that I expected.

LISTENING AND SPEAKING
The best things in life are free

1 What pleasures are there in life that don't cost anything? Think of three things you love that are free. Compare your ideas with a partner, then the class. Make a list.

2 **T 6.9** Listen to five people talking about the best things in their lives that are free. Put these photos in the order you hear them. Compare them with your list. Are any of them the same?

3 **T 6.9** Listen again and complete the chart. Compare your answers with a partner.

	What?	**Why?**	**Is it free?**
Ben, 15			
Mary, 55			
Michael, 36			
Laura, 8			
Kiera, 24			

4 Choose one of your favourite free things. Make some notes about the reasons why you like it.

Work with a partner. Now talk about it for one minute without stopping. Your partner will time you.

READING AND SPEAKING
London: the world in one city

1 What is the capital city of your country? Write down two things that you like about your capital and two things that you don't like. Tell the class.

> I like the shops, but I don't like all the traffic.

2 Describe your capital city. What is it like? How big is it? Is it old or modern? Is it very cosmopolitan? Which nationalities live there?

3 Read the introduction to the article on this page. Are these sentences true (✓) or false (✗), according to the article?

1 London is more cosmopolitan than Toronto.
2 New York is the most diverse city ever.
3 Londoners don't work as hard as people in other cities.
4 Immigrants want their children to learn English.
5 Londoners are the friendliest people in the world.
6 Londoners only like eating English food.
7 Most Londoners want to leave the city eventually.

4 Work in two groups to answer the questions about your texts.

Group A Read texts 1 and 3.
Group B Read texts 2 and 4.

1 Who are the people in the photo?
   Where are they?
   What are they doing?
2 What nationality are they?
3 Write the names of …
   the owner/manager
   the shop/café/restaurant
   the area of London where it is
4 What other nationality is mentioned?
5 Are/Were there any problems between nationalities?
6 What food is mentioned?
   What's it called?
   What's it like?

5 Work with a partner from the other group. Compare the communities, using your answers to exercise 4.

What do you think?

• Why do so many nationalities choose to live in London?
• Are there any groups of foreigners living in your town? Where do they come from? What do they find different? Do they mix with other groups, or keep themselves apart?

 **WRITING** Describing a place **p108**

London:

GREATER LONDON
Green Lanes
CENTRAL LONDON
River Thames
Peckham
Stockwell
New Malden

Leo Benedictus spent months interviewing the immigrant communities that give the city of London its vitality and, more importantly, its food!

New York and Toronto may think they are more cosmopolitan, but London in the 21st century is certainly the most diverse city ever. This is one of the reasons why it was chosen to host the 2012 Olympic Games. More than 300 languages are spoken by the people of London, and it has 50 nationalities with populations of more than 10,000.

Why is this? Firstly, London is a place of business. Londoners have the fewest bank holidays in Europe and work the longest hours. People come for jobs and money. But that is not why they stay. Language is one reason. Fluency in English is a great gift for their children. Another surprising reason is the character of the London people. They are not as friendly as some other nationalities. But this has advantages – people leave you alone, and you are free to live your own life. Finally, the most delicious reason is – food. You can have dinner in more than 70 different nationalities of restaurant any night of the week. Londoners' enthusiasm for foreign food creates thousands of jobs for new communities.

All Londoners, old and new, have the same principles. They work hard, love their children, and move out of the city centre as soon as they can afford it!

1 Posh Daddy from Nigeria

Posh Daddy is the manager of the Big Choice Barber's on Peckham High Street. It is a West Indian and African hairdresser's. These two black communities haven't always got on well together. 'When I first came here, we just wanted to be accepted by the West Indian community, but they weren't very friendly,' he says. 'Now it is getting better. These days most of my West Indian brothers in the barber's like eating African food like me, pepper soup and *kuku paka*, which is chicken with coconut – very hot and spicy.'

2 Staff in the kitchen of the Asadal

'This restaurant was a little bit of Korea brought into a very English town,' says Young-il Park, the manager of the Asadal restaurant in New Malden. The Asadal is famous for its *kimchi* – salty, spicy chilli peppers and vegetables. Young-il's father opened the Asadal in 1991 – the first Korean restaurant in the town. Young-il was the only Korean in his school. 'The thing I noticed most was that people stared,' he says. 'Now you see a lot of Koreans here.'

3 The staff in the Yasar Halim Bakery

Yasar Halim, a Turkish grocer's and baker's, is known all over London. It was opened in Green Lanes in 1981 by Mr Halim, a Turkish Cypriot. At that time, no one was selling food from his homeland. Now the shop is famous for its *baklava*, a sweet cake made with nuts and honey. The shop is very busy, and the staff working there – both Turkish and Greek Cypriots – look like they're having a great time together. In their homeland of Cyprus, there are still problems between the two communities. But in this area of London, they live together as good neighbours.

4 Portuguese football fans in the FC Porto Fan Club in Stockwell

'Football is a passion for us,' says José Antonio Costa, the president of the Porto Fan Club which meets in Stockwell. 'Many people come for friendship – you know, in a foreign country, you feel more comfortable with your own people.'

Eric Santos, the owner of Santos's café near the club, says, 'People come for my wife's *bacalhau* – salted cod, made with potatoes and onions. Delicious!' There is quite a big Portuguese-speaking community here, from Portugal, Brazil and Madeira, but they do not always stick together. 'Everyone looks after their own interests.' The Portuguese and the Madeirans, in particular, are very separate groups in London, because Madeira wants independence from Portugal.

VOCABULARY AND PRONUNCIATION
Synonyms and antonyms in conversation

Synonyms

1 **T 6.10** We often use synonyms in conversation because we don't want to repeat words. Listen and repeat. Practise with a partner.

Isn't it a lovely day!

Yes, its really beautiful.

2 Complete the conversations, using a synonym from the box.

| generous   fed up   fantastic   messy   rude   modern |

1 **A** Look at all these **new** buildings!
  B Yes. Paris is much more _____ than I expected.

2 **A** Wasn't that film **brilliant**?
  B Absolutely! It was _____ . We loved it.

3 **A** Your bedroom's really **untidy**. Again!
  B What do you mean? It doesn't look _____ to me.

4 **A** I couldn't believe it, their son was so **impolite** to me.
  B Don't worry. He's _____ to everyone.

5 **A** Dan doesn't earn much, but he's always so **kind**.
  B He is, isn't he? He's one of the most _____ people I know.

6 **A** I'm **bored** with this exercise!
  B I know. I'm _____ with it, too!

T 6.11 Listen and check. Practise the conversations with your partner. Pay particular attention to stress and intonation.

Antonyms

3 **T 6.12** We can also use antonyms in conversation to avoid repeating words. Listen and repeat.

Ugh! My soup's cold!

I know, mine's not very hot either.

4 Write a synonym and an antonym for the adjectives.

Adjective	Synonym (same)	Antonym (opposite)
bored	fed up	interested
wonderful		
modern		
impolite		
untidy		
generous		
cold		
miserable		

Music *of* English – stress and intonation ♪♫

Sometimes we use *not very* with an antonym because it sounds more polite.

T 6.13 Listen and repeat. Practise the stress and intonation.

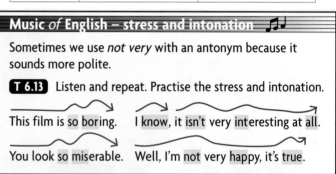

This film is so boring.   I know, it isn't very interesting at all.

You look so miserable.   Well, I'm not very happy, it's true.

---

5 Reply to these sentences in a polite way.
1 Tokyo's such an expensive city.
2 Paul and Sue are so mean.
3 Their house is always so messy.
4 That sales assistant was so rude!
5 Jim looks really miserable.
6 This exercise is so boring!

T 6.14 Listen and check. Practise the conversations with your partner.

EVERYDAY ENGLISH
A city break

1 Rolf has booked a city break. He is going for three nights with his friend, Jonas. Look at the pictures and complete the online booking form.

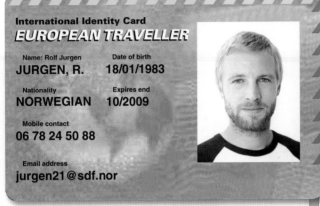

International Identity Card
EUROPEAN TRAVELLER

Name: Rolf Jurgen
JURGEN, R.

Date of birth
18/01/1983

Nationality
NORWEGIAN

Expires end
10/2009

Mobile contact
06 78 24 50 88

Email address
jurgen21@sdf.nor

Metropole Hostel Online Booking

Booking details

Check in date	12 July
Number of nights	
Number of people	

Please select a room

Price per person per night
6 bed mixed dorm	20€	
6 bed female dorm	25€	

Customer details

First name: Rolf   Last name:
email: Phone number:
Gender M ☐ F ☐   Nationality:

Credit card details

Card holder's name:
Credit card number: 257868
Card type: Visa   Expiry date: 07/12 MM/YY

Total cost of rooms: ☐ €
Booking fee: 10 €
Total: ☐ €

I have read and accept the <u>Terms and Conditions</u> ☐

---

2 Rolf and Jonas are in the Tourist Office. Make questions from columns A and B. Match a question with a leaflet.

Where can I buy a new backpack?   *Orchard Shopping Centre – c*

A	B
	can I buy a new backpack?
	exhibitions are showing this week?
Where	's the nearest cashpoint?
	does the metro stop running?
How much	can I get something to eat?
	does the tour take?
What time	play is on this week?
	is a travel card for a week?
How long	can I get a battery for my camera?
	is there a bar with live music?
What	

3 **T 6.15** Listen to a conversation between Rolf, Jonas, and someone who works in the tourist office. What do Rolf and Jonas want to do and see? What problems are there?

4 **T 6.15** Listen again and complete the lines of conversation with the exact words.

1 Excuse me. _____ help me?
2 _____ a trip on one of those buses …
3 _____ does the tour _____ ?
4 How much _____ ?
5 … it's best _____ advance.
6 I _____ for my mother.
7 Is there a _____ here?
8 There's a good _____ .

5 In pairs, ask and answer the questions in exercise 2 about your town or city.

> **Where's the nearest cashpoint?**
>> Go out of the building and turn left. Walk to the post office. It's about five minutes.

Planning a break

6 Plan a two-day break for someone coming to your town. Include information on:
- Where to stay/eat/shop …
- What to see/do …
- How to get around

7 Fame!

Present Perfect · *for, since* · Word endings · Making conversation 2

STARTER

What is the Past Simple and the past participle of these verbs? Are they regular or irregular?

write	be	make	win	have
read	do	get	know	become

▶▶ **Irregular verbs *p158***

FAMOUS FAMILIES
Present Perfect and Past Simple

1 Look at the photographs. How do you think the people are related?

2 Who are the sentences referring to? Write the names.

1 _____ invented psychoanalysis to help his patients.

2 _____ governed the tiny principality for nearly 56 years.

3 _____ has made clothes for many famous people, including Madonna.

4 _____ was a founder member of *The Beatles*.

5 _____ has modelled for *Vogue* and Yves Saint Laurent.

6 _____ has been in the music business since 1984.

7 _____ wrote many children's books, including *Charlie and the Chocolate Factory* and *The BFG (The Big Friendly Giant)*.

8 _____ has been married three times and has four children.

T 7.1 Listen and check.

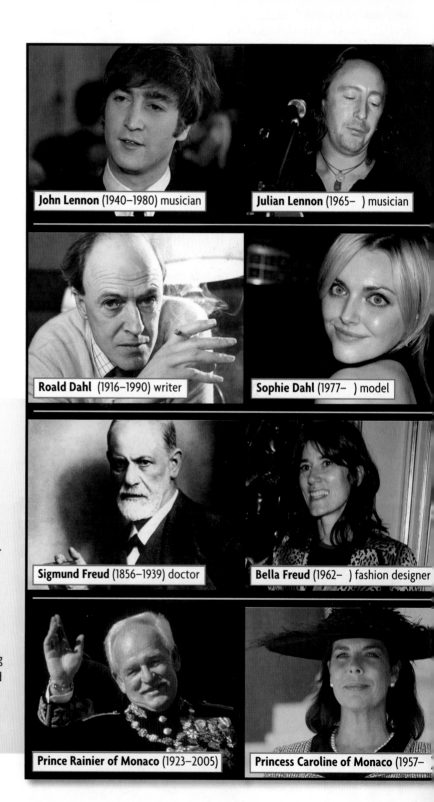

John Lennon (1940–1980) musician

Julian Lennon (1965–) musician

Roald Dahl (1916–1990) writer

Sophie Dahl (1977–) model

Sigmund Freud (1856–1939) doctor

Bella Freud (1962–) fashion designer

Prince Rainier of Monaco (1923–2005)

Princess Caroline of Monaco (1957–

1 Find examples of the Past Simple in the sentences in exercise 2. Find examples of the Present Perfect.

2 Why are the different tenses used in these sentences?

*John Lennon **made** a lot of records.*
*Julian Lennon **has made** a lot of records.*

Why is this sentence wrong?

John Lennon has played with the Beatles for 12 years.

3 *For* and *since* are often used with the Present Perfect. Look at the examples. When do we use *for*? When do we use *since*?

for *two hours/six weeks/ten years*
since *six o'clock/yesterday/last week/1997*

▶▶ **Grammar Reference 7.1 and 7.2 p135**

3 Put the verbs in the Present Perfect or Past Simple.

1 **John Lennon** __started__ (start) his first band when he was 15. His eldest son, **Julian,** __has been__ (be) in the music business since he was 19. He _____ (make) five albums. He _____ (not know) his father very well.

2 **Roald Dahl** _____ (write) the story *The BFG* in 1982 for his granddaughter, Sophie. It is about a little girl called Sophie. **Sophie Dahl** _____ (be) a model since she was 17, but she also likes writing. She _____ (write) some short stories and one novel.

3 **Sigmund Freud** _____ (work) in Vienna for most of his life. His great-granddaughter, **Bella Freud,** _____ (be born) in London and _____ (work) there since 1990. But when she was a fashion student, she _____ (live) in Rome.

4 **Prince Rainier of Monaco** _____ (marry) American film star Grace Kelly in 1956. Their daughter, **Caroline,** _____ (have) quite a tragic life. She _____ (divorce) her first husband after only two years and both her mother and her second husband _____ (die) in terrible accidents. She _____ (be) married to her third husband, Prince Ernst of Hanover, since 1999.

T 7.2 Listen and check.

4 Write questions using the prompts. Ask and answer with a partner.

1 When / John Lennon / start his first band?
2 How long / Julian Lennon / be in the music business?
3 When / Roald Dahl / write *The BFG*?
4 How many novels / Sophie Dahl / write?
5 Where / Sigmund Freud / work?
6 Where / Bella Freud / work since 1990?
7 Who / Prince Rainier / marry?
8 How many times / Princess Caroline / be married?

T 7.3 Listen and check.

PRACTICE

Discussing grammar

1 Choose the correct verb form.

1 *Have you ever been / Did you ever go* to a rock concert?
2 I *saw / have seen* U2 last week.
3 I love rock music. I *like / have liked* it all my life.
4 U2's concert *was / has been* fantastic.
5 I *have bought / bought* every record they *have made / made*.
6 U2 *have been / are* together since 1976.

Speaking

2 Your teacher will give you a card which begins *Find someone who …* .

Decide on the question, beginning *Have you ever … ?* Stand up, and ask everyone in the class.

Have you ever met a famous person?

No, I haven't.   Yes, I have.

Ask questions to find out more.

Who did you meet? What was he/she like?

3 Report back to the class.

Clara and Jacques have never met a famous person, but Mayumi has. She saw Tom Cruise at a film première.

for and *since*

4 Complete the time expressions with *for* or *since*.

1 _____ a year   4 _____ nine o'clock   7 _____ months
2 _____ August   5 _____ I was a student   8 _____ 1996
3 _____ a couple of days   6 _____ half an hour   9 _____ ages

5 Match the lines in **A**, **B**, and a sentence in **C**. There is more than one answer. Read them aloud to a partner.

A	B	C
1 I've known my best friend	from 2001 to 2005.	It's not bad. I quite like it.
2 I last went to the cinema	for an hour.	I went camping with some friends.
3 I've had this watch	two weeks ago.	We met when we were 10.
4 We've used this book	since 1999.	I really need a cup of coffee.
5 We lived in Edinburgh	since the beginning of term.	My dad gave it to me for my birthday.
6 We haven't had a break	for years.	We moved because I got a job in London.
7 I last had a holiday	for three years.	The film was terrible.
8 This building has been a school	in 2003.	Before that it was an office.

T 7.4 Listen, check, and practise. Make similar sentences about you using the lines in **A**.

Asking questions

6 Complete the conversation. What tenses are the three questions?

A Where _____ live, Anna?
B In a flat in Green Street.
A How long _____ there?
B Only for -er, ... three months. Yes, since June.
A And why _____ move?
B Well, we wanted to live near the park.

T 7.5 Listen and check. Practise the conversation with a partner.

7 Make more conversations, using the same tenses.

1 **A** What ... do?	2 **A** ... got a car?	3 **A** ... know Alan Brown?
B I work	**B** Yes, we	**B** Yes, I ... .
A Really? How long ... ?	**A** How long ... ?	**A** How long ... ?
B For	**B** Since	**B** For ... .
A And what ... do before that?	**A** ... pay a lot for it?	**A** Where ... meet him?
B I worked	**B** Not really, it was	**B** We ... .

T 7.6 Listen and compare.

8 With a partner, ask and answer questions beginning *How long ... ?*

> How long have you lived / worked / known / had ... ?

Then get some more information.

> Why did you move?   What did you do before ... ?   Where did you meet ... ?

how long ? *where ?* *why ?* *why ?* *when* *where ?* *why ?* *how long ? what* *what ?* *how much* *when ?*

LISTENING AND SPEAKING
The band *Goldrush*

1 What kind of music do you like? Who are your favourite bands and singers? If you could meet them, what would you ask them? Write some questions.

From left to right: Robin, Garo, Hamish, Graham, and Joe

2 Look at the photos. What kind of music do you think *Goldrush* play? What musical instruments can you see?

3 Read the questions to *Goldrush*. Are any of them similar to your questions from exercise 1?

1 Which two members of the band are brothers? How long have they played together?
2 How long have *Goldrush* been together as a band?
3 How did Robin's musical career begin?
4 Who has influenced the band? In what ways?
5 Why is touring the United States such an amazing experience?
6 How many albums have they made since 2002?
7 What are their future plans?

T 7.7 Listen to an interview with the members of the band and answer the questions.

4 **T 7.7** Listen again. Tick (✔) the correct boxes. Check answers with a partner.

Instruments they play	Bands/musicians they have played with	Places they have visited
☐ guitar	☐ Whispering Bob	☐ the United States
☐ piano	☐ Neil Young	☐ Poland
☐ bass	☐ The Flaming Lips	☐ Spain
☐ violin	☐ Bob Dylan	☐ South Africa
☐ trumpet	☐ Mark Gardener	☐ Hong Kong
☐ keyboards	☐ Six by Seven	☐ Azerbaijan
☐ saxophone		☐ Uzbekistan
☐ drums		☐ Australia

Language work

5 Make sentences about *Goldrush* with the time expressions.

Robin and Joe have had a band since they were teenagers.

A	B
since they were teenagers	in 1999
Robin/recently/Bob Dylan	Graham and Garo/2002
Spain twice so far	Hamish/two years ago
the US a few times	Robin/when he was at school
just finished/Ozona	Uzbekistan/last year

Which tense are all the verbs in **A**? Which tense are they in **B**? Why?

Roleplay

6 Work in groups of four. Three of you are members of a band. One is a journalist. Look at p151.

READING AND LISTENING
Davina Moody – Drama Queen

1 Write down the name of two celebrities who are in the news at the moment. Read the names aloud round the class. Say why they are in the news. What have they done?

2 Look at the photos and the title of the article about a famous film star. What is a 'drama queen'? Which of these adjectives do you think describe her?

> temperamental   easy-going   moody   spoilt   selfish
> thoughtful   kind   bad-tempered   talented

3 Read the first part of the article.
  1 How did Davina travel?
  2 Who did she travel with?
  3 Is Davina the first famous star to stay in the hotel?
  4 Did the hotel staff enjoy looking after her?

4 Look at the headings for the series of disasters. Work with a partner. What do you think the five disasters were? Share ideas with the class.

5 Read the article quickly. Whose ideas were most like the disasters? What were they?

6 Read the article again. Are these sentences true (✔) or false (✗)? Correct the false sentences.
  1 Davina Moody has hired 40 rooms in the hotel.
  2 The hotel manager has had a nervous breakdown.
  3 She has been a star for many years.
  4 She always wears yellow dresses.
  5 She didn't like the lighting in her room.
  6 She was very angry when the staff woke her up.
  7 She met hundreds of important people at the champagne reception.
  8 Her film was not successful.
  9 She sacked her manicurist.

What do you think?

What is your opinion of this movie star? Why does she behave like this?

T 7.8 Listen to Davina talking to a reporter about the article. What does she say? Who do you believe?

Project

Find an article about a celebrity from a newspaper or magazine. Is it a kind or an unkind article? Bring it into class and tell the class about it.

 **WRITING** A biography *p109*

Davina Moody
Drama Queen

Los Angeles
Wednesday, February 8th

She arrived by private jet on Sunday morning with a 20-strong entourage, including her PA (personal assistant), the PA to the PA, her hairdresser, make-up artist, manicurist, chef, dietician, masseuse, personal trainer, chauffeur, six bodyguards and, of course, a vet for her six-month-old King Charles Spaniel, Pooksie.

By Sunday evening the staff at California's Hollywood Hills Hotel, who have met and looked after some of the world's most famous and most temperamental film stars, felt that this star deserved an Oscar for her off-screen performance. Davina Moody was very moody, the moodiest of them all.

A Series of Disasters

MISS MOODY is in Hollywood to attend the première of her latest movie. She has hired 17 rooms in the hotel at a cost of $40,000 a night. Unfortunately, since her arrival, there have been a series of disasters. These have given the usually calm and patient Arnold Baglioni, hotel manager, a near nervous breakdown and played havoc with the normal running of his hotel.

1 No red carpet!

The first disaster came very soon after her arrival. Davina climbed out of her white stretch-limousine onto … the sidewalk. There was NO RED CARPET and Miss Moody NEVER walks on sidewalks. She hasn't walked on a sidewalk since she became a child star nearly 30 years ago.

2 No white roses!

Worse was to follow. The corridor leading to her rooms was lined with roses. Davina loves roses but these were yellow roses. She wanted *white* roses. She hates yellow roses. In fact Miss Moody hates anything yellow. She has never worn anything yellow in her life.

3 The wrong lighting!

Davina travels with a 'lighting director'. She has just employed a new lighting director. He has the job of organizing the lighting in any room to show her face to its best advantage. She likes pink lights. She looks younger with pink ones. The lights in her hotel room were … yellow! Miss Moody has now moved rooms and fired the lighting director.

4 Fire! Fire!

A real disaster! At midnight on Monday there was a fire in the hotel kitchens. The fire brigade arrived and ordered everyone to leave the building. However, the hotel staff were too afraid to wake Miss Moody. They decided to let her sleep. Fortunately the fire was small. After ten hours' sleep, Miss Moody woke in a bad mood. No one has had the courage to inform her of the danger she was in.

5 The worst disaster of all!

Tuesday was the big day – the première of *The Lady Loves To*. Before it, there was a special champagne reception. Hundreds of important people from the movie industry were invited to greet the beautiful star. They came and they waited … and waited. Three hours and 500 bottles of champagne later, Miss Moody's PA to the PA rushed into the room. The explanation? Davina was too upset to attend – she had a broken finger nail and nobody could find the manicurist.

A happy and not so happy ending!

Davina Moody missed the première. Perhaps this was fortunate. This morning's newspaper headlines read: DAVINA'S $10,000,000 MOVIE DISASTER. So her movie has flopped, and apparently the manicurist and Mr Baglioni have run away together to start a new life.

VOCABULARY AND SPEAKING
Word endings

1 Look at the common noun endings.

-er	-or	-ist	-ian	-ant

Find a job with each ending in the text on p59.

2 Use the endings to make more jobs from these words.

art	politics	music	account	decorate	photograph
reception	interpret	science	library	electric	law

T 7.9 Listen, check and repeat.

3 Look at the noun and adjective endings.

nouns	-ation	-sion	-ment	-ness	-ence	-al
adjectives	-y	-ly	-ous	-ful	-less	-al

Complete the charts. There are some spelling changes.

Noun	Verb
ar'rival	_____
'trainer	_____
invi'tation	_____
_____	'organize
_____	ex'plain
de'cision	_____
_____	em'ploy
im'provement	_____
dis'cussion	_____
_____	ag'ree
_____	i'magine
_____	'advertise

Noun	Adjective
mood	_____
friend	_____
fame	_____
_____	'patient
_____	'happy
_____	kind
_____	'different
'danger	_____
di'saster	_____
'beauty	_____
use	_____
help	_____

It's O.K. I'm not really in the mood, either.

Pronunciation – word stress

4 **T 7.10** Read the groups of nouns, adjectives, and verbs aloud. After each group listen, check, and repeat. Pay attention to the word stress.

1 Two-syllable **nouns** and **adjectives**. Where is the stress?

nouns	beauty	kindness	lawyer	artist	difference

adjectives	noisy	friendly	famous	different

2 Two-syllable **verbs**. Where is the stress?

arrive	invite	explain	improve	discuss	employ	agree

3 **Nouns** ending in *-tion* and *-sion*. Where is the stress?

invitation	explanation	information
ambition	decision	discussion

4 What is the difference in stress on these pairs of words? Say them aloud.

imagine / imagination	advertise / advertisement
politics / politician	photograph / photographer

Talking about you

5 Work with a partner. <u>Underline</u> the correct word in the questions. Ask and answer the questions.

1 Has your teacher got a lot of *patience* / *patient*?

2 Who is the most *patience* / *patient* person you know?

3 What puts you in a bad *mood* / *moody*?

4 Have you ever done anything very *danger* / *dangerous*?

5 What's the *difference* / *different* between an exam and a test?

6 Does your school *employ* / *employment* many teachers? How many?

7 Have you made much *improve* / *improvement* in your English over the last year?

8 What is your main *ambition* / *ambitious* in life?

9 Would you like to be a *politics* / *politician*?

10 What do you think is the secret of *happy* / *happiness*?

EVERYDAY ENGLISH
Making conversation 2 – short answers

1 **T 7.11** Listen to the conversations. Which answer sounds more polite? What are the differences?

Music *of* English – sounding polite

1 To sound polite, don't just answer *Yes* or *No*. Use the short answer.

Do you like cooking?   *Yes, I do.*

Have you ever been to Venice?   *No, I haven't.*

T 7.12 Listen and repeat. Pay attention to stress and intonation.

2 It's also a good idea to add more information.

Do you like cooking?   *Yes, I do, especially Italian food.*

Have you ever been to Venice?   *No, I haven't, but I'd love to go one day.*

T 7.13 Listen and repeat.

---

2 Complete the short answers. Practise with a partner.

1 'Are those new jeans you're wearing?' 'No, they _____?'
2 'Have you got the time, please?' 'No, I _____?'
3 'Can you play any musical instruments?' 'Yes, I _____ actually.'
4 'Do you like learning English?' 'Yes, I _____?'

T 7.14 Listen and check. What other information did you hear? Choose some of the conversations and practise them with your partner.

3 Complete the short answers. Then continue the conversation with the correct line from the box.

1 **A** Is it still raining?
  B No, _____ . _____ .
2 **A** Did you see the football last night?
  B Yes, _____ . _____ .
3 **A** Have you got change for a pound?
  B No, sorry, _____ . _____ .
4 **A** Have you tried the new pizza place?
  B Yes, _____ . _____ .
5 **A** Are you ambitious?
  B Yes, _____ . _____ .
6 **A** Are you doing anything tonight?
  B No, _____ . _____ ?

I've only got a ten-pound note
Why? What are *you* doing
It was a great game
It's just stopped
I went there last weekend with Frank
I want to have my own business one day

T 7.15 Listen and check. Choose one of the conversations. Continue it with a partner. Act it out to the class.

4 Think of questions to ask each other. Use these ideas to help you.

- Do you … like/play/go/have … ?
- Can you … ride/speak/run/use … ?
- Did you … go/have/win/do … last night?
- Have you ever … been/seen/tried/had … ?
- Are you … good at/afraid of … ?
- Have you got … a car/a CD player/a pet … ?

5 Stand up and ask your questions. Use short answers and give more information in your replies.

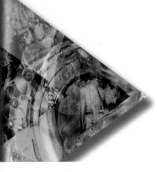

8 Do's and don'ts

have to • **should/must** • **Words that go together** • **At the doctor's**

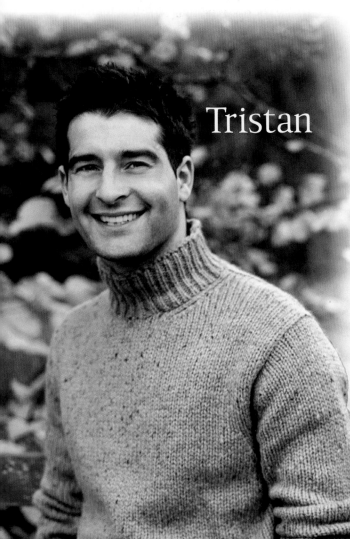

Tristan

> ### STARTER
>
> What's true for you? Make sentences about your life.
>
> **I have to …**   **I don't have to …**
> - get up early every morning   • do the housework
> - work at the weekend   • go to school
> - pay bills   • do homework

WHAT'S HIS JOB?
have to

1 **T 8.1** Listen to Tristan talking about his job. What do you think hi[s] job is? Does he work in the town or the country? Does he like his job[?]

2 Complete the lines from Tristan's interview with words from the box[.]

have to	don't have to	Do you have to	had to	didn't have to

I sometimes <u>have to</u> work at night.
<u>Do you have to</u> work at weekends?
When I'm on call, I <u>don't have to</u> stay in the surgery.
I <u>had to</u> study for five years.
I <u>didn't have to</u> look for a job.

3 Talk about Tristan. Change the sentences in exercise 2 using *he*.

> He sometimes has to work at night.
>> Does he … ?

4 Complete the questions and answers about Tristan.
  1 'How long <u>does</u> he have to <u>work</u> ?'
    'About 8 to 10 hours a day.'
  2 <u>Does</u> he <u>hdesto</u> work at night?'
    'Yes, he does.'
  3 'How long did he <u>have</u> to study?'
    'Five years.'
  4 'Why was he lucky?'
    'Because he didn't <u>have to</u> look for a job.'
  5 'What other things _____ Tristan _____ do?'
    'He has to _____.'

62 Unit 8 • Do's and don'ts

PRACTICE

Pronunciation

1 **T 8.2** Listen to these sentences. Notice the different pronunciations of *have/has/had*.

   1 I **have** /hæv/ a good job.
      I **have** /hæf/ to work hard.
   2 He **has** /hæz/ a nice car.
      She **has** /hæs/ to get up early.
   3 I **had** /hæd/ a good time.
      I **had** /hæt/ to take exams.

   T 8.2 Listen again and repeat.

Talking about jobs

2 Work with a partner. Choose a job from the box, but don't tell your partner. Ask and answer *Yes/No* questions to find out what the job is.

   | architect taxi-driver dentist farmer lawyer nanny |
   | photographer accountant optician mechanic soldier |
   | hairdresser chef politician nurse housewife plumber |

   Use these questions to help you.

Do you ... ?	Do you have to ... ?	Did you have to ... ?
• work inside • earn a lot of money • work with people • use a computer	• wear a uniform • work unsocial hours • use your hands • get up early • speak English	• study at college • do a lot of training

   Do you have to wear a uniform?   *No, I don't.*

3 Which of the jobs *wouldn't* you like to do? Why?

   I wouldn't like to be a farmer because they have to work outside all year.

Talking about you

4 In groups, discuss the questions. If you live at home with your parents, use the present tense. If you've left home, use the past tense.

   1 What do/did you have to do to help in the house? What about your brothers and sisters?
   2 Can/Could you stay out as long as you want/wanted? Or do/did you have to be home by a certain time?
   3 Do/Did you always have to tell your parents where you are/were going?
   4 What other rules are/were there in your family?

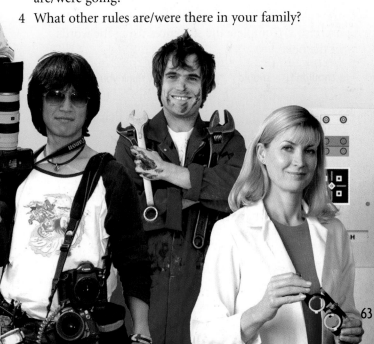

63

PROBLEMS, PROBLEMS
should/must

1 Read the problems from a magazine problem page. Match the problems and advice. What other advice would you give?

Problems

1 My ex-boyfriend is going to my best friend's wedding. He was horrible to me. Should I go?

2 There's a group of bullies at school. They're making my life miserable.

3 I've fallen in love with my boss. Should I tell him?

4 I'm 16. I chat to a boy on the Internet. He wants to meet me. Should I go?

Advice

a No, you shouldn't. It will only cause problems at work.

b Of course you should. But look happy and wear a fantastic dress!

c I don't think you should. You have no idea what he's really like.

d You must tell your parents and your head teacher about this.

2 Here is some more advice for the problems in exercise 1. Complete the sentences using the words in the box.

shouldn't   should   must   don't think you should

1 I think you _____ show your ex that you're fine without him.

2 If you do go to meet him, you _____ take a friend with you. This is really important.

3 You _____ let these cowards ruin your life.

4 I _____ have relationships with people you work with.

T 8.3 Listen and check. Practise the conversations with a partner.

GRAMMAR SPOT

1 Look at the sentences.

You **should** go to the wedding.   You **must** see a doctor.

Which expresses strong obligation *(it's really necessary)*?
Which expresses a suggestion *(I think it's a good idea)*?

2 *Should* and *must* are modal verbs.

Should I go?   You **shouldn't** see him.   He **must** be careful.

Do we use *do/does* in the question and negative?
Do we add *-s* with *he/she/it*?

▶▶ **Grammar Reference 8.2–8.4 p136**

3 Work in groups. Read aloud the problems and give advice.

• I can't sleep at night.

> You must take more exercise.

> You shouldn't drink too much coffee.

• I think I've twisted my ankle.
• I've got exams next week, and I'm really nervous.
• I like my job, but I don't like the people I work with.
• My computer's behaving very strangely.
• I argue a lot with my parents.
• My car's making a funny noise.

PRACTICE

must or *should*?

1 Work in groups. Complete the sentences with *must* or *should*.

When you're driving …,

1 you _____ stop at red lights.
2 you _____ be kind to other drivers.
3 you _____ wear a seat belt.
4 On a long journey, you _____ have a rest from time to time.
5 In Britain, you _____ drive on the left.

What do you think?

2 Work in groups. Make sentences from the chart.

If you want to …		
learn English, do well in life, keep fit,	you have to you don't have to you should you shouldn't you must	work hard. do some sport. learn the grammar. go to university. buy a dictionary. smoke. speak your language in class.

LISTENING AND SPEAKING
Leaving home

1 Discuss the questions.

1 When do young people in your country leave home?
2 What problems are there for young people living away from home for the first time?
3 Look at the photos. Who are the people? Why do you think Ian Mitchell looks worried?

2 **T 8.4** Listen to Ian Mitchell, who lives in the North of England. He is talking about his daughter, Evie, who has left home to live in London. Answer the questions.

1 How old is Evie? When did she move to London?
2 Is she enjoying living there? What does she think of London?
3 Why did she move there?
4 Where is she living?
5 Who is she living with?
6 What does her boyfriend do? What's his name?
7 What does she do at the weekend?
8 Why does she have to earn extra money?
9 How often does she phone home?
10 What does she say to her parents?

3 **T 8.5** Listen to Evie talking about her life in London and answer the same questions. Which of her answers are different?

What do you think?

• Should Evie's father be so worried about his daughter?
• Was Evie right to leave home at 18?
• What advice can you give to Evie and her father?

Roleplay

Work in two groups.

Group A: Parents
Discuss your worries about Evie.

Group B: Evie
Discuss what to tell your parents about your life in London. What can you say to stop them worrying about you?

Find a partner from the other group. Roleplay a conversation. Start:

> Evie it's so good to have you home again. We've been so worried about you.
>
> I'm fine. Living in London is great. You shouldn't worry.
>
> But …

▶▶ **WRITING** Letters and emails **p110**

Ian Mitchell

Evie Mitchell

READING AND SPEAKING
Jobs for the boys ... and girls

1 Discuss these questions.

1 Which of these jobs are traditionally done by men, and which by women? Which are done by both?

> nurse builder teacher plumber soldier
> computer programmer secretary chef gardener
> painter firefighter detective nanny

2 Do you believe *all* the jobs in exercise 1 can be done equally well by both sexes? If not, why not?

3 In Britain, the Equal Opportunities Commission (EOC) fights sexism, racism, and prejudice in the workplace. What does this mean?

2 Read the first part of the newspaper article on this page. Answer the questions.

1 What was the EOC report called? What does this mean?

2 What does the report say schools and employers are still doing?

3 What school subjects do you think are 'traditional for their gender'? Give examples.

4 What examples does the EOC give of jobs which are 'traditional for their gender'?

3 Work in two groups.

Group A Read about Jenny.
Group B Read about Alex.

4 Answer the questions about your person.

1 What did she/he study?

2 What is she/he doing now? Why?

3 Who has she/he had problems with? Why?

4 Does she/he like the career she/he finally chose?

5 What advice does she/he give to other people who want to do the same thing?

Compare your answers with a partner from the other group.

What do you think?

- Who has had the more difficult time? Jenny or Alex?
- Would you like to do what they did?
- Is it more difficult for women to do men's jobs or men to do women's jobs?
- Is this a problem in your country? Why?/Why not? Can you give any examples?

Jobs for the boys ... and girls

Can you imagine ringing for a plumber and a woman arriving at the door? Or paying a man to look after your children? Does this seem unusual?

Sally Rice, social affairs correspondent, investigates.

A recent report by the Equal Opportunities Commission, called 'Free to Choose', says that schools and employers are still recommending some careers only for boys and others only for girls. The government has to take action on this, says the EOC.

At school, boys and girls continue to study subjects that are traditional for their gender, and they continue to get poor careers advice. Employers for some jobs still choose young people because of their gender, not their ability.

For example, less than 3% of men work in childcare in Britain, and only 1% of women work in building, engineering, and plumbing. So what's it like for someone to cross the gender gap at work?

'We don't want **women** here.'

Jenny Boland – plumber

Jenny, a plumber from Harrow, says she has to fight sexism and prejudice every day in her job.

A few years ago, while Jenny was studying psychology at college, she had a problem in her bathroom and had to call a plumber. 'I watched the plumber while he was working, and I was fascinated. I wanted to learn how to do it.' But she has had a lot of problems with male plumbers from the very beginning.

Jenny says, 'Some of them have been really horrible. It's been so difficult to change their negative opinion of me. They are so sure that I can't do plumbing just because I'm female. One employer told me, "This is a job for big strong men. We don't want women here."'

But what do the customers think? 'Oh, the customers have been great!' she says. 'A lot of them actually prefer a female plumber!' Jenny loves her job. 'I get so much satisfaction from plumbing. I just love fixing things!'

What is her advice to other women who want to try non-traditional careers? 'You should definitely try it, but you have to be tough,' she says.

me **nanny agencies** didn't want me at all.'

Alex Karlsson – nanny

Alex was an engineering student in Sweden until three years ago. But he found it boring and decided to change careers.

He has always loved children, and now he is a qualified male nanny (or 'manny'!) to 18-month-old Jack. But he has had some problems. 'There is prejudice. A lot of people don't think that a man can look after a child as well as a woman. Some nanny agencies didn't want me at all,' he said. 'Some parents didn't want a man looking after their children. I had to wait nearly a year for my first job.'

But does he like his new career? 'I love it!' says Alex. 'Jack was 10 weeks old when I started looking after him. I don't think it's strange to feed him and change his nappy – it's my profession. It's wonderful to be part of his development. I love playing with him, and teaching him things as well.'

What is his advice for other men who want to work in childcare. 'You should go for it!' he says. 'Ignore the prejudice. Just show them you can do it!'

VOCABULARY AND PRONUNCIATION
Words that go together – applying for a job

1 Verbs often go together with certain words and phrases.

apply *for a job*

    give *somebody advice*

        go *for an interview*

Work with a partner. Match the verbs in **A** with the phrases in **B**. Sometimes more than one answer is possible.

A	B
interview	hard
study	engineering
earn	somebody for a job
take care of	a lot of training
do	career
change	children
work	time with someone
spend	a lot of money
get on	together/with somebody

2 **T 8.6** Alex has applied for the job of nanny to baby Jack. Jack's mother, Rachel, is interviewing him. Listen and answer the questions.

1 Why did Alex choose a career as a nanny?
2 How long did he have to train?
3 How many boys were on his course?
4 What did he learn on the course?
5 What does Rachel want Alex to do before she offers him the job?
6 What question does Alex ask?

3 Listen again. Use the phrases from **A** and **B** in exercise 1 to talk about Alex with your partner.

Rachel is interviewing Alex for the job of ...   *Alex was studying ...*

Compound nouns

4 Two nouns can go together to make a new noun.

child + care = childcare

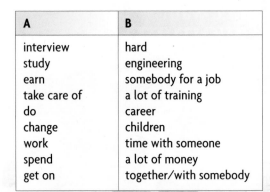

> **Music of English** – word stress 🎵
>
> **T 8.7** Listen and mark the stress. Is it on the first or second word?
>
>   *childcare*   *job interview*   *training course*
>
> Listen again and repeat.

5 Match the nouns from **A** with nouns from **B** to make compound nouns. They are all from this unit.

A		B	
hair	flight	message	journey
country	house	page	attendant
text	train	wife	side
problem	fire	fighter	dresser

T 8.8 Read them aloud with your partner. Listen, check, and repeat.

6 Choose a compound noun and give a definition to the class. Can they guess the word(s)?

> This is what you have to have before you get a job.

> That's right.

> A job interview.

EVERYDAY ENGLISH
At the doctor's

1 Match these illnesses with the pictures.

a sore throat	diarrhoea /daɪəˈrɪə/
a cold	'flu
food poisoning	a twisted ankle

2 Read the symptoms and complete the illnesses.

Symptoms	Illnesses
1 I can't stop sneezing and blowing my nose.	I've got _____ .
2 I keep being sick, and I've got diarrhoea.	I've got _____ .
3 It hurts when I walk.	I've _____ .
4 I've got stomach-ache and I keep going to the toilet.	I've got _____ .
5 My glands are swollen, and it hurts when I swallow.	I've got _____ .
6 I've got a temperature, my whole body aches, and I feel awful.	I've got _____ .

T 8.9 Listen and practise saying the symptoms and illnesses in pairs.

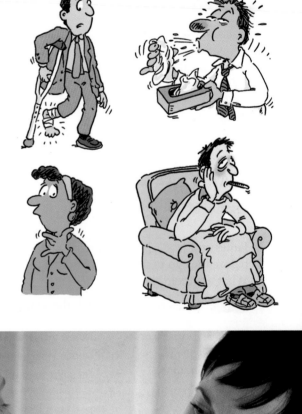

3 **T 8.10** You will hear a conversation between Manuel, a student from Chile, and a doctor. Answer the questions.

1 What are Manuel's symptoms?
2 What is the doctor's diagnosis?
3 What advice does she give him?
4 What does she prescribe?

4 **T 8.10** Listen again and complete the lines of conversation with the exact words you hear.

1 What _____ the matter?
2 I haven't _____ for a few days.
3 I've got _____ temperature, ...
4 I've _____ a few times.
5 Let me _____ at you.
6 Have you _____ which might have disagreed with you?
7 Well, you _____ a day or two in bed, ...
8 Drink _____ liquids, and just take _____ for a while.
9 Seeing me is _____ , but you'll _____ for the prescription.

Compare answers with a partner.

5 Look at the tapescript on p123. Practise the conversation with a partner.

6 Make similar conversations with other symptoms.

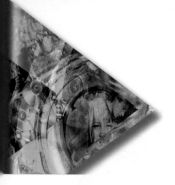

9 Going places

Time clauses · if · Hot verbs *make/do/take/get* · Directions

STARTER

Make sentences about you using the phrases in the box. Tell the class.

If the weather is nice this weekend,	I think I'll …
If the weather isn't nice this weekend,	I'll probably …
When I get home tonight,	I'm going to …

A GAP YEAR
Time and conditional clauses

1 James and Jessie, both 18, are going to have a 'gap year' before they go to university. Look at the photos. What are their plans?

2 **T 9.1** Listen to James. Match the sentence halves.

Before I go to university,	I know my parents will worry!
As soon as I have enough money,	I'll phone home twice a week.
	I'm going to travel round South America.
When I'm travelling around,	
If I don't keep in touch,	I'll book a flight to Rio de Janeiro.

3 Cover the orange box. Try to say the full sentences.

4 **T 9.2** Listen to Jessie and do the same.

I'm going to work in an old people's home	after the job ends.
	as soon as I finish school.
I'll also live in the home	if I have a holiday before term starts!
I'll work	
I'm going to Greece with some friends	until I've saved enough money for a holiday.
I won't be tired	while I'm working there.

5 **T 9.1** and **T 9.2** Listen again to James and Jessie and check.

James

Jessie

ASHGROVE
Retirement home

PRACTICE

What if ... ?

1 Look at these hopes for the future. Make sentences using *If ... , I'll ...*

If I don't go out so much, I'll do more work.
If I do more work, I'll ...

If ...

I don't go out so much
↓
do more work
↓
pass my exams
↓
go to university
↓
study medicine
↓
become a doctor
↓
save people's lives

If ...

I spend less on new clothes
↓
have more money
↓
save some every week
↓
be rich when I'm thirty
↓
start my own business
↓
make a lot of money
↓
retire when I'm fifty

What will you do if ... ?

2 Work with a partner. One of you is going on safari to Africa. The other sees lots of problems. Use the ideas below to help you.

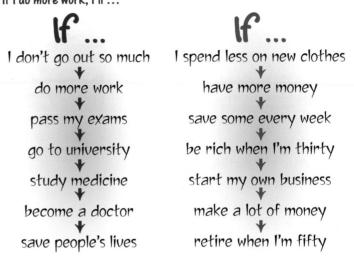

I'm going on safari to Africa.

Oh dear, what will you do if you get chased by wild animals?

It'll be OK. I won't get chased. But I hope I'll see lots of wild animals.

- you get chased by wild animals
- it's the rainy season
- there are lots of insects
- you get sunburnt
- you get lost in the bush
- your car breaks down
- you have to sleep in a tent

T 9.3 Listen and compare. Look at the tapescript on p123 and practise the conversation with a partner.

3 Make a similar conversation about one of these topics.

> learning to snowboard   going mountain climbing
> giving up your job to travel the world   joining the army

Discussing grammar

4 Complete the sentences with *when, if, before, as soon as,* or *until*. Sometimes more than one answer is possible. Compare answers with a partner.

1 I'll have a bath _____ I go to bed.

2 I'm coming to London tomorrow. I'll ring you _____ I arrive.

3 We're planning a barbecue _____ it's nice at the weekend.

4 Wait here _____ I get back.

5 _____ you have any problems, just ask for help.

6 I'm going to give up this job _____ I find a better one.

7 I'm only going to do this job _____ I find a better one.

8 I want to get home _____ it gets dark.

9 I'm going to study English _____ I'm completely fluent.

10 Don't forget to give me your address _____ you leave.

Talking about you

5 Complete the sentences with your ideas. Compare your ideas with a partner then the class.

1 As soon as this lesson finishes, I'm going to …

2 If I have time this evening, I'll …

3 If our teacher gives us a lot of homework, I won't …

4 While I'm doing my homework, I'll …

5 I won't go to bed until …

6 If I have a holiday this summer, I'll probably …

7 When my English is fluent, I'm going to …

8 As soon as I'm earning a good salary, I'll …

9 Before I get old, I'm going to …

10 When I'm old, I won't …

When I get to Rio …

6 James (from p70) is leaving for Rio de Janeiro. He's saying goodbye to his mum. Put the verbs in brackets in the correct tense. Put *if, when, while,* or *as soon as* into each box.

Mum Bye, my darling. Have a good flight to Rio. Remember, we **'re expecting** (expect) a phone call from you this evening ⌈when⌉ you get there!

James I _____ (ring) you ⌈   ⌉ I arrive at Diego's house.

Mum Good. What time will you get there?

James Well, the flight takes 12 hours. ⌈   ⌉ the plane _____ (arrive) on time, I _____ (be) there about 11.30 – Rio time, of course. ⌈   ⌉ you _____ (be) asleep when I ring, I _____ (leave) a message on the answerphone.

Mum I won't be asleep!

James OK! OK! Don't worry, Mum. I'll be fine.

Mum All right. But ⌈   ⌉ you _____ (travel) around the country, _____ you _____ (remember) to call us regularly? Make sure you phone twice a week.

James Of course! And I _____ (phone) you ⌈   ⌉ I _____ (run out of) money!

Mum Cheeky! But you must look after yourself, darling. Give my best wishes to Diego's parents, and don't forget to give them this present ⌈   ⌉ you _____ (get) to their house.

James Don't worry. I won't. Oh, they _____ (call) my flight! Love you, Mum. Bye!

Mum Love you, James. Take care!

T 9.4 Listen and check. Practise the conversation with a partner.

VOCABULARY AND SPEAKING
Hot verbs – *make*, *do*, *take*, and *get*

The verbs *make*, *do*, *take*, and *get* are very common in English. Read these examples from exercise 6 on p72.

What time will you **get there**?
… the flight **takes 12 hours**.
Make sure you phone twice a week.
Take care!

make and *do*

1 Add the words and phrases to the correct columns.

| friends | the washing-up | up your mind | a course |
| me a favour | my best | a fortune | a noise |

MAKE	DO
friends	

2 Complete the sentences with a phrase and *make* or *do* in the correct form.

1 I _____ last night. It's your turn tonight.
2 Please tell the children not to _____ . I'm trying to work.
3 I _____ , but I still failed the exam.
4 I don't know if I want the chicken or the fish. I just can't _____ .
5 My sister's very popular. She _____ very easily.
6 Could you _____ and give me a lift to the station? Thanks.
7 My grandfather _____ in business. He's a rich man.
8 I'm going to _____ in Spanish before I go to Spain.

T 9.5 Listen and check.

'This song is for Dad, who thinks I'm doing my homework.'

take and *get*

3 Add the words and phrases to the correct columns.

| a photo | a cold | angry | a long time | care | better |
| two tablets a day | on well with someone | | ready | | |

TAKE	GET
a photo	

4 Complete the sentences with a phrase and *take* or *get* in the correct form.

1 Everybody smile! I want to _____ of you all.
2 I know my bedroom's a mess, but don't _____ I'll tidy it soon.
3 Bye-bye! See you soon. _____ of yourself.
4 Atishoo! Oh dear. I think I'm _____ .
5 The doctor told me to _____ until I _____ .
6 I like Ingrid very much. I _____ with her.
7 It _____ to become really fluent in a foreign language.
8 If you don't hurry up and _____ , we'll be late for the party.

T 9.6 Listen and check.

Talking about you

5 Complete the questions with the correct form of *make*, *do*, *take*, and *get*.

1 How long does it _____ you to _____ ready in the morning?
2 What time did you _____ to school today?
3 Do you always _____ your homework?
4 Do you sometimes _____ mistakes in English?
5 When did you last _____ angry?
6 Who usually _____ the washing-up in your family?
7 Did you _____ many photos on your last holiday?
8 Do you know anyone who has _____ a lot of money?
9 Is your English _____ better?
10 Would you like to _____ a course in another language?

T 9.7 Listen and check. Ask and answer the questions with a partner. Give true answers.

READING AND SPEAKING
Travel addicts

1 Write down three reasons why people travel abroad. Compare ideas with the class. Do you think travelling can become addictive?

2 Read the title and the introduction to the article. When do people usually have gap years? Why do you think it's hard to come home after a year away?

3 Read the article. Put these lines in the right space *a–d*.

1 until we find a way to escape
2 As soon as I have enough, I'll be off on my next trip round the world
3 If I see just one travel brochure,
4 And when I've finished that, I'll start Portuguese

4 Work with a partner. Read about Ben and his friends. <u>Underline</u> the mistakes in the summaries. Correct them.

BEN
Ben returned from his travels just three months ago and now he wants to go travelling again. He spent two years travelling with his girlfriend, Jane. They visited 31 countries, including Australia, Fiji and Vietnam and got married on a beach in Thailand. It was the best time of their lives but now they are happy to settle down back home.

SANDIE and IAN
Ben met Sandie and her boyfriend, Ian, when he was in Sydney. They are hoping to marry next year and spend a year travelling again on their honeymoon. They both have stressful jobs as lawyers but they enjoy their work.

REBECCA
Ben met Rebecca when she was working for a computer company in Australia. Now she's back home and looking for work. She's enjoying telling all her friends and family about her time abroad.

What do you think?

- Why do people become travel addicts? Do you think they are looking for something or running away from something?
- Why are travellers' friends and family often not interested in their experiences?

Discussion

1 Make a list of five places in the world you'd like to go to. Say why.
2 In groups compare your lists. Discuss as a class which are the most popular places.

TRAVEL ADDICTS

'Gap years are not just for young people. But before you give up your job, remember that coming home is the hardest part,' says travel addict **Ben Williams**.

My name is Ben. I am 32 years old and I am a travel addict. I've been back home now for almost six months, but I know that I will always be an addict. (a)_____ I know I will want to go away again.

Two years ago I was on an island in Fiji, at the start of a year-long break that took me and my girlfriend, Jane, to 14 countries. We watched fireworks over the Sydney Opera House at New Year, saw the sun rise over the temples of Angkor Wat in Cambodia, and spent my 31st birthday on a Thai beach.

It was without doubt the best year of our lives. No work, no boss, no worries. No grey skies of Britain, just carefree months going into the distance. True, there wasn't much money, but it didn't matter.

We loved having the freedom to go where we wanted, when we wanted. If we liked a place, we stayed. If not, we just got the next bus out. We only had one worry in the world. We knew we had to return to Britain.

> **'We loved having the freedom but coming back was awful.'**

Coming back was awful. We had huge debts, and we had to find work. The routine of getting up, going to work, going home, eating, sleeping, and getting up again is just about killing me. I'm finding it difficult to do what other people tell me to do.

Before I went travelling, I worried about earning more money, buying a bigger car, a house, etc. Now that I'm back, I don't care about those things any more. I'm living like a student again, and saving all my money. (b)_____ .

Sandie & Ian's story ...

While I was travelling, I met other people like me. Sandie, 28 and Ian, 33, got married and spent a year travelling on their honeymoon. We met on a beach in Thailand. They were both IT consultants with stressful jobs. Now that they are home, they are making big changes to their lives. 'Work just isn't so important anymore,' says Sandie. 'But I suppose we'll have to stay in these jobs (c)_____ .'

Rebecca's story ...

I met Rebecca, 26, in Australia during her round-the-world trip. Now she's back home, and she's also having trouble readjusting to life. 'It's terrible,' she says. 'During the first couple of weeks back at work, I couldn't sit at my computer. Nobody understands. My parents and friends just aren't interested in my experiences. I don't know why. It was such an important time in my life. I keep looking at my photos, so that I won't forget.'

For me too, I wonder if life back home will ever feel normal again. Next week I'm starting an evening course to learn Spanish. (d)_____ . They'll be very useful languages in South America!

LISTENING AND SPEAKING
Going nowhere

1 Do you know anybody that *doesn't* like travelling abroad? Who? Why? In groups write a list of reasons why people don't want to travel.

Some people are afraid of flying.
People who have pets don't want to leave them.

2 Look at the photos. Why do you think these people don't want to travel?

T 9.8 Listen to a radio programme about them called *People and Places*. Answer the questions.

1 Were any of their reasons on your list?
2 What main reason does each person give?

3 Who gives these reasons? Write **R** (Roger), **A** (Annabel), or **J-C** (Jean-Claude).

☐ Tourism is destroying our planet.

☐ Going away is too much trouble. It's not worth it.

☐ I would be hungry all the time.

☐ You can see everything on TV these days.

☐ I don't like being a tourist.

☐ When you get home you have a mountain of mail.

☐ My country can give me everything.

☐ Travelling by plane is bad for the environment.

☐ I love Europe for its history and traditions.

T 9.8 Listen again and check.

4 Answer the questions.
1 Which places abroad have they been to? When and why? What did they think of them?
2 What do their partners think about their unwillingness to travel?

What do you think?

Discuss the questions.
- What are the tourist destinations in your country?
- Are they being ruined by too many visitors?
- Think of a place that is very popular in the world, but which you have no desire to visit. Why don't you want to go there?

▶▶▶ **WRITING** Discussing pros and cons *p112*

Roger

Mary

Annabel

Jean-Claude

EVERYDAY ENGLISH
Directions

1 Look at the map of the small town of Modbury and find these things:
- a farm
- a wood
- a pond
- a bridge
- a path
- a hill
- a river
- a gate

2 Read the descriptions and add the places to the map.
1 The <u>hotel</u> is **opposite** the car park.
2 The <u>bank</u> is **on the corner** of Lower Road and Hill Road. It is **next to** the <u>baker's</u>.
3 The <u>supermarket</u> is **between** the <u>chemist's</u> and the <u>greengrocer's</u>.
4 There is a bus stop **in front of** the <u>newsagent's</u> **in** Station Road.
5 There are two pubs. The <u>Red Lion</u> is in Station Road, **opposite** the newsagent's **near** the railway bridge, and the <u>Old Shepherd</u> is in Church Street, **behind** the school.

3 **T 9.9** Listen and repeat the questions and answers. Pay attention to stress and intonation.

4 Ask and answer questions about other places on the map with your partner. Use the prepositions from exercise 2.

> **Excuse me, is there a supermarket near here?**
>> **Yes. It's in ..., between the ... .**

5 Find the farm and the church on the map. Complete the directions from the farm to the church with the prepositions in the box.

up   down   over   past   through (x2)
out of   into   across   along

You go _____ the hill, and walk _____ the path, _____ the pond, _____ the bridge, and _____ the gate. Then you go _____ the road and take the path _____ the wood. When you come _____ the wood, you walk _____ the path and _____ the church. It takes ten minutes.

T 9.10 Listen and check.

6 Give your partner directions to get to your house from your school.

10 Things that changed the world

Passives · Verbs and nouns that go together · Telephoning

STARTER

1 Make true sentences from the chart.

2 What is made in your country?

Nikon cameras Champagne Ferrari cars Whisky IKEA furniture	is are	made in	Scotland. Sweden. France. Italy. Japan.

A PHOTOGRAPH THAT CHANGED THE WORLD
Passives

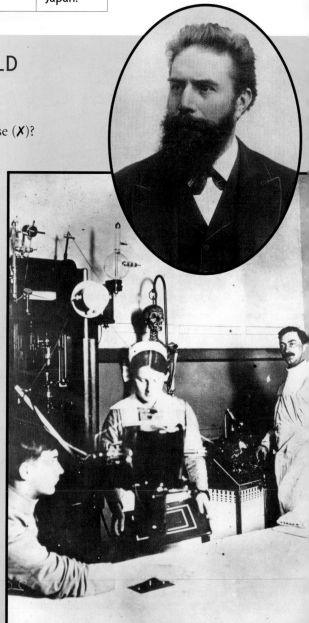

1 Read the story of X-rays on p79. Are these sentences true (✓) or false (✗)?

1 X-rays were discovered by Wilhelm Roentgen in 1986.
2 The first X-ray photograph was taken by Roentgen's wife.
3 The first X-ray machine was also invented by Roentgen.
4 It is called 'the window into the human body'.
5 X-rays are only used in medicine.

GRAMMAR SPOT

1 Nearly all the verb forms in the text are in the passive. The passive is formed with the verb **to be** and the **past participle**.

*X-ray machines **are used** every day.*
*The first X-ray machine **was built** in 1896.*

2 Read the text again. Write the passive verb forms in the chart.

Present Simple	Past Simple	Present Perfect	*will* Future
are seen			

3 What is the main interest of sentences **a** and **b**? X-rays or Wilhelm Roentgen? Which sentence is active? Which is passive?

a *Wilhelm Roentgen discovered X-rays.*
b *X-rays were discovered by Wilhelm Roentgen.*

When we are more interested in the object of the active sentence, we use the passive.

▶▶ **Grammar Reference 10.1 p139**

A photograph that changed the world

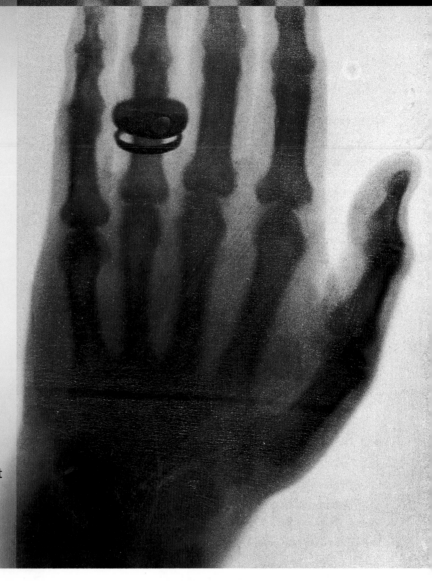

This is the first X-ray photograph. It was taken by a German scientist, Wilhelm Konrad Roentgen, in 1896. It is his wife's hand. The bones in her hand (and also her wedding ring!) are clearly seen in the photo.

X-rays were discovered by accident, while Roentgen was experimenting with electricity. Soon after, he built the first X-ray machine. Immediately, hospital operations were made much safer. For the first time, doctors could see inside people's bodies before they cut them open! In 1901, Roentgen was awarded the very first Nobel Prize in Physics. His invention is still used every day by doctors and dentists, and is called 'the window into the human body'.

Since the introduction of computer imaging in the 1970s, X-ray machines have been used for other things, too. At airports, many criminals have been caught with illegal items in their luggage. Also, lost works of art have been discovered underneath other paintings. In factories, many faults in new products are found every day, using X-rays. There is no doubt that new uses for X-rays will be developed in the future.

Active and passive

2 Complete the sentences with an active or passive form.

	Active	Passive
1	They make Rolls Royce cars in Britain.	Rolls Royce cars _are made_ in Britain.
2	Over 5 million people _____ the Eiffel Tower every year.	The Eiffel Tower is visited by over 5 million people every year.
3	Alexander Graham Bell invented the telephone in 1876.	The telephone _____ by Alexander Graham Bell in 1876.
4	Thieves _____ 'The Scream' by Edvard Munch in 2004.	'The Scream' by Edvard Munch was stolen in 2004.
5	They have sold a Van Gogh painting for $82 million.	A Van Gogh painting _____ for $82 million.
6	More than 2,000 people _____ Mount Everest.	Mount Everest has been climbed by more than 2,000 people.
7	BMW will produce 200,000 Mini cars next year.	200,000 Mini cars _____ by BMW next year.
8	_____ Leonardo da Vinci _____ the helicopter?	Was the helicopter invented by Leonardo da Vinci?
9	Bell didn't invent television.	Television _____ by Bell.

PRACTICE

Active and passive

1 What is paper made of? Who invented it? Read *The history of paper* and check your ideas.

2 Read the text again. Put the verbs in brackets in the correct tense, active or passive.

    T 10.1 Listen and check.

Questions and answers

3 Match the question words and answers.

	Ts'ai Lun.
When? (x2)	About 300 kg.
Where? (x2)	In Spain.
Who / by?	In AD 105.
How long?	Since the 18th century.
How much?	In China.
	In the 10th century.

4 Write the questions, using the passive. Ask and answer them with a partner.

> When was paper invented?
>> In AD 105.

    T 10.2 Listen and check.

5 Correct these sentences.

  1 Paper is only used to make newspapers and books.

    No, it isn't. It's used to make hundreds of everyday things.

  2 All clothes are made out of paper.

    No, they aren't. Only some ...

  3 Before paper, people wrote on trees.

  4 Paper was invented by a Chinese scientist.

  5 The Chinese gave their invention to the world immediately.

  6 They made paper out of wood.

  7 The first paper mill in Europe was built in France.

  8 Paper has been made out of cloth since the 18th century.

    T 10.3 Listen and check.

Check it

6 Underline the correct word or words in each sentence.

  1 Where *was* / *were* these shoes made?

  2 I was given this watch *by* / *from* my uncle.

  3 Someone *has stolen* / *has been stolen* my bag!

  4 The newsagent *sells* / *is sold* stamps.

  5 British policemen *don't carry* / *aren't carried* guns.

  6 All the beer was *drank* / *drunk* by nine o'clock.

  7 Have all the sandwiches *eaten* / *been eaten*?

The history of paper

Today, paper (1)_____ (use) for hundreds of everyday things – books and newspapers, of course, but also money, stamps, cups, bags, and even some clothes.

Long ago, before paper, people (2)_____ (write) on animal skins, bones and stones. Then in 2700 BC, the Egyptians (3)_____ (start) to make papyrus, which was similar to paper. But the first real paper (4)_____ (invent) in AD 105 by a Chinese government official, Ts'ai Lun. It (5)_____ (make) from a mixture of plants and cloth. The Chinese (6)_____ (keep) their invention secret for centuries.

Finally, in the 10th century, paper (7)_____ (bring) to Europe by the Arabs. The first European paper mill (8)_____ (build) in Spain in 1150. Since the 18th century, most paper (9)_____ (make) out of wood, because it is much stronger than cloth.

Nowadays, each person (10)_____ (use) about 300 kg of paper every year. That's a lot of paper!

VOCABULARY AND SPEAKING
Verbs and nouns that go together

1 Around each verb, *one* noun does *not* go with it. Which one?

a cure   the truth

discover

gold   paper
DNA

cars   a discovery

make

homework   a phone call
£1,000

hello   a story

tell

the truth   a joke
a lie

advice   a present

give

information   a complaint
a lift

the bus   weight

lose

money   the game
the way

an umbrella
a watch

carry

a gun   passengers
a briefcase

the peace   a diary

keep

a secret   a promise
an idea

the family   the ball

miss

the bus   the way
school

2 Work with a partner. Choose a noun from each group, and write a sentence using the verb. Read your sentences to the class.

> BMW cars are made in Germany.

> An Airbus can carry 555 passengers.

3 There are eight nouns that do *not* go with the verbs in exercise 1. Complete the sentences with the correct verbs.

1 Paper was __invented__ by a Chinese goverment official in AD 105.
2 I _____ my homework very quickly, then I went out.
3 This is my father's watch. He _____ it every day until he died.
4 _____ hello to your parents from me when you see them.
5 Are you the manager? We'd like to _____ a complaint.
6 I was late for work because I _____ the bus.
7 I'm no good at reading maps so we completely _____ our way.
8 I've just _____ a really good idea! Do you want to hear it?

Talking about you

4 Answer these questions about yourself. Then ask and answer them with a partner.

1 Do you always wear a watch?
2 Are you good at telling jokes?
3 What was the last present you gave? Who to?
4 What was the last phone call you made? Who to? Why?
5 Do you keep a diary?
6 Have you or a friend ever made a complaint in a restaurant?
7 Have you ever been homesick? Did you miss your family or your friends?
8 What is the best advice you've ever been given?

T 10.4 Listen and compare answers.

READING AND SPEAKING
A discovery and an invention that changed the world

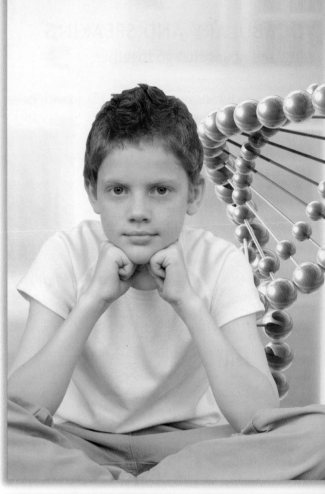

1 Which of these are discoveries and which are inventions?
- the telephone
- television
- the atom
- radium
- the Internet
- the electric light
- penicillin
- DNA
- *Google*

2 Work in groups. Add more discoveries and inventions to the list in exercise 1.

Which things changed the world the most? Compare your ideas with other groups.

3 You are going to read texts about DNA and *Google*. The words in the box all appear in the texts. Which words go with each text? Use a dictionary to help you guess.

nouns	weblink	structure	company	cure
	disease	result	search engine	cell
verbs	contain	borrow	commit (a crime)	
	dream	be related to		

4 Work in two groups.

Group A Read about DNA.
Group B Read about *Google*.

Which words from exercise 3 are in your text?

5 Answer the questions.
1 Who made the discovery/invention?
2 How long did it take to develop?
3 Were there any problems in the beginning?
4 What are important dates in its history?
5 How useful is the discovery/invention now? Give an example.
6 What could happen with it in the future?

6 Find a partner from the other group. Tell your partner about your discovery/invention, using your answers from exercise 5.

What do you think?

- Have there been any stories in the news recently where DNA was involved? What about?
- What were the last three Internet searches you made? Which search engines do you use regularly? Have you ever used *Google*?

▶▶ **WRITING** A review *p113*

The discovery of DNA

Did you know that a tiny piece of your hair gives us information about ... ?

— who you are related to
— which career you could be successful in
— any crimes you have committed
— what illnesses you could get
— how and when you could die

This is possible thanks to the information in DNA (or deoxyribonucleic acid). Your hair and every cell in your body contains your own unique DNA. It can tell you a lot about your family, health, and personality.

DNA was discovered by a German scientist, Friedrich Miescher, in 1869, but nobody realized its importance then. Other scientists thought that it was too simple to contain the map of how we are made! In 1953, a group of British scientists at Cambridge University finally discovered the structure of DNA and how it worked. They were given the Nobel Prize for Medicine in 1962.

Gradually, scientists learned to 'read' more and more of the information in DNA. In 1986, for the first time DNA testing was used by the police. Some DNA is usually left by a criminal at the place where the crime was committed. This can be matched with DNA from a suspect. The test shows if the suspect is guilty.

In 1990 the Human Genome Project was begun. Scientists wanted to make a map of the 3 billion chemical letters in human DNA. Over 1,000 scientists all over the world worked on the project, and it took 10 years. With this information, it is possible that a cure for many diseases will be found in the future. But it also brings with it many questions. Do we want to be able to choose what our babies will look like, or pick the best person for a job with DNA tests?

The invention of Google

'How many common English words were invented by Shakespeare?'
How long did it take people to find the answer to this question 15 years ago? And now? You can *google* it and find the answer immediately!

Google is the most popular Internet search engine in the world. It was invented by two students, Larry Page and Sergey Brin. They met in 1995, when they were both studying computer science at Stanford University, USA. They were also both fans of the science fiction TV programme *Star Trek*, and they loved the spaceship computer. They dreamed of producing something that could also answer any question in seconds.

Internet search engines at the time were slow and gave many websites that weren't useful. In January 1996, Page and Brin decided to make a better and faster search engine. They thought the results should be based on the popularity of each website – the most popular ones have the highest number of 'weblinks' (links to other websites).

Nobody would give them money for their project, so they used their credit cards and bought as much computer memory as possible. They also borrowed money from family and friends. Then, in 1998, they were given a cheque for $100,000, and they started their own company. Their first office was in a friend's garage! The company name Google comes from mathematics. A 'googol' is a very high number – 1 followed by a hundred zeros.

The Google search engine was soon used by thousands of people worldwide because it was fast, easy and accurate. By 2002 it was the biggest search engine on the Internet. Now, more questions have been answered by Google than any other Internet service, from sport to science, and from music to medicine. Google hopes that in the future all the world's information will be put on the Internet, so that everybody can find everything.

LISTENING AND SPEAKING
Things that really annoy me

1 Write down on a piece of paper three things that really annoy you. Give the paper to your teacher.

2 Look at the cartoons. What problems is the man having?

3 **T 10.5** Listen to two old men complaining about modern life. What problems do they have with … ?

- automated answer phones
- domestic machines
- car radios
- choosing a computer
- computer printers
- last year's technology
- too much choice

How are their problems similar to the ones in the cartoons?

What do you think?

1 What complaints could people have about these things?

> flat-pack furniture
> people who use mobiles in public places
> opening plastic packets
> people who drop litter

2 Here are some more things that annoy people. How old do you think the people are?

- I want a mobile, but my mum says 'No'.
- I've no idea how you turn this television on.
- Me want sweeties NOW!
- Young people don't say 'Please' and 'Thank you' any more.
- I can never stay out late, even at weekends.
- Families don't sit down and eat together these days.
- I really want those trainers, but I'm broke – again!

3 Your teacher will read out some of the things that annoy you. Can you guess who wrote them?

Roleplay

In pairs, write a dialogue between two people complaining. You can choose how old they are. It could be you and your friend, two young children, your parents, or your grandparents …

Act your dialogues out in class.

EVERYDAY ENGLISH
Telephoning

1 **T 10.6** Listen and practise saying the telephone numbers.

020 7927 4863	633488
01923 272 994	061 44 501 277
07971 800 261	07881 905 024

How were these numbers expressed?

0   00   55   99   33   88

2 **T 10.8** Listen to four phone conversations and decide …

- who is speaking to who.
- what they are talking about.
- how well they know each other.

3 **T 10.8** Listen again and complete the expressions from the conversations.

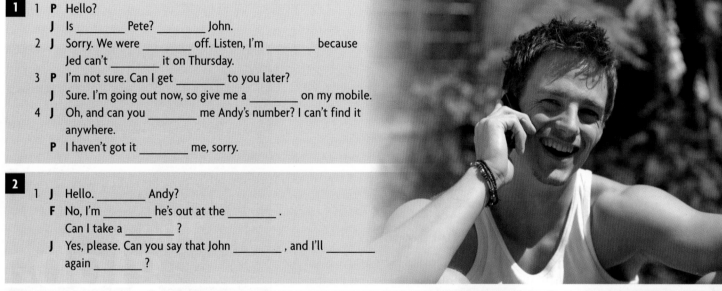

1

1 **P** Hello?

   J Is _____ Pete? _____ John.

2 **J** Sorry. We were _____ off. Listen, I'm _____ because Jed can't _____ it on Thursday.

3 **P** I'm not sure. Can I get _____ to you later?

   J Sure. I'm going out now, so give me a _____ on my mobile.

4 **J** Oh, and can you _____ me Andy's number? I can't find it anywhere.

   P I haven't got it _____ me, sorry.

2

1 **J** Hello. _____ Andy?

   F No, I'm _____ he's out at the _____ . Can I take a _____ ?

   J Yes, please. Can you say that John _____ , and I'll _____ again _____ ?

3

1 **R** The line's _____ . Would you like to _____ ?

2 **R** It's _____ for you now.

3 **S** Who's _____ please?

   D _____ is Darshan Gandhi.

4 **S** Yes, I'll put you _____ .

4

1 **S** _____ I speak to Dawn Edwards, please?

   D _____ .

2 **S** Great! I'll _____ you a call on Friday, then.

3 **S** OK. Speak _____ you soon. Bye for _____ !

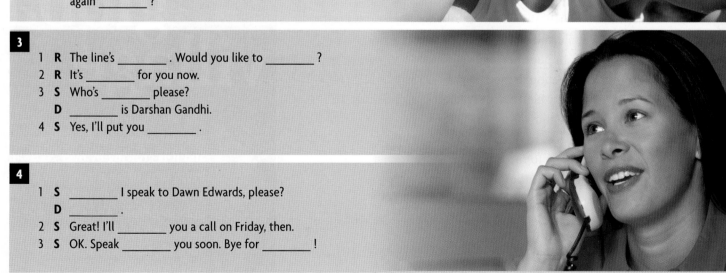

4 Look at the tapescript on p124. Practise one of the conversations with a partner.

5 Your teacher will give you a role card. Prepare what you are going to say alone, then be ready to make a call or answer the phone.

11 What if ...?

Second conditional · *might* · Phrasal verbs · Exclamations with *so* and *such*

STARTER

1 Who is the leader of your country? Who do you think is the most important leader in the world? Why?

2 What would you do if you were leader of the world? Share your ideas with the class. Whose ideas do you think are best?

> I would give all the poor people $1,000.

> I'd send a spaceship to explore Mars.

> I would ban football, because it's all my boyfriend talks about!

THE GLOBAL VILLAGE
Second conditional

1 Read about the global village. Complete the sentences below with the verbs in the box.

> would live   ~~would be~~   would be   would control
> wouldn't have   would die   wouldn't know

If the world were a village of 100 people ...

1 there __would be__ 60 Asians, 14 Africans, 12 Europeans, 8 Latin Americans, 5 North Americans, and 1 from the South Pacific.

2 51 would be male and 49 _____ female.

3 80 _____ in poor housing.

4 50 wouldn't have enough food.

5 24 _____ any electricity. (And most of the other 76 would only use it at night.)

6 17 _____ how to read.

7 7 would have access to the Internet.

8 5 _____ 32% of the village's money.

9 only 1 would have a college education.

10 1 person _____ every year, but 2 babies would be born.

2 Ask and answer questions about the global village with a partner.

• How many people ... be women?
• How many people ... live in poor housing?
• ... everybody have enough food?
• ... most people have electricity?
• How many people ... be very rich?
• ... most people have access to the Internet?

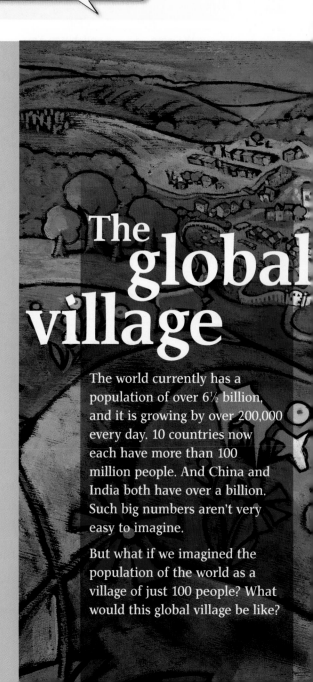

The global village

The world currently has a population of over 6½ billion, and it is growing by over 200,000 every day. 10 countries now each have more than 100 million people. And China and India both have over a billion. Such big numbers aren't very easy to imagine.

But what if we imagined the population of the world as a village of just 100 people? What would this global village be like?

GRAMMAR SPOT

1 Look at these two sentences. Which describes the real world? Which is imagined?

   China and India have over a billion people.

   If the world were a village of 100 people, 51 would be male, and 49 female.

2 Notice that *was* can change to *were* in the *if* clause.

   *If the world **were** a village, ...* (You can also say *If the world **was** a village, ...*)

3 Read these sentences. Which sentence is more probable?

   If I have time, I'll (will) ...

   If I had a lot of money, I'd (would) ...

   Which tenses are used in the *if* clauses? How are the result clauses formed?

▶▶ **Grammar Reference 11.1 p140**

PRACTICE
Discussing grammar

1 Work with a partner. How many sentences can you make from the chart?

If I	were had found knew didn't know didn't live	a politician, the answer, you, the time, a £50 note, in a big city,	I'd I wouldn't	tell you. travel the world. keep it. always tell the truth. accept the job. be bored. help you. ask the teacher.

2 Put the verbs in the correct form.

   1 If I _____ (be) rich, I _____ (travel) round the world. First I _____ (go) to Canada, then I _____ (go) to New York.

   2 If he _____ (work) harder, he _____ (have) more money.

   3 I _____ (go) to work if I _____ (feel) better, but I feel terrible.

   4 If I _____ (can) speak perfect English, I _____ (not be) in this classroom.

   5 What _____ you _____ (do) if a stranger _____ (give) you £1 million?

   6 What _____ you _____ (say) if I _____ (ask) you to marry me?

If I were you ...

3 We can give advice using *If I were you, I'd ... .*

   Work with a partner. Give these people advice.

   1 I found a wallet in the street.

   > If I were you, I'd take it to the nearest police station.

   2 I don't like my sister's boyfriend.
   3 I've had a row with my mother.
   4 I never have enough money.
   5 My neighbours make a lot of noise.
   6 I really need to do more exercise.

   T 11.1 Listen and compare.

WHO KNOWS?
might

1 Look at the pictures of Nisa and Viktor. They are both students. Where do they come from? What differences do you think there are between their lives?

2 **T 11.2** Listen to them talking about their ambitions and complete the texts.

3 Answer the questions.

1 Who is certain about what they want to do? Who is not?
2 Who is more ambitious? What makes you think this?
3 Where does Nisa live? What do her parents do?
4 What does Viktor enjoy studying?
5 Who wants to live in another country?
6 What jobs are they thinking of doing?

4 What are some of Nisa's plans and ambitions?

* <u>She's taking</u> her high school exams next year.
* _____ a job in an office in town.
* _____ to university.
* _____ save some money.
* _____ an architect.

5 What are some of the possibilities in Viktor's life?

* <u>He might</u> go to art college.
* _____ a designer.
* _____ Russian language and literature at university.
* _____ in Germany for a while.

GRAMMAR SPOT

1 *Might* means the same as *perhaps ... will ...* .

'What are you doing tonight?'

'I don't know. I **might** go out, or I **might** stay at home.'

2 *Might* is a modal auxiliary (like *can* and *must*).

I **might** study at university.

I **might not** pass my exams.

Do we add *-s* with *he/she/it*?

Do we use *do/does* in the negative?

▶▶ **Grammar Reference 11.2 p140**

Nisa Isaacs, 14
Cape Town, South Africa

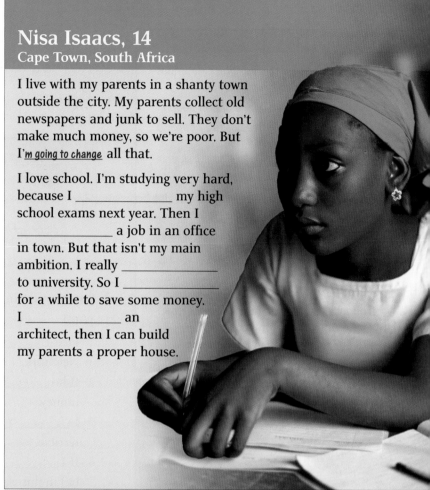

I live with my parents in a shanty town outside the city. My parents collect old newspapers and junk to sell. They don't make much money, so we're poor. But I <u>'m going to change</u> all that.

I love school. I'm studying very hard, because I _____ my high school exams next year. Then I _____ a job in an office in town. But that isn't my main ambition. I really _____ to university. So I _____ for a while to save some money. I _____ an architect, then I can build my parents a proper house.

Viktor Panov, 16
St Petersburg, Russia

I'm studying for my Certificate of Education, but I'm not sure what I want to study afterwards. I love doing art at school, so I <u>might go</u> to art college. That would be fun. I _____ a designer.

But I also enjoy Russian language and literature, so I _____ that at university. I'll have to get good exam results to do that. I'd also like to try living in another country. I've got family in Germany, so I _____ there for a while. Perhaps I could study art and design in Berlin. That would be great!

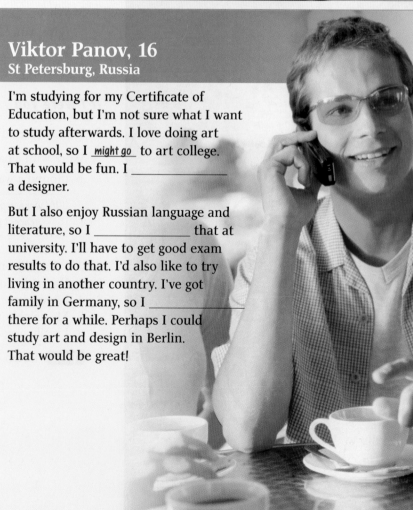

PRACTICE

Discussing grammar

1 Work with a partner. Choose the correct verb in the sentences.

1 **A** What's for supper?
  B *We're having / we might have* lamb. It's in the oven.

2 **A** What time are we eating?
  B Don't worry. *It'll be / it might be* ready before your TV programme.

3 **A** Who's eating with us?
  B I've invited Jerry, but *he'll be / he might be* late. It depends on the traffic.

4 I'm going into town tomorrow. *I'm having / I might have* lunch with Jo at 1.00.

5 **A** Are you going to have a winter holiday this year?
  B *I am / I might.* I haven't decided yet.

T 11.3 Listen and check. Practise the conversations.

Possibilities

2 Make conversations with your partner about these future possibilities. One of you isn't sure about anything.

> **What sort of car are you going to buy?**

> **Well, I might get a Fiat or a Toyota.**

1 **A** What sort/car/buy?
  B Fiat/Toyota

2 **A** Where/on holiday?
  B Scotland/Spain

3 **A** What/have to eat?
  B steak/takeaway pizza

4 **A** Who/going to the dance with?
  B ask Tony/ask Richard

5 **A** What/do if/won the lottery?
  B give it all away/travel the world

T 11.4 Listen and compare. What else do the people say?

3 Ask and answer questions with a partner about your possible future plans …

- after the lesson.
- this evening.
- at the weekend.
- for your next holiday.

LISTENING AND SPEAKING
At a crossroads in life

1 Look at the picture. What do you do at a *crossroads*? What do you think the expression 'at a crossroads in life' means? Can you give any examples?

2 **T 11.5** Listen to three people who have reached a crossroads in their lives. Complete the chart.

Andy 31   Lucy 23   Maureen 68

	What has happened?	What choices do they have?
Andy		
Lucy		
Maureen		

3 **T 11.5** Listen again and check your answers. What reasons do they have for and against their possible choices?

What do you think?

What would you do if you were … ?

- Andy
- Lucy
- Maureen

Discuss each situation with a partner, and then with the class. Does everybody agree what they should do?

4 **T 11.6** Listen to Andy, Lucy, and Maureen a year later. Were you right?

Discussion – Dilemmas

Work in small groups. Look at the situations on p151 and discuss what you would do.

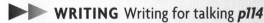 **WRITING** Writing for talking *p114*

READING AND SPEAKING
Supervolcano

1 Discuss the questions.

  1 What famous volcanoes are there in the world? How many can you name?

  2 Are they active or extinct? What do you know about them?

2 What do you think a 'supervolcano' is? Read the first half of the article about them. Check the highlighted words in your dictionary. Mark the sentences true(✔), false(✗), or don't know (**?**).

  1 A supervolcano is a volcano which has recently erupted.

  2 Not many people know that Yellowstone Park is a supervolcano.

  3 Yellowstone Park is an extinct supervolcano.

  4 About 40 supervolcanoes have been found on our planet.

  5 The most recent eruption of a supervolcano was in Yellowstone Park.

  6 It is unlikely that another supervolcano will erupt.

3 Read the second half of the article. Check the highlighted words, and put the events in the correct order.

If Yellowstone volcano erupted, …

☐ there would be no summer in Europe.

[1] 87,000 people would die immediately.

☐ the tropical forests would die.

☐ Iceland might start to help feed the world.

☐ warmer countries would have famines.

☐ only 10% of our sunlight would reach the earth.

Check the answers in class, and then read them aloud to a partner.

If Yellowstone … , then …

4 Read the last part of the article. Why is there no need for us to worry?

5 What do these numbers refer to in the article?

3 million	1960s	9,000	40	74,000
640,000	250kmph	87,000	¾	90%

What do you think?

- Where do you think there might be other volcanic eruptions in the future?

- Do you think scientists will one day find ways of stopping these disasters? How best could they help us?

- If an eruption did happen, what do you think you could do to try and survive? Work in groups, and think about food, housing, heating, and clothing. Tell the class your ideas.

Yellowstone National Park

A geyser erupting in Yellowstone National Park

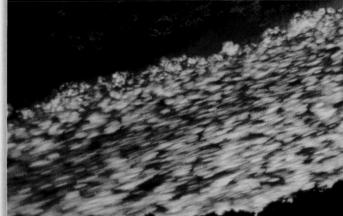

Supervolcano!

If this volcano erupted, the world would freeze ...

Yellowstone National Park, Wyoming, USA. A hot July day, and some of the 3 million visitors who come to the park every year are watching one of the geysers erupt. Everyone is impressed, but as they chatter excitedly and eat their ice-creams, not many of them realize that they are standing on top of the largest active volcano in the world. Scientists have known for a long time that Yellowstone is a volcanic area. But the strange thing is that until the 1960s, none of them could find a volcano anywhere in the park. Then, new photos taken by NASA showed the reason why – the whole park, 9,000 square metres of it, is a volcano!

Volcanoes like Yellowstone are called 'supervolcanoes', because they are so huge and dangerous – 1,000 times more powerful than ordinary volcanoes. There are about 40 of them on Earth, but none of them has erupted recently. The most recent was 74,000 years ago in Indonesia. The last time Yellowstone Park erupted was 640,000 years ago.

But what would happen if the Yellowstone volcano erupted again today? Here are the events that might follow:

Day 1 – Yellowstone Park, USA

If the volcano erupted, hot ash and rock would shoot up into the air at 250kmph. The cities of Denver and Salt Lake would be destroyed immediately, and 87,000 people would die. Eventually the ash would cover ¾ of the USA, and drinking water and food crops would be contaminated.

Week 1 – Europe

The whole of Europe would be covered by a grey cloud. Summer would turn to winter, and in some places the sea would freeze. No European country would be able to grow food for four or five years.

The next 3 months – Worldwide

90% of our sunlight would be blocked and a volcanic winter would cover the Earth. The tropical forests would die and food crops in warm countries, such as India and China, would fail. Only countries near the North and South Poles could carry on as usual. Iceland would do well, because most of its food is grown in special greenhouses. It might be able to send food to the rest of the world.

How likely is it?

Fortunately, scientists at the Yellowstone Volcanic Observatory say that there is no evidence that the volcano will erupt in the near future. They say 'such events are unlikely to happen in the next few centuries'. So we can all get on with our lives and stop worrying, which is good to know.

VOCABULARY AND SPEAKING

Literal phrasal verbs

1 Phrasal verbs consist of a verb + adverb/ preposition. Some phrasal verbs are literal.

> *I want to **go away** and travel.* (= go + away)
> ***Take off** your coat.* (= take + off)
> *She **gave away** all her money.* (= give + away)

2 Complete the sentences with a word from the box.

out	at	down	on	back

1 Put _____ something warm. It's cold today.
2 There's some ice-cream in the freezer. Can you get it _____ ?
3 Dave! Come here and sit _____ next to me.
4 Look _____ the countryside. Isn't it beautiful?
5 When are you going _____ to your country?

3 Do or mime the actions to a partner. Can your partner guess the phrasal verb?

You're picking something up.

> pick something up
> look for something
> turn something off
> lie down
> turn round
> try something on
> throw something away

4 Complete the sentences with a phrasal verb from exercise 3.

1 I'm _____ my glasses. Have you seen them anywhere?
2 I like these jeans. Can I _____ them _____ ?
3 You shouldn't drop litter on the floor! _____ it _____ !
4 Don't _____ the newspaper. I haven't read it yet.
5 If you don't feel well, go and _____ .
6 'Do you like my dress?'
  'Let me see. _____ . Yes. Very nice.'
7 Why are all these lights on? _____ them _____ .

T 11.7 Listen, check, and repeat.

Idiomatic phrasal verbs

5 Some phrasal verbs are idiomatic.

> *I **gave up** my job because it was boring.* (= stop)
> *The plane **took off**.* (= leave the ground)
> *Let's **put off** today's meeting till next week.* (= postpone)

6 Do or mime the actions. Can your partner guess the phrasal verb?

> look after someone
> my car's broken down
> get on with somebody
> run out of milk
> look up a word
> Look out!

You're looking after a baby.

7 Complete the sentences with a phrasal verb from exercise 6.
1 Can I _____ this word in your dictionary?
2 I've _____ milk, so I can't have any cereal.
3 My boss is a great guy. I _____ well _____ him.
4 Leave little Ela here. I'll _____ her while you're out.
5 Oh no! Our car's _____ , and there isn't a garage for miles!
6 _____ ! There's some broken glass on the floor.

T 11.8 Listen, check, and repeat.

Talking about you

Complete the sentences with one of the phrasal verbs on this page in the correct form.

1 How do you _____ your parents?
2 When did you last catch a plane? Did it _____ on time?
3 Have you ever _____ a baby? Whose?
4 Do you _____ all your rubbish, or do you recycle some of it?
5 When did you last _____ something _____ in a clothes shop? Did you buy it?
6 When you see litter in the street, do you _____ it _____ ?
7 Have you ever _____ petrol? What did you do?
8 If you won a lot of money, would you _____ any of it _____ ? Who to?

T 11.9 Listen and check. Ask and answer the questions about you with a partner.

EVERYDAY ENGLISH
Exclamations with *so* and *such*

1 **T 11.10** Read and listen to the sentences.

> I was scared.   I was very scared.   I was so scared!

Do you think *so* is used more in written or in spoken English?
What effect does it have?

2 Look at the sentences. When do we use *so*,
such a(n), *such*, *so many*, and *so much*?

> I was **so** surprised!
> It was **such a** shock!
> It was **such an** awful idea!
> He has **such** crazy friends!
>
> We had **such** terrible weather!
> There were **so many** problems!
> I've got **so much** work!

▶▶ **Grammar Reference 11.3 p141**

Music *of* **English** – sentence stress   ♫♪

Read these sentences aloud. <u>Underline</u> the main stress.

I was so worried!   It's such a nice day!   We had so much fun!

T 11.11 Listen, check, and repeat. Practise saying the
sentences in exercise 2.

---

3 Complete the sentences in **A** with *so*, *such a*, *such*, *so many*, or *so much*.
Then match them with the sentences in **B**.

A	B
1 Their house is _____ mess!	I could eat a horse.
2 There were _____ people at the party!	I don't know where it's all gone.
3 I'm _____ hungry!	You really didn't have to.
4 Jane and Pete are _____ nice people!	She understands every word I say.
5 I've spent _____ money this week!	There was nowhere to dance.
6 A present! For me? You're _____ kind!	Thank you so much for inviting us.
7 We've had _____ nice time!	But I can't stand their kids.
8 Molly's _____ clever dog!	I don't know how they live in it.

T 11.12 Listen and check. Practise the exclamations.

4 Use *so* and *such*.
What can you say … ?

> That was such a good party!
>
> We had so much fun!

* at the end of a party
* at the end of a long journey
* when you finish an interesting book with a sad ending
* as you go round a friend's new flat
* at the end of a wonderful meal
* in a row with your boyfriend/girlfriend/husband/wife

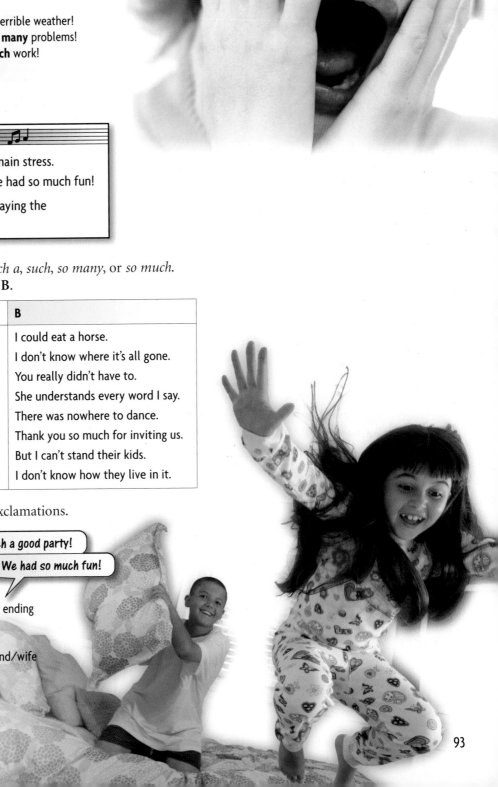

12 Trying your best

Present Perfect Continuous • Hot verbs *bring/take/come/go* **• Social expressions 2**

 STARTER

1 Ask and answer these questions.

- How long have you been learning English?
- When did you start?

2 Ask your teacher the same questions about teaching English.

STREET LIFE
Present Perfect Continuous

1 Read Al's story. Answer the questions.
   1 What went wrong in Al's life?
   2 Where does he sleep?
   3 How is he trying to help himself?

2 Match and write questions *a–f* from p95 with answers 1–6 in the article.

   T 12.1 Listen and check. Finish Al's answer in question 4.

3 With a partner, cover the questions and practise the conversation.

GRAMMAR SPOT

1 Which are the questions in the Present Perfect Continuous? What are the other tenses?

2 Look at the two questions. What are the different tenses? Why are they used?

   How long have you been selling Street News?

   How many copies have you sold today?

   Which tense asks about the activity of selling?

   Which tense asks about the number sold?

3 Complete the sentences with the Present Perfect Simple or Continuous.

   I _____ (read) this book all week.

   I _____ (read) two books this month.

▶▶ **Grammar Reference 12.1 p142**

STREET NEWS
AL'S STORY

Al Brown, 31, from a small town in Pennsylvania, USA, had his own delivery business for five years. When he lost it, he also lost his home and his family. He now sleeps on the streets in New York. *Street News* is a magazine that is sold by homeless people in the city. Selling newspapers gives them a small income, so they can begin to save money for somewhere to live.

1 [_____]?

For a year. It was very cold at first, but after a while you get used to it.

2 [_____]?

I came here to look for work, and I never left.

3 [_____]?

For six months. I'm outside the subway station seven days a week selling the magazine.

4 [_____]?

Lots. But I get fed up with people who think I drink or take drugs. My problem is I'm homeless. I want a job, but I need somewhere to live before I can get a job. So I need money to get somewhere to live, but ...

5 [_____]?

Usually about 70. But I've brought 100 with me.

6 [_____]?

So far, ten. But it's still early. Here, take one!

a How many copies do you sell a day?

b How long have you been selling *Street News*?

c Have you made many friends?

d How many copies have you sold today?

e How long have you been sleeping on the streets?

f Why did you come to New York?

4 Make more questions to ask Al.
- How long/trying to find a job?
- How many jobs/had?
- How long/standing here today?
- How/lose your business?
- How long/had your dog?
- Who/best friend?
- Where/meet him?
- How long/known each other?

T 12.2 Listen and check.

5 Ask and answer the questions with a partner. Invent Al's answers.

T 12.3 Listen and compare your answers.

PRACTICE

Discussing grammar

1 Choose the correct tense.

1 How long *have you been living* / *do you live* in Paris?

2 Anna *has been finding* / *has found* a good job.

3 Pete and I *have gone out* / *have been going out* for over six months.

4 I *bought* / *have bought* a new flat a few months ago.

5 How long *have you had* / *have you been having* your car?

6 Tom *worked* / *has been working* as a postman for the past month.

7 I *'ve written* / *'ve been writing* an essay all day.

8 I *'ve written* / *'ve been writing* six pages.

Talking about you

2 Put the verbs in the Present Perfect Simple or Continuous, or the Past Simple.

1 How long _____ you _____ (study) at this school?

2 How long _____ you _____ (use) this book?

3 Which book _____ you _____ (have) before this one?

4 How long _____ you _____ (know) your teacher?

Ask and answer the questions.

What have they been doing?

3 Make a sentence about the people, using an idea from the box. Add *because* and say what they've been doing.

> He's hot because he's been running.

~~hot~~	back hurts	paint on her clothes		dirty hands
no money	tired	eyes hurt	wet	red face

4 Complete these sentences with the Present Perfect Simple about some of the people in exercise 3.

1 (a) He _____ (run) five miles.
2 (c) She _____ (paint) three walls.
3 (e) They _____ (spend) all their money.
4 (f) They _____ (play) six games.
5 (i) He _____ (make) a cake and a pie.

Exchanging information

5 Look at the picture of Stelios Haji-Ioannou. What do you know about him? What is he famous for? What companies has he started?

6 Work with a partner. You have different information about Stelios. Take it in turns to ask and answer questions.

Student A
Look at p145.
Stelios was born ... *(Where?)* in 1967.

Student B
Look at p148.
Stelios was born in Greece ... *(When?)*.

> Where was Stelios born?

> In Greece.

> When was he born?

> In 1967.

VOCABULARY AND SPEAKING
Hot verbs – *bring*, *take*, *come*, and *go*

The verbs *bring*, *take*, *come*, and *go*, are very common in English. Look at the examples. Some are from this unit.

I **came** here to look for work.	I never **went** back home.
He **brought** his dog with him.	**Take** one of these!

1 Underline the examples of the verbs in these questions. Ask and answer them with a partner.

1 What did you bring with you to school today?
2 When you are invited to a friend's house, do you usually take something?
3 Who comes to visit you at home most often?
4 Where do you usually go after school?

2 The choice between *bring* / *take* and *come* / *go* depends on where the speaker is.

I'm going to France on holiday. I must remember to take my French dictionary.

I came to Britain to study English. Fortunately, I brought an umbrella.

She uses *take* and *go* for a movement away from her.	He uses *bring* and *come* for a movement towards him.

3 Complete the conversations with *bring*, *take*, *come*, and *go* in the correct form.

1 A Goodbye, everyone! I'm _____ on holiday tomorrow.
   B Where are you _____?
   A Australia. I'm _____ my family to visit their cousins in Sydney.
   B Lucky you! When you _____ back, _____ me a T-shirt!

2 A Listen, class! Please finish your work before you _____ home. And tomorrow, don't forget to _____ in your money for the school trip. We're _____ to the Natural History Museum.
   B Oh, Miss Jones! Can't you _____ us somewhere more exciting?

3 A Daniel, you were very late last night. What time did you _____ home?
   B It was before midnight, Mum, honest. Mick _____ me home in his car.

4 A I've been decorating my new flat. You must _____ and visit me on Saturday. And _____ Emma and Jake with you. I'll cook you a meal.
   B Great! We'll _____ some champagne to toast your new home!

5 (*In London*)
   A I'll miss you when I _____ back home to Spain. You must _____ and visit me at Christmas.
   B I'd love to! I want you to _____ this photo with you. It will remind you of the day we _____ to Oxford together.
   A OK. And when you visit, _____ me some more English books to read!

6 (*In France*)
   A I'm _____ to London tomorrow, so tonight my best friend is _____ round to my house to say goodbye. She's _____ a present she wants me to _____ to her sister in London.
   B Well, have a good trip!

T 12.4 Listen and check your answers.

READING AND SPEAKING
In her father's footsteps

1 Do you know any famous explorers? Why do some people do dangerous and difficult things?

2 Read the first part of the article. Can you explain the title?

3 Read the complete article. Answer the questions.

1 Has Alicia been to the North Pole before?
2 Who is she going to walk with?
3 What has she been doing to prepare for the journey?
4 What has her father done in his exploring career?
5 What does he think about her trip? And what does he think her main problem will be?
6 How do Alicia's mother and great-grandmother feel about it?

4 Discuss these questions with a partner, and then with the class.

1 Should Mr Hempleman-Adams let his daughter go on the trip?
2 Why is his advice to her 'Take it easy'? What does he mean?
3 What do you think will happen on the trip?
4 Do you think she'll be successful?
5 How will her father feel if she fails? If she succeeds?

Tense review

5 Complete the sentences with the verbs in brackets in the correct tense.

1 Alicia _____ (fly) to the North Pole when she was eight.
2 She _____ (not walk) to the North Pole yet.
3 She _____ (start) the 200-mile trip next month.
4 She _____ (plan) the trip for a long time.
5 Her father _____ already _____ (make) the journey twice in his life.
6 He also _____ (climb) Mount Everest in 1993.
7 At the moment he _____ (try) not to worry about his daughter's trip.
8 He _____ (hope) that she will enjoy it.

6 Read a second newspaper article on p151. Compare your ideas for questions 3–5 in exercise 4 with Alicia's experience.

What do you think?

• Why do you think Alicia wanted to do the trip?
• Why do you think she wants to do something different in the future?
• Would you do something like this? Why? / Why not?

 **WRITING** Linking ideas **p115**

In her

When Alicia Hempleman-Adams was eight years old, she became the youngest person to travel to the North Pole. But that was on a plane when she visited her father, the British explorer David Hempleman-Adams. Now the 15-year-old has decided to follow in her dad's frozen footsteps. Next month, Alicia is going to set off on a journey to the Arctic that could put her in the record books, as the youngest person to walk to the North Pole.

Alicia won't be alone. Four others, including her physical education teacher, are also going to walk the 200-mile route across Baffin Island in northern Canada.

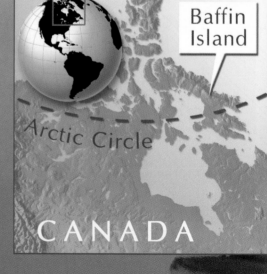

Baffin Island

Arctic Circle

CANADA

father's footsteps

She has been training hard for the journey. She has been walking a lot with a heavy backpack, and she has also been practising pulling a sled long distances. 'It's going to be pretty cold,' she said. 'It's −20°C at the moment, and it might get to −30°C. But I think we're prepared.'

'She's half my size and a teenager.'

Alicia has to be well-prepared if she wants to be like her dad. David Hempleman-Adams, 48, has been travelling in the Arctic and Antarctic for 25 years. He has walked to the South Pole once, and the North Pole twice. In 2000 he was the first to fly in a balloon over the North Pole. He has also climbed the highest mountains in all seven continents.

Mr Hempleman-Adams said that it took a long time before he agreed to let his daughter go on the trip. 'I am a little worried. It's going to be very hard. She's half my size and a teenager, so I think the cold will be a big problem.'

Alicia's mother is also trying to stay calm about the trip. She thinks that Alicia is too young to make the journey. Mr Hempleman-Adams said, 'My wife has always thought I'm silly to be an explorer.' And when his 90-year-old grandmother heard of the latest plan, she shouted, 'Oh, no, not again!'

He said, 'If Alicia doesn't finish, it's not a problem. She's got the rest of her life to do it. You've got to enjoy it. There's no other reason for doing adventure.'

What advice does he give his daughter? 'Take it easy,' he said.

Alicia and her father

Alicia training for the trip

ifyoucomeback

For all this time I've been _____ you, girl	following / loving
Oh yes I have	
And ever since the day you left me here alone	
I've been _____ to find, oh, the reason why	trying / asking
So if I did something _____	right / wrong
Please tell me	
I wanna _____	understand / say sorry
'Cause I don't want this love to ever _____	finish / end

Chorus

And I swear	
If you come back in my life	
I'll be there till the end of _____	time / the road

(Come back to me
Come back to me
Back into my life)

And I swear	
I'll keep you right by my _____	self / side
'Cause baby, you're the one I _____	want / 'll marry

(Come back to me
Come back to me
Back into my life)

Oh yes you are

I watched you go	
You've taken my _____ with you	keys / heart
Oh yes you have	
Every time I tried to reach you on the _____	mobile / phone
Baby you're never there	
Girl you're never _____	home / alone
So if I did something _____	right / wrong
Please tell me	
I wanna _____	understand / say sorry
'Cause I don't want this love to ever _____	finish / end
No, no, no, no	

Chorus

Maybe I didn't know how to _____ it	show / explain
And maybe I didn't know what to say	
This time I won't disguise	
Then we can build our _____	house / lives
Then we can be as one	

Chorus

1 **T 12.5** Close your books and listen to a song by the band *Blue*. Who is the boy singing to? What's he trying to do?

Glossary	
wanna	want to
I swear	I promise
I won't disguise	I won't hide my feelings
be as one	be together

2 Work with a partner. Choose the best words in *italics* to complete the song.

T 12.5 Listen again and check your answers.

What do you think?
- Does the boy know why the girl left him?
- What does he think the reason might be?
- If she comes back, what does he promise to do?
- Do you think she will come back?

EVERYDAY ENGLISH
Social Expressions 2

1 Complete the conversations with the correct expressions.

1

I'm sorry	Excuse me	of course	Pardon

A _____ ! Can I get past?

B _____ ?

A Can I get past, please?

B _____ . I didn't hear you. Yes, _____ .

A Thanks a lot.

2

That's right	Oh, what a pity	Congratulations	Never mind	I hear

A _____ you're getting married soon. _____ !

B _____ , next July. July 21st. Can you come to the wedding?

A _____ ! That's when we're going away on holiday.

C _____ . We'll send you some wedding cake.

A That's very kind.

3

Good luck	See you later	Same to you	Good idea
What about you	No, of course not		

A _____ in your exam!

B _____ . I hope we both pass.

A Did you go out last night?

B _____ . I went to bed early. _____ ?

A Me, too. _____ after the exam. Let's go for a drink.

B _____ .

4

Well	Don't worry	Bye	Safe journey
Thank you for having me		You're welcome	

A Here's my train!

B _____ . It doesn't leave for another five minutes.

A _____ , I'd better get on, anyway, and find my seat.
It was lovely staying with you. _____ .

C _____ . It was a pleasure.

A Goodbye, then. See you again soon, I hope.

B and C _____ ! _____ !

2 **T 12.6** Listen and check. Practise the conversations with a partner. Remember stress and intonation!

3 **T 12.7** Listen. Reply using one of the expressions.

4 Make more conversations for these situations.
- being sympathetic to a friend who's just failed an exam
- trying to get off a crowded bus
- leaving a friend's house where you've just had dinner
- saying goodbye to teachers/schoolfriends when you leave school

Writing

UNIT 1 DESCRIBING FRIENDS – Correcting common mistakes

1 Look at the symbols often used to correct mistakes in writing. Correct the mistakes in the sentences. Compare your answers with a partner.

Sp	Spelling	1	I'm <u>enjoing</u> the party. (Sp)
WW	Wrong word	2	My brother has a good <u>work</u>. (WW)
WO	Word order	3	I have <u>two brothers younger</u>. (WO)
Gr	Grammar	4	She's got some new <u>reds</u> shoes. (Gr)
T	Tense	5	He <u>arrive</u> yesterday. (T)
P	Punctuation	6	They <u>arent</u> coming. (P)
⋏	Word missing	7	She's ⋏ doctor.
Prep	Preposition	8	They went <u>in</u> Italy on holiday. (Prep)

2 Work in two groups. In each of the sentences below there is one mistake.

Group A Find the mistakes in **A.** Use the symbols to mark them, but don't correct them.

Group B Find the mistakes in **B.** Use the symbols to mark them, but don't correct them.

A

1 I like Rome because is a beautiful city.
2 She studied for three years psychology.
3 There aren't any milk.
4 He's speaking French, German and Spanish.
5 I watched TV than I went to bed.
6 Did you by any bread at the supermarket?

B

1 I lost my all money.
2 What did you last night?
3 He always wear jeans.
4 My town is quite at the weekend.
5 I want that I pass the exam.
6 They arrived at London.

3 Find a partner from the other group. Correct each other's sentences.

4 Correct this piece of student writing.

My best friend was my best man when I <u>get</u> married (T) two <u>year</u> ago. (Gr) <u>He's</u> name is Mario and we met <u>in</u> (Gr) (prep) university in Bologna. In fact, we met on our very first day <u>their</u>. (Sp) Mario was ⋏ first person I spoke <u>with</u> and we (prep) discovered we were both studying Spanish and that we were both football fans. When we left university, we went <u>together travelling</u> for six <u>month</u>. (WO) (Gr) We had a fantastic time touring <u>north</u> and <u>south america</u>. (P) (P) The <u>travel</u> through Chile was amazing. (WW) When we were in Mexico, we met two sisters <u>of</u> London, Tamsin and (prep) Tanya. Now I'm married <u>with</u> Tanya, and next year (prep) Mario and Tamsin ⋏ going to get married. I like Mario because he ⋏ very funny and we <u>has</u> really good times (Gr) together. He <u>live</u> in a different town now, but we text (⋏Gr) or call <u>often each other</u>. (WO) I'm very lucky that he's my friend.

5 Write about your own best friend.

6 Swap with a partner and see if you can find any mistakes. Read some examples of your work aloud to the class.

1 Imagine that you receive an email from an old friend. It is many years since you last heard news from them. Make notes about what you want to tell them about you and your life in your reply.

but, although, and *however*

2 Read these sentences. They all mean the same. How are they different?

> • I don't write many letters **but** I send emails a lot.
> • **Although** I don't write many letters, I send emails a lot.
> • I don't write many letters. **However**, I send emails a lot.

3 Join these pairs of sentences in three different ways using *but, although,* and *however*.

1. He's a good friend. We don't meet often.
2. She isn't English. She speaks English very well.
3. It rained a lot. We enjoyed the holiday.

so and *because*

4 Read these sentences.

> 1 He lived in France for many years, **so** he speaks French well.
> 2 He speaks French well **because** he lived in France for many years.

Which pattern goes with which sentence?

a Result ◄─────────── Cause
b Cause ──────────► Result

5 Join the pairs of sentences in two different ways, using *so* and *because*.

1. She went home. She was tired.
2. We didn't enjoy our holiday. The weather was bad.
3. He worked hard. He passed all his exams.
4. I enjoy history lessons. I like the teacher.
5. It started to rain. We stopped playing tennis.

6 Read the email. Who is writing to who? Why? What news does she give? Complete the email with one of these linking words.

> but   although   however   so   because

From:	"rebecca king" <bec.king5@wana.com>
Date:	Wed, 27 Apr. 20:07:36 +0100 (BST)
To:	"Martha Baines" <m@baines.fsnet.co.uk>
Subject:	Re: Do you remember me?

Dear Martha,

How wonderful to hear from you. Of course I remember you, (1)_____ it's over ten years since we last met. Who gave you my email address? It was great to learn a bit about you and your family. You asked what I'm doing these days, (2)_____ here's some of my news.

First things first – I married George! I know you never liked him much, (3)_____ you'll probably be pleased to hear that we're now divorced. (4)_____ , we still see each other a lot (5)_____ we have two children, twins, Sam and Toby. They're six now and they're good boys, (6)_____ of course, they're sometimes a bit of a handful. We moved from Birmingham (7)_____ I didn't want the boys to grow up in a big city. We now live in a big, old farmhouse in Wales. It's really beautiful (8)_____ it's expensive to look after (9)_____ it's so old. George still lives in Birmingham, (10)_____ he often visits and the boys always spend part of their holidays with him.

I know you're busy (11)_____ I'd love you to visit us soon and meet my new husband. Yes, I'm married again. Do you remember Hugo King? He was older than us and I think you liked him a lot! Well, we got married a year ago. Can you believe it?

I can't wait to hear more of your news, (12)_____ write very soon.

Love

Rebecca (Becca) x

7 Write an email to your old friend. Use your notes from exercise 1 and the phrases below.

> Dear X
> How wonderful/amazing to hear from you.
> I was so surprised./What a wonderful surprise!
> How did you get my email address?
> It was great to hear your news.
> Let me tell you something about my life.
> I can't believe that ...   Let's keep in touch.
> Guess what!   Best wishes/All the best
> Do you remember...?

Swap emails with a partner. Read your partner's email.

1 Write the sentences with the adjectives and adverbs in the correct place.

1 A dog jumped up at me.
   (large, suddenly)
   A large dog suddenly jumped up at me.

2 Thank you for your invitation. I can't come.
   (kind, unfortunately)

3 I got out of bed and went to make a cup of tea.
   (downstairs, nice)

4 We had a meal and went to the theatre.
   (lovely, then)

5 I was sitting at home when something happened.
   (last Thursday evening, very strange)

6 He's got three sisters and I've got three sisters.
   (older, too)

7 There was a documentary on TV last night. I enjoyed it.
   (good, very much)

8 I worked all week.
   (really hard, last)

2 Work with a partner. Look at the pictures. What do you think the story is about?
Use the prompts for pictures 1–4 to write the story of **Aunt Camilla's Portrait**. Take it in turns to read it aloud to the class.

Picture 1
My Aunt Camilla ... old and very ... . One day ... in the mirror ... suddenly decided that ... a portrait of herself. Immediately, she ... the world-famous portrait painter, Rolf Unwin.

Picture 2
Twice a week she ... his studio. Rolf ... painted her ... . He didn't want ... see the picture until ... .

Picture 3
Finally, ... the portrait ... ready. My aunt ... excited and hurried ... . The portrait ... exactly like my aunt. Unfortunately, she ... and refused ... . She ordered him to ... .

Picture 4
This time ... didn't visit the studio ... . After another three months, the portrait ... ready and my aunt ... see it. The face ... a beautiful ... girl. It didn't ... like my aunt at all, ... she ... loved it. She paid Rolf ... .

Turn to p149 and compare your stories. What are some of the differences?

Aunt Camilla's Portrait

3 Here's another picture story – 'The French Burglar'. It's a true story! Write the story, using the prompts for each picture. Use as many adverbs and adjectives as you can.

> 1 One ... summer's evening last June, a burglar broke into a ... house in Paris. First he ... living room and ... put ... .
>
> 2 Next ... kitchen to ... . He opened ... and saw ... cheese.
>
> 3 ... feeling hungry, so he took ... and sat ... . Then he remembered ... .
>
> 4 He went back ... and quickly ... .
>
> 5 After that ... upstairs to ... , but suddenly ... really tired, so ... .
>
> 6 Unfortunately, ... asleep ... , and the next morning when ... .

4 Compare your story with a partner's. Read some aloud to the class.

Then turn to p150 and compare your stories. What are the differences?

The French Burglar

1 Read the postcard. Where are Richard and Sandy? Are they enjoying their holiday? Where did their friend go on holiday? What is wrong with the style of the writing?

Dear Sam,
Here we are in New York having a nice time. The weather is very nice. We're staying in quite a nice hotel in a nice part of town, Lower Manhattan. We have nice views of the Chrysler and Empire State Buildings from our bedroom window. We think all the skyscrapers are nice. Yesterday we went on a really nice helicopter tour of the city and then in the evening we saw a nice show on Broadway. Today we are going shopping for clothes in Bloomingdales. I want to buy some nice designer jeans. They are much cheaper here. Did you have a nice time in the South of France? We hear that the markets there are nice.
   See you soon,
      Love,
         Richard and Sandy

POSTCARD

Samantha Troy

10 Wallasey Road

Brentwood

ESSEX CM15 7LE

ENGLAND

'New York city at night'

2 Richard and Sandy use *nice* eleven times. Complete the sentences below with more descriptive adjectives from the box. Use as many different ones as possible. Careful! Sometimes more than one word is possible, but not always!

| great   warm and sunny   interesting   good   wonderful |
| luxurious   spectacular   amazing   exciting   brilliant   beautiful |

1 We're having a _____ time here in New York.

2 The weather is _____.

3 We're staying in a _____ hotel in a/an _____ part of town.

4 We have _____ views of the Empire State Building.

5 We think the skyscrapers are _____.

6 We went on a/an _____ helicopter ride.

7 In the evening we saw a/an _____ show.

8 I bought some _____ designer jeans.

9 Did you have a _____ time in the South of France?

10 We hear that the markets there are _____.

3 Work with a partner. Read the postcard aloud with a variety of adjectives. Use *nice* once only. Where do you think is the best place to use it?

4 Think of a holiday you once had. Imagine you are still there. Write a postcard to an English friend about it, but use the adjective *nice* once only! You can write about some of these things.

- the journey
- the weather
- the accommodation
- the food
- some things you did yesterday
- some things you are going to do today

Read your postcard to the class.

UNIT 5 FILLING IN A FORM

1 When do you fill in forms? Give some examples.

2 Match the expressions and questions.

1	First name	a	Are you married or single?
2	Surname	b	What do you do in your free time?
3	Date of birth	c	What's your phone number?
4	Place of birth	d	What's your first name?
5	Permanent address	e	What do you do?
6	Marital status	f	Where were you born?
7	Occupation	g	When were you born?
8	Qualifications	h	What's your family name?
9	Hobbies/Interests	i	Where do you live?
10	Tel. no.	j	What degrees, diplomas, certificates, etc. do you have?

3 Follow these instructions. Write about you.

1 Write your name in capital letters.
2 Sign your name.
3 Delete where not applicable.
(Mr/Mrs/Miss/Ms)
4 Write your postcode.

4 Complete the form.

5 Compare the information on your form with other students.

The Global School of English

PLEASE WRITE IN CAPITAL LETTERS

Mr/Mrs/Ms*   Family name [   ]   First name [   ]

Sex [   ]   Date of birth [   ]   Nationality [   ]

First language [   ]   Level of English [   ]

Address in your country

[   ]   Occupation [   ]

Email address [   ]

Where did you hear about the school? [   ]

Have you been to ... before? [   ]   If yes, when? [   ]

Date of arrival [   ]   Date of departure [   ]

Reason for learning English: Business/pleasure/exams/other* (If other, please specify.)

[   ]

How many hours a day do you want to study? [   ]

Signature [   ]   *Delete where not applicable.

1 Complete this sentence in any way you can.

   The town where I was born is / has ...

Share the information with the class.

GRAMMAR SPOT

1 We use *who*, *that*, *which*, and *where* to join sentences. Look at these sentences.

I met a man. He comes from my town.
I met a man **who** comes from my town.

I bought a house. It's in the High Street.
I bought a house **which / that** is in the High Street.

The hotel was very comfortable. We stayed in it.
The hotel **where** we stayed was very comfortable.

2 *Who*, *which*, *that* and *where* are relative pronouns. Complete the rules with a relative pronoun.

   • _____ is for people.

   • _____ or _____ is for things.

   • _____ is for places.

---

2 Join the sentences with the correct relative pronoun.

   1 There's the boy. He broke the window.
   2 That's the palace. The Queen lives in it.
   3 There are the policemen. They caught the thief.
   4 I bought a watch. It stopped after two days.
   5 Here are the letters. They arrived this morning.
   6 That's the hospital. I was born in it.

3 Read the description of a town. Complete the text with *who*, *which*, or *where*. Then answer the questions.

   1 Where is the town?
   2 Why is it called Newcastle?
   3 What was it like 50 years ago?
   4 What is it like now?
   5 How many bridges are there?
   6 What are the people like?
   7 What is 'The Angel of the North'?
   8 What is a 'Geordie'?

4 Write a similar description of your home town in about 200 words. First write some notes about it.

   • Where is it? • What's its history? • What's it like now?

Next write some personal opinions.

   • Do you like it? • Why?

5 Read some aloud and compare your towns.

THE TOWN WHERE I WAS BORN

I was born in Newcastle, a city in the north-east of England. Newcastle is on the banks of the River Tyne, (1)_____, in the 12th century, a 'new castle' was built, (2)_____ gave the city its name.

   Today Newcastle is one of Britain's biggest cities, with a population of about 260,000. 50 years ago, it was very industrial. The main industry on the Tyne was shipbuilding, but now, this river, (3)_____ once ships and coal barges sailed, is lined with fashionable hotels, bars, and restaurants.

   There are seven bridges over the Tyne, (4)_____ link Newcastle to the next town, Gateshead. The most recent is the beautiful Millennium Bridge, (5)_____ was built in 2001. Next to it is an old flour mill, now the famous Baltic Art Centre, (6)_____ you can see the work of contemporary artists, (7)_____ produce many of their paintings and sculptures on site.

   I moved from Newcastle ten years ago but I often return. I miss the people, (8)_____ are so warm and friendly, and I miss the wild, beautiful countryside to the north of the city. I also miss my favourite sculpture, 'The Angel of the North', (9)_____ greets you as you arrive in the North East.

   People (10)_____ are born near the River Tyne have a special name. They are called 'Geordies'. I am very pleased to be a 'Geordie'!

1 Write down the names of three people alive today who were born famous, and three who have become famous. Share your ideas with the class. Why are they famous?

2 What do you know about Princess Caroline of Monaco? Discuss with a partner.

3 Read these six paragraphs about Princess Caroline. Work together to put the paragraphs in the correct order. Did you find any of the facts you and your partner discussed?

4 Here are some facts about the life of Caroline's sister, Princess Stephanie of Monaco. Divide the information into five paragraphs. Use this and the text about Caroline to help write Stephanie's biography. Use *and*, *then*, *but*, and relative pronouns to help link your ideas.

THE LIFE OF A PRINCESS (1)

Caroline

a [ ] However, just one year after her mother's death, Caroline married Italian businessman Stefano Casiraghi and, with the birth of their three children, found real happiness. Then tragedy struck again. In October 1990, Stefano died in a powerboat accident. The shock caused Caroline to lose her hair. She moved from Monaco to St Rémy and for five years she stayed at home with her children.

b [ ] *Princess Caroline of Monaco* was born on January 23, 1957. She was the first child of Prince Rainier III and Princess Grace of Monaco. Her brother Albert followed 14 months later, and seven years after that her sister Stephanie was born. Prince Rainier and Princess Grace wanted their children to have a normal life. However, this proved impossible. The paparazzi have followed their lives since they were small. The activities of the two princesses have been of particular interest.

c [ ] The divorce was the first of many misfortunes in Caroline's life. In 1982, her mother, Princess Grace, died in a terrible accident while she was driving with Stephanie down the narrow Monaco roads. The death of this once famous film star was a huge tragedy for the family.

d [ ] Caroline was a bright, beautiful child, and after school in England, she went to study in Paris. She adored the Paris nightlife but of course, the paparazzi followed her everywhere. Her parents were furious. They became even more upset when Caroline met and wanted to marry French banker and playboy Philippe Junot, aged 38. When Caroline, aged 21, married Junot in 1978, Princess Grace said, 'This won't last two years', and she was absolutely right. They divorced in 1980.

e [ ] However, the pain of the past showed again on her face when her father, Prince Rainier, died in 2005. Prince Albert is now Monaco's head of state. Caroline's son, Andrea, is the heir. Her eldest daughter, Charlotte, who looks very like her mother, already stars in celebrity magazines. The paparazzi have started again with the next generation.

f [ ] Then, in 1995, she met Prince Ernst of Hanover again, the man her mother had always wanted her to marry. Although he was already married, they began a relationship and finally married in 1999. Caroline's happiness seemed complete with the birth of a daughter, Alexandra.

THE LIFE OF A PRINCESS (2)

Stephanie

★ Born: 1 February 1965 … third and last child of …

★ Often called the 'wild-child princess'

★ Aged just 17 in 1982 when her mother died while … . She was a passenger in the car.

★ Some people said that Stephanie was driving.

★ After crash … went wild

★ Had two children by her bodyguard, Daniel Ducret:
Louis, b. 1992,
Pauline, b. 1994

★ Married Ducret 1995

★ Divorced 1996 … paparazzi photographed Ducret with Belgian beauty queen

★ Third child 1998, Camille. She has never named the father.

★ Stephanie has always loved circuses. Next boyfriend an elephant trainer, Franco Knie.

★ In 2003, married again – Adans Lopez Peres, a Portuguese acrobat 10 years her junior, from the same circus as Knie.

★ Divorced 2004

★ Father died 2005. Stephanie distraught. She was his favourite.

5 Write a biography of a celebrity that interests you.

1 Work with a partner. Discuss which beginnings can go with which endings. More than one is sometimes possible. Which are formal? Which are informal? Which are usually only used in emails?

1 Dear Peter,	a Lots and lots of love, Harry xxx
2 Dear Ms Lombard,	b Love, Concetta
3 Hello Cathy,	c Yours, George
4 Dear Sir or Madam,	d Bye for now, Sammy
5 Dear Mum,	e Yours faithfully, Daniel Miles
6 Hi Rob,	f Yours sincerely, Kay Macey
	g Best wishes, Dave

A formal letter

2 Read the formal letter. Complete it with the words or phrases from the box.

> frequently   advertisement   However   interested in
> sincerely   to hearing   some information   to improve
> application form

3 Look at the different parts of the letter. Compare it with formal letters in your country.
Are the names, addresses, and the date in the same place? Do you have many different greetings and endings for formal and informal letters and emails?

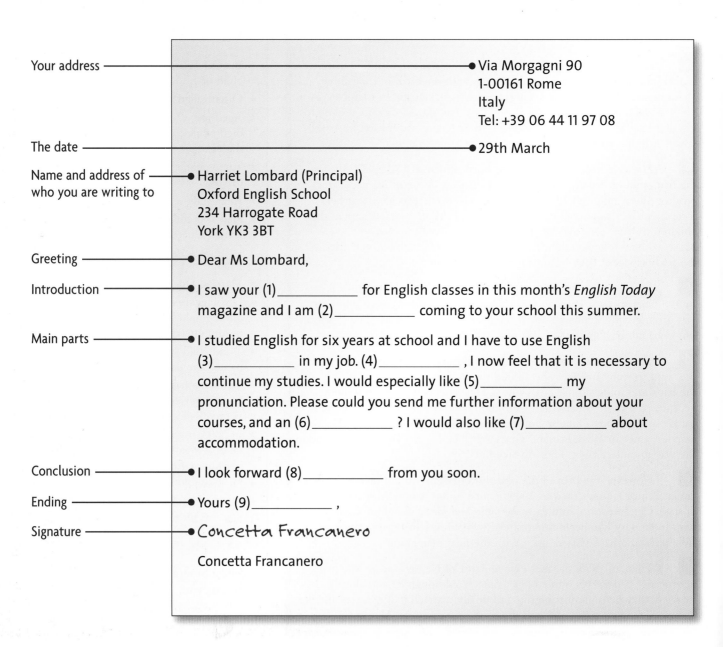

Your address → Via Morgagni 90
1-00161 Rome
Italy
Tel: +39 06 44 11 97 08

The date → 29th March

Name and address of who you are writing to → Harriet Lombard (Principal)
Oxford English School
234 Harrogate Road
York YK3 3BT

Greeting → Dear Ms Lombard,

Introduction → I saw your (1)_____ for English classes in this month's *English Today* magazine and I am (2)_____ coming to your school this summer.

Main parts → I studied English for six years at school and I have to use English (3)_____ in my job. (4)_____ , I now feel that it is necessary to continue my studies. I would especially like (5)_____ my pronunciation. Please could you send me further information about your courses, and an (6)_____ ? I would also like (7)_____ about accommodation.

Conclusion → I look forward (8)_____ from you soon.

Ending → Yours (9)_____ ,

Signature → Concetta Francanero

Concetta Francanero

An informal email

4 Read Concetta's email to her English friend Rob. Compare it with the letter. How does she express the highlighted lines from the email more formally in the letter?

5 Match these lines from an email and a formal letter.

A	B
It was great to hear from you.	Please find enclosed a photocopy of ...
Thanks for ...	I apologize for ...
I want to ask about ...	Thank you for your letter of 1st November.
I'm sorry about ...	If you require further assistance, ...
I'm sorry to have to tell you that ...	I regret to inform you that ...
I'm sending you a copy of ...	I would like to enquire about ...
If you need any more help, ...	Thank you for ...

From: "Concetta Francanero " <cetta.nero@aol.com>
Date: Sat, 21 May 07:50:28 -0700 (PDT)
To: robbojon@ntlworld.co.uk
Subject: Coming to England

Hi Rob,

Just to let you know that I'm thinking of coming to England this summer. You know I have to use English a lot at work now, and I think I need some extra lessons. I especially want my pronunciation to be better – you're always telling me it's bad! Anyway, I saw an ad in a magazine for a school in York. Isn't that quite near you? Can you send me some more information about language schools in your area? It would be great to see you while I'm there, and I'd also love to meet some of your friends.

Can't wait to hear from you. See you soon I hope.
Love

Concetta

6 Write a similar letter about yourself to the school in York. Then write an email to an English friend and tell them about it.

1 Do you sometimes travel by train? Write down three things you *like* and three things you *don't like* about travelling by train. Compare your ideas with the class.

2 Read these notes. How many of your ideas are here?

Advantages of train travel	Disadvantages of train travel
• fast	• sometimes expensive
• comfortable	• sometimes crowded
• not stressful	• sometimes delayed
	• not door to door
You can ...	**You must ...**
• relax (read / look out of the window)	• travel at certain times
• work	• use other transport to get to
• eat	the station

3 Now read the text. What is the purpose of each paragraph?

4 Put the linking words on the right into the correct place in each paragraph. Sometimes you will need to change the punctuation.

5 Make notes about the advantages and disadvantages of one of these topics. Then write a text similar to the one below, giving your own opinions. Write about 150 words.
- Travelling by car
- Travelling by plane
- Holidays abroad

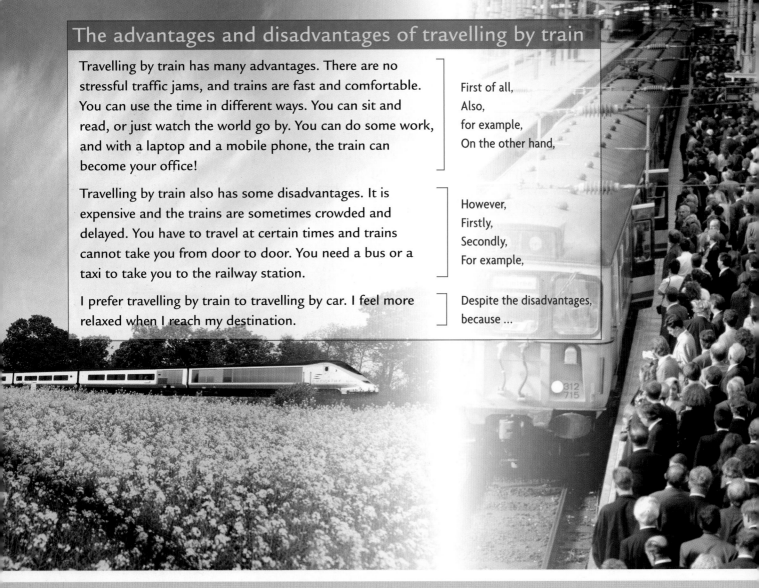

The advantages and disadvantages of travelling by train

Travelling by train has many advantages. There are no stressful traffic jams, and trains are fast and comfortable. You can use the time in different ways. You can sit and read, or just watch the world go by. You can do some work, and with a laptop and a mobile phone, the train can become your office!

First of all,
Also,
for example,
On the other hand,

Travelling by train also has some disadvantages. It is expensive and the trains are sometimes crowded and delayed. You have to travel at certain times and trains cannot take you from door to door. You need a bus or a taxi to take you to the railway station.

However,
Firstly,
Secondly,
For example,

I prefer travelling by train to travelling by car. I feel more relaxed when I reach my destination.

Despite the disadvantages,
because ...

1 Which films are popular at the moment? What have you seen recently? Complete these sentences. Then talk to a partner about it.

- The last film I saw was …
- It starred …
- It was about …
- I really enjoyed/didn't enjoy it because …

2 Read the paragraph below. What do the words in **bold** refer to?

I saw a really good film last week. **It** was a horror movie. I went with two friends. **They** didn't enjoy **it** at all. They said the acting was terrible. **That** surprised me, because I thought **it** was excellent. My parents rarely go to the cinema. **This** is because **they** wait until the film comes out on DVD, and then they watch **it** at home.

3 What do you know about the story of Frankenstein? Share your ideas with the class. Answer the questions.

1 Is *Frankenstein* a book or a film? Or both?

2 What kind of story is it? Is it …
- a detective story?
- a horror story?
- a science fiction story?
- a romance?

3 Who or what is Frankenstein? Is he …
- a doctor?
- a scientist?
- a monster?
- a student?

4 Read the review of the novel *Frankenstein*. Check your answers to exercise 3.

5 Read the review again. What do the words in **bold** refer to?

6 Complete the review with the past participles in the box.

| translated written published made |
| said told terrified used |

7 Look at the headings. Find the information in the review of *Frankenstein*.

- title and author
- type of book / film
- characters
- the plot

Make some notes under the same headings about a book or film that you have read or seen recently. Then write a short review. Read it aloud to the class and answer questions about it.

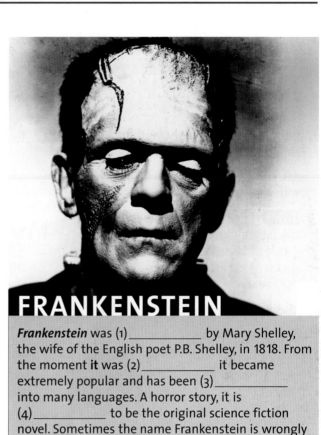

FRANKENSTEIN

Frankenstein was (1)_____ by Mary Shelley, the wife of the English poet P.B. Shelley, in 1818. From the moment **it** was (2)_____ it became extremely popular and has been (3)_____ into many languages. A horror story, it is (4)_____ to be the original science fiction novel. Sometimes the name Frankenstein is wrongly (5)_____ as the name of the monster, but in fact, Frankenstein is the name of the scientist who created it.

The story is (6)_____ through the letters of a man called Walton, an English explorer. We learn of Victor Frankenstein, a student of science from Geneva, **who** discovers the secret of life and decides to make a human being. So at night he visits graveyards and collects bones and bodies. With **these** he creates a person who is more monster than man.

The monster is huge and ugly, and of course, people are (7)_____ when they see it. As a result, the poor creature has no friends and feels lonely and depressed. Finally, it asks Frankenstein to make it a wife. **This** he refuses to do. So the monster attacks and kills not only Frankenstein's brother, but also his friend, and his bride, Elizabeth. Frankenstein is heartbroken and is determined to kill the monster.

Unfortunately, while chasing **it**, **he** dies. The monster then kills **itself**.

Over 40 movies have been (8)_____ of the story of Frankenstein, **the first** as long ago as 1910. It is a fascinating story because of the character of the monster, **which** is both sad and frightening at the same time.

1 Think about your future life. How do you see your life … ?

- next year
- in five years' time
- in ten years' time

Write some notes about your hopes and ambitions at each of these times.

Ask and answer questions about them with a partner.

2 **T 11.13** Read and listen to Susannah talking about her future. What are her definite plans? What is she not sure about? What are her hopes, ambitions, and dreams?

3 Now read Susannah's talk again carefully. There are six paragraphs. In each one <u>underline</u> any words or expressions that would be useful when you write a talk about your future. Compare with your partner.

4 Rewrite the first paragraph about you. Read it aloud to your partner.

5 Write a talk about your future plans and dreams. Mark pauses and words you want to stress. Practise reading it aloud. Give your talk to the class. Answer any questions.

My dreams for the future

Hello everyone. My name's Susannah, Suzie for short. I'm 20 years old. At the moment I'm in my second year at art school and I often dream about my future. I have big plans and I'd like to tell you a bit about them.

My most immediate plans are holiday plans. I'm going to visit my brother, who's working in Australia. My mother and I are going to spend Christmas with him in the summer sun. I'm very excited about that.

When I return, I have to make a final decision about which course I'm going to study next year. I'm still not sure – I might do fashion design or I might do landscape design. It's difficult because I'm interested in both clothes and gardens. If I choose landscape, I'd like to work with my friend Jasper. He's brilliant with gardens and we've already worked on two together. It was great fun and we get on very well.

In five or ten years' time I would like to have my own business and work for myself, like my father. He has his own building business. I might even do a business course after I finish art school.

Of course, one day I hope to marry and have children – ideally, before I'm 30, but I can't plan when I'll meet the right person and I haven't got a boyfriend at the moment.

In my dreams I see myself at 40 running a successful gardening company with about 20 employees. I'll design beautiful gardens for beautiful people. I'll have a beautiful house, two beautiful children and, of course, a husband who's as successful as I am. Who knows, it might even be Jasper!

1 Join each pair of sentences with the words in *italics*. Make any changes necessary. Check with a partner.

1 *and/still*
He's been learning English for five years. He still can't speak a word.

He's been learning English for five years and he still can't speak a word.

2 *although/only*
She's 15 years old. She walked to the North Pole.
_____

3 *eventually/who*
We found someone. He could speak Russian.
_____

4 *which/unfortunately,*
I sent you an email. You didn't receive it.
_____

5 *but/especially*
I love all ice-cream. I love strawberry ice-cream.
_____

6 *when/suddenly*
We were having a picnic. It started to rain.
_____

7 *just/so/of course*
They've had a baby girl. They're delighted.
_____

8 *However, usually*
He's always giving me advice. I don't follow it.
_____

2 Quickly read the brief biography of the explorer David Hempleman-Adams. How did he become interested in the outdoor life? How many of his achievements can you remember? What is 'the impossible grand slam'?

3 Read the biography more carefully. Put the words on the right in the correct places in the lines and make any necessary punctuation changes.

4 Write a list of the most important events that have happened in your life. Show your list to your partner and ask and answer questions about them.

5 Write your autobiography. Swap them with others in the class. Decide whose is the most interesting and/or the most well-written. Read those aloud.

DAVID HEMPLEMAN-ADAMS
explorer and adventurer

David Hempleman-Adams was born in the railway town of Swindon, Wiltshire in 1956. When he was 9 years old, his parents divorced and he had to make a big decision. Should he live with his father or move to a small village with his mother? He chose to go with his mother. He loved country life and being outside in the fresh air.

Unfortunately, just

Eventually, Fortunately especially

He became interested in climbing. He climbed in the Welsh mountains, in North America, and in 1981, he climbed Kilimanjaro, Africa's highest mountain. His dream was to climb Everest, and this he did in 1993. Everest was not enough and David wanted other challenges. He wanted to climb the highest peaks in all seven continents, and to walk to the North and South Poles. He fell through the ice and was attacked by a polar bear. He succeeded in all his challenges. On 29 April, 1998, he became the first man in history to complete the so-called 'impossible grand slam' of peaks and Poles.

Soon, First of all then

eventually, However

Although

Not satisfied, he took up ballooning and broke three more records. In 2000, he ballooned solo to the North Pole, in 2003, he crossed the Atlantic, and in 2007 he broke the world altitude record.

Still
First, next
finally

In 2004, David's amazing achievements were recognized worldwide in New York. Astronaut Buzz Aldrin presented him with the Explorer's Club medal. He was a world hero.

Also
when
At last

David married in 1992 and has three daughters. The eldest, Alicia, has followed in her father's footsteps. At 15, she became the youngest person to walk to the North Pole.

Incredibly
just

Tapescripts

UNIT 1

T 1.1 **Marija Kuzma** Hello! My name's Marija Kuzma and I come from Zagreb, the capital city of Croatia. I'm 20, and I'm studying medicine at the University of Zagreb. The course lasts six years and it's all in English! It's hard work, but I'm enjoying it a lot. I live at home with my mother, father and grandmother. I can speak three foreign languages – English, French, and Italian. I speak Italian because my grandmother's from Italy, and she always spoke to me in Italian when I was very young. I speak English because I went to an English-speaking high school. After I graduate, I'm going to work for *Médecins sans Frontières* in West Africa, because I want to travel and help people.

T 1.2 **Jim Allen** Hello. My name's Jim Allen and I come from the north of England, near Manchester. I live in a village just outside the city. I live alone now, because my wife died three years ago. But I'm near my daughter and her family, so that's OK. Until last year, I worked in a paper factory, but now I'm retired. I never liked my job much but now I'm really enjoying life! I'm a student again. I'm studying with the *University of the Third Age*. It helps retired people like me who want to study again, and it's really wonderful. You see, I left school when I was 15 and started work in the factory, because we needed the money. Now I'm studying Spanish. I love it. My son lives in Spain with his Spanish wife. Next year I'm going to visit them for six months, so I want my Spanish to be good!

T 1.3 **I = Interviewer   J = Jim**
1 I Do you have a job?
   J No, I don't. I'm retired. I'm a student now.
2 I Which university do you go to?
   J I don't go to university. I study at home.
3 I Are you enjoying the course?
   J Yes, I am. It's wonderful.
4 I What are you doing at the moment?
   J I'm writing an essay about *Don Quixote*.
5 I Why did you leave school at 15?
   J Because my family was poor. We needed the money.
6 I Who are you going to visit next year?
   J My son and his wife. They live in Spain now.

T 1.4
1 Do you like listening to music?
2 What sort of music do you like?
3 Do you often wear jeans?
4 What's your teacher wearing today?
5 Where did you go on your last holiday?
6 What did you do yesterday evening?
7 What are you doing this evening?
8 What are you going to do after this course?

T 1.5 **Best friends**
Shona I have three or four good friends, but I think my best friend is Kirsty. We first met when we were 12. She started at my school, and the teacher asked me to look after her. We soon became friends. We looked quite funny together. She's very tall, and I'm quite small! Because we grew up together, we know everything about each other. So Kirsty knows me better than anyone else. I can always talk to her about my problems. She always listens and then gives me good advice! I hope I do the same for her. We are both married now, and – er, we live quite near each other, but in different towns. We talk on the phone all the time, especially now, because we are both having a baby this summer!

Dominic My best friend is called Sammy –er and he often comes to play at my house after school. A long time ago –er when I was four –er we went to Busy Bee Nursery School together. Me and Sammy are both six now. I like him 'cos he's funny and he plays football. I like going to play at his house, too. He's got a big garden, and a nice dog called King.

Michael I have two very good friends from university called Dave and Azam. We stayed in the same house near the university. I don't know why we became friends. We were all very different. Dave was very quiet and always worked hard, and Azam was, well, a bit crazy! He never remembered his house keys. He climbed in through the window at least once a week. He loved cooking Indian food and having parties. We had parties all the time in our house. Now, of course, life is very different. Dave is a writer and lives in France. He sends me long, funny emails every month. Azam is an international lawyer. He's working in Hong Kong at the moment. But we still meet once a year with our families. We usually meet at Dave's house in France and have a holiday together.

Brianna My best friend is my neighbor, Caleb. He's 16. Our moms are good friends, and I call Caleb's mom Auntie Janine. We grew up together. When we were kids, we always liked the same games. Now we're into the same music. Weekends, we usually go on the Internet, or sometimes we go downtown to the music stores to listen to our favourite artists. Caleb's cool. He's like a brother to me.

T 1.6 **Blind Date**
I = Interviewer   M = Matt
I So, Matt, which lovely lady did you choose and why did you choose her?
M Well, they all looked lovely and at first I thought 'Oh I'll choose Holly, she sounds sporty and good fun'. But in the end I chose Beth. I chose her because I liked her eyes, and because she seemed a bit different from the other London girls. Best of all, I liked the fact that she couldn't think of anything that she hated.
I So tell us about the date. What happened when you met?
M Well, I arrived first at the restaurant – an Indian restaurant, of course, and when Beth walked in –er I could see she was nice-looking, but she seemed quite nervous, –er, shy, and perhaps a bit embarrassed by being on a date with a stranger… but I liked that. We ordered our meals, and she tried to tell me why she was vegetarian. I felt a bit guilty because I ordered chicken curry, but it was OK, we laughed about it, and after that she started to relax and we began to really enjoy ourselves. I told her that she was very brave to cycle in London, because you know I can surf and swim in rough seas, but I really couldn't ride a bike in the London rush hour. But she said it's fine if you're careful. She was really interested in my job and my time at sea. We both agreed that one day we'd like to move out of London and live in the country – I'd like to be beside the sea, of course. Suddenly it was midnight and time to part. We're going to meet again next week. There's a lot more I'd like to know about Beth.

T 1.7 **I = Interviewer   B = Beth**
I And now Beth. What did you think of the date, Beth?
B Oh, I liked Matt a lot, the moment I saw him, but I felt so nervous. I was amazed he chose me and at first I just couldn't speak, but he was really kind. He asked me about my job and said how brave I was, cycling in London – it's not really brave – anyway, soon we were laughing like old friends. I think he's very good-looking. He has a really interesting job and he's very funny. I hope I'm interesting enough for him. Anyway, he's coming to see me at the bookshop next week and we're going to have lunch together. Who knows? I'd love to go camping with him one day.

T 1.8
1 I'm reading a good book.
   I booked my flight online.
2 What kind of music do you like?
   My mother's a very kind person.
3 What does this mean?
   Some people are very mean. They don't like spending their money.
4 I live in a flat.
   Holland is a very flat country.
5 Can you swim?
   I'd like a can of coke.
6 Do you want to play football?
   We saw a play at the theatre.
7 The train's coming.
   Athletes have to train very hard.
8 The phone's ringing.
   What a lovely ring you're wearing!

T 1.9 **T 1.10** **T 1.11** and **T 1.12** see p13

UNIT 2

T 2.1

Anne-Marie Boucher has a small family hotel with her husband, Pascal, near Quebec City, Canada. It's situated on the coast outside the town, and near two national parks. She says, 'Our hotel has got wonderful views of the St Lawrence River and the Isle of Orleans.'
She has visitors from all over the world. She says, 'We speak French, English, and a little Italian, which is very useful! Our guests keep us busy both summer and winter, so we've always got lots to do.'
They don't have much free time. 'But I like it that way,' she says. 'And I love meeting new guests.' In winter it's very cold, –10° C. Their guests go skiing or snowmobiling in Mont Sainte-Anne Park.
It's January now, and she is enjoying her favourite sport, dog-sledding. She's got twelve dogs, and she's racing them across the snow. She says 'I'm working the dogs very hard at the moment. Next year I want to race in a dogsled competition. It's really exciting.'

Lien Xiaohong is 22. She lives and works in a toy factory in Guangdong province, China.
She lives in a room with 14 other women in the factory dormitory, seven hundred miles from her family. The factory where she works employs 15,000 workers, nearly all of them women in their twenties. She works from 8 a.m. to 7 p.m. She has just an hour for lunch. She says, 'I work five and a half days a week, but I usually do overtime in summer. It's very tiring. When I'm not working or studying, I sleep.' Her monthly wage is about $65, enough to send a little back home to her family, and to pay for computer classes and English classes in town. She says, 'I haven't got any money left to buy things for myself.'
It's the evening now, and she is having a computer lesson in a private school. 'There are two skills that are essential these days,' she says. 'English and computers. One day I want to be my own boss.'

T 2.2
1 'Do you like your job, Lien?'
   'No, I don't like it much. My hands hurt all the time.'
2 'What are you doing at the moment?'
   'I'm having a computer lesson.'
3 'Have you got any brothers or sisters?'
   'I've got a brother. He lives with my parents in Hunan province.'

4 'Where do you go on holiday, Anne Marie?'
   'Well, we don't usually go on holiday, so we're
   lucky to live in this beautiful place.'
5 'Why are you working the dogs so hard at the
   moment?'
   'Because I want to race in a competition next year.'
6 'How many dogs have you got?'
   'I've got twelve! They don't live in the hotel, of
   course.'

T 2.3 see p16

T 2.4 I = Interviewer M = Miguel

I Thank you for agreeing to do this interview,
   Miguel.
M No problem.
I First of all, where exactly do you come from?
M I'm from Valencia in Spain.
I And where do you live in Valencia?
M I live with my parents. They've got a restaurant
   in the old town centre.
I Have you got any brothers or sisters?
M I've got two brothers. They're both older than
   me, and they don't live at home.
I And what do you do?
M I work in my parents' restaurant. I'm a waiter.
I And what do you like doing in your free time?
M I love sailing. We've got a small boat in the marina.
I Where do you go on holiday?
M I usually go to stay with my brother, Rolando. He
   lives in Madrid.
I And what are you doing here in Oxford?
M I'm studying English at a language school here.
I Oh, really? Well, your English is very good!
M Thank you! And thank you for the practice!

T 2.5

Chantal
'Where does Chantal come from?' 'Marseilles, in
France.'
'Is she married?' 'No, she isn't.'
'Does she have any brothers and sisters?' 'Yes, she has
one brother.'
'Has she got any children?' 'No, she hasn't.'
'What does she do?' 'She's a fashion buyer.'
'What does she do in her free time?' 'She goes to the
gym.'
'Where does she go on holiday?' 'She goes to her
holiday home in Biarritz.'
'What's she doing at the moment?' 'She's buying
clothes in Milan.'

Mario and Rita
'Where do they come from?' 'Siena, in Italy.'
'Are they married?' 'Yes, they are.'
'Do they have any children?' 'Yes, one daughter.'
'Have they got any grandchildren?' 'Yes, they've got
one grandson.'
'What do they do?' 'He's retired and she's a housewife.'
'What do they do in their free time?' 'They go to the
opera.'
'What are they doing at the moment?' 'They're
preparing to go to the USA.'

T 2.6 see p17

T 2.7

1 I never have breakfast on weekdays, only at
   weekends.
2 I have a hot shower every morning and every
   evening.
3 My sister washes her hair at least four times a
   week.
4 She didn't have time to put on any make-up this
   morning.
5 My brother never reads books or newspapers, he
   only reads music magazines.
6 I don't often do the washing-up because we've
   got a dishwasher.
7 I'm going to make a cup of coffee. Does
   anybody want one?

8 My dad always watches the ten o'clock news on TV.
9 My mum says I text my friends too much.
10 You made this mess, so you clear it up!
11 Can I send an email from your computer, please?
12 How can you listen to music while you're working?
13 I'm always so tired after work I just want to
   relax in front of the TV.
14 I cooked a meal for ten people last night.
15 I didn't forget to do my homework, I forgot to
   bring it.
16 Can you wait a minute? I need to go to the toilet.

T 2.8 A 24/7 society

P = Presenter I = Interviewer Je = Jerry
Ja = Jackie Do = Doreen Da = Dan

P Good morning, and welcome to today's lifestyle
   programme *A 24/7 society*. Over eight million
   people now work at night. What do they do, and
   why do they do it? Our reporter, Richard Morris,
   finds out.
I Well, it's 8pm on a Thursday night, and I'm in a
   BMW car factory, where they make the Mini. The
   night workers are arriving now. With me is Jerry
   Horne. Jerry, tell me, what hours do you work?
Je I work 12 hours a night, four times a week.
I And do you like it?
Je Well, it was difficult at first, but it's OK now. And
   the money's good. I can earn much more
   working at night.
I Why do people work at night here?
Je Because the robots do! The robots make a lot of
   each car, but we finish them. And the Mini is
   very popular, so we need to make 200,000 a year!
I That's amazing! Are there any problems working
   at night?
Je Well, the main problem is that you need to be
   very careful between the hours of 1 o'clock and 3
   o'clock in the morning. That's when accidents
   happen.
I Right. Thanks, Jerry. And have a good night!
   …
I It's 10.30pm, and a lot of people are going to bed
   now. But I'm in a hairdresser's called Hairwear
   with Jackie Wilson, the manager. Jackie, is this
   the country's first 24-hour hairdresser's?
Ja Yes, it probably is! We're only open for 24 hours
   on a Friday night at the moment. But I think
   that will change in the future, because people
   want it. And I think it's a good idea.
I What sort of people come in?
Ja All sorts! Young mothers come in when their
   husbands get home. A lot of people come in
   before they go to a night club. A politician comes
   in after work at midnight. And of course, other
   night workers come in after work between 2
   o'clock and 6 o'clock in the morning. It helps
   them relax before they go to bed.
I Any problems?
Ja Not really. The main problem is that most of the
   customers fall asleep under the hairdryer!
   …
I It's now 1 o'clock in the morning and I'm in the
   Co-op bank. I'm sitting next to Doreen. At night
   this telephone banking centre only has six
   workers. Doreen, what hours do you work?
Do I work from Sunday to Wednesday from 10pm to
   7am.
I Aha. And what do you think of the job?
Do I love it! We're like a family at night. We're all good
   friends, and the work is more relaxed. Customers
   aren't in a hurry at 2 o'clock in the morning!
I Are there any disadvantages?
Do Well, it's bad for you! You need to look after your
   health. If you don't, you get ill. But it's OK for
   me – I could never sleep at night, anyway!
   …
I Well, it's 4 o'clock in the morning, and I'm
   feeling very sleepy! I'm in the local supermarket
   with Dan. So, Dan, when did you start work?

Da At midnight. And I finish in two hours' time at 6
   o'clock. But some weeks I work during the day.
   The difficult thing is changing from day working
   to night working.
I Any other problems?
Da Well, often it isn't easy to see my friends or my
   girlfriend. They're going out and I'm going to
   work! And at weekends, sometimes I sleep all
   day. My girlfriend doesn't like that much!
I So why do you do it?
Da For the money, really. And I don't mind working
   at night.
I Thanks, Dan. So there you are. These are just some
   of the many people who have a different sort of
   lifestyle. Well, I'm off to bed now. Good night!

T 2.9

1 J = James N = Nicole
J Hello. What's your name?
N Nicole.
J I'm … James. I'm a teacher. And – er, where are
   you from?
N Paris. I come from Paris.
J How lovely. Paris is so beautiful.
N Yes, I like it.
J Er … What … what do you do – er, in Paris?
N I'm a student.
J Mm. And … how do you find living in London,
   Nicole?
N It's OK.
J Are you having a good time?
N Yes.
J Can I get you a coffee?
N No.
J Er … Are you missing your family at all?
N No.
J Have you got any brothers or sisters?
N Yes. I've got a brother.
J Er … Oh! Er … what does he do?
N He's a student, too.
J Oh well, I've got a class now. Goodbye, Nicole.
N Bye.

2 C = Catherine M = Marco
C Hello. What's your name?
M I'm Marco. And what's your name?
C Catherine.
M What a pretty name. In Italy, we say Caterina.
C Oh, that's lovely! So, you're from Italy, Marco.
   Where exactly are you from?
M I come from 'Roma' – or as you say in English,
   Rome.
C Oh, yes of course, 'Roma'! That sounds so nice.
M That's right. And you, Catherine, where do you
   come from?
C I'm from Dublin, in Ireland.
M Oh, I'd love to visit Ireland one day.
C You must. It's really beautiful. And what do you
   do in Rome, Marco?
M I'm a student. I'm studying to be an architect.
C Oh, really?
M Yes. I want to design beautiful, modern buildings
   for my beautiful, old city.
C How interesting! I just love Rome.
M Do you know Rome?
C Not really. I once had a weekend there and I just
   loved it.
M Ah, you must visit again.
C I'd love to. And how do you find London? Are
   you enjoying it here?
M Oh yes, I am, very much indeed. I'm making a
   lot of good friends and even the food's not bad.
C But not as good as Italian food!
M Aaah! What can I say? Caterina – er Catherine,
   can I get you a coffee?
C Yes, please. I'd love one. There's still ten minutes
   before class.
M OK. Why don't we s........

T 2.10 **T 2.11** and **T 2.12** see p21

UNIT 3

T 3.1 see p22

T 3.2

1 It happened every morning.
  It didn't happen every morning. It happened every night.
2 Red locked all the doors.
  He didn't lock all the doors. He opened them.
3 Amy Watson started the home.
  Amy Watson didn't start the home. Mary Tealby started it.
4 They saw a man on the film.
  They didn't see a man on the film. They saw a dog.
5 He opened the doors with his nose.
  He didn't open the doors with his nose. He opened them with his teeth.
6 Reporters came to film Amy.
  Reporters didn't come to film Amy. They came to film Red.

T 3.3

1 What did Red do?
  He opened all the cage doors.
2 Why did he open the doors?
  Because he wanted to go to the kitchen.
3 How often did he do it?
  Many times.
4 Who did Amy think it was?
  The ghost of Mary Tealby.
5 What did they put in the cages?
  Cameras.
6 How did he open the doors?
  With his teeth.
7 Did they have a good time?
  Yes, they did. They had a great time.
8 Why did 400 people phone the dogs' home?
  Because they wanted to give Red a home.

T 3.4

a looked, played, wanted
b tried, studied
c arrived, used, decided
d stopped, planned

T 3.5

/t/ looked, stopped
/d/ played, tried, arrived, used, planned
/ɪd/ wanted, studied, decided

T 3.6

1 The phone rang, so I answered it.
2 I felt ill, so I went to bed.
3 I made a sandwich because I was hungry.
4 I had a shower and washed my hair.
5 I lost my passport, but I found it later.
6 I called the police because I heard a strange noise.
7 The printer broke, so I mended it.
8 I forgot her birthday, so I said sorry.
9 I took my driving test and I passed it!
10 I told a joke but nobody laughed.

T 3.7 **The thief, his mother, and $2 billion**

Stephane Breitweiser, 33, from Alsace, in France, is the greatest art thief in Europe. For over six years, while he was working as a lorry driver, he stole 239 paintings from museums in France, Austria, and Denmark. He went into the museums just as they were closing and hid the paintings under his coat. Nobody looked at him because he was wearing a security guard's uniform.
Back in his apartment, where he was living with his mother, he filled his bedroom with priceless works of art. His mother, Mireille, 53, thought all the paintings were copies. One day while they were having supper, the police arrived, and they took Stephane to the police station. Mireille was so angry with her son that she went to his room, took some paintings from the walls, and cut them into small pieces. Others she took and threw into the canal. Altogether she destroyed art worth two billion dollars! Both mother and son spent many years in prison.

T 3.8 see p24

T 3.9 **The man with the golden gun**

N = Narrator   B = Bond   M = Mary   S = Scaramanga

N James Bond got back to his hotel room at midnight. The windows were closed and the air-conditioning was on. Bond switched it off and opened the windows. His heart was thumping in his chest. He breathed in the air with relief, then he had a shower and went to bed.
  At 3.30 Bond suddenly woke up. There was a noise. It was coming from the window. Something was moving behind the curtain.
B Mary Goodnight! What the hell are you doing here?
M Quick, James! Help me in!
B Oh, my g . . . !
M I'm terribly sorry, James!
B Sh! Sh! Sshh!
B What the hell are you doing here? What's the matter?
M James, I was so worried. A 'Most Immediate' message came from HQ this evening. A top KGB man, using the name Hendriks, is staying in this hotel. He knows you're here. He's looking for you!
B I know, Hendriks is here all right. So is a gunman called Scaramanga. Mary, did HQ say if they have a description of me?
M No, they don't. They just have your name, Secret Agent James Bond.
B Thanks, Mary. Now, I must get you out of here. Don't worry about me, just tell HQ that you gave me the message, OK?
M OK, James. Please take care, James.
B Sure, sure. Now, come on!
S This is not your lucky day, Mr Bond. Come here both of you and put your hands up!
N Scaramanga walked to the door and turned on the lights. His golden gun was pointing directly at James Bond.

T 3.10

1 I was dreaming peacefully when suddenly a loud noise woke me up.
2 My Grandma is nearly 75 and she still goes swimming regularly.
3 I unlocked the door quietly and went outside into the night.
4 She whispered softly in his ear, 'Do you really love me?' 'Of course I do,' he replied.
5 I was just relaxing with a really good book when someone knocked loudly on the door.
6 First break the eggs into a bowl and then mix them together with the flour.
7 I got up quickly and crept downstairs to the front door.
8 I work hard and I do my homework carefully, but I still don't get good marks.

T 3.11 see p28

T 3.12

A Did you send Oliver a birthday card?
B I had no idea it was his birthday. When was it?
A On October the 11th.
B The 11th of October! That's a week ago. I'll phone him this evening and apologize.

T 3.13 and **T 3.14** see p29

T 3.15

A What star sign are you?
B I'm Aries.
A Hey, so am I! When's your birthday?
B The 11th of April.
A I don't believe it! Same as me. Which year?
B 1990.
A That's amazing! We're like twins!

T 3.16

1 A When's Easter this year?
  B It's early, I think. Easter Sunday's on the 27th or the 28th of March.
  A Yes, you're right. Look, it's the 27th. That is early!
2 A Judy, can you tell me when the next meeting is?
  B Let me see. Ah, yes. It's next month. Wednesday, the 16th of June.
  A What time?
  B It starts at 2.30.
  A So Wednesday, the 16th at 2.30?
  B That's right.
  A Thanks.
3 A Miss Lomax, I've scheduled your flight for Tuesday, May 7th at 7.40 a.m.
  B Let me put that in my computer diary. So … that's Tuesday the 7th of May at 6.40.
  A No 7.40 a.m., Miss Lomax.
  B Oh yeah. Thanks Sally. →

UNIT 4

T 4.1 see p30

T 4.2 N = Nick   S = Sarah

N Is that everything?
S Er, let's have a look. We've got some apples, but there aren't any bananas. And we've got some tea, but there isn't any coffee.
N OK, bananas and coffee. What about orange juice? Is there any orange juice left?
S Let's see. There's a little, but not much.
N Orange juice, then. And vegetables? Have we got many vegetables?
S Well, we've got some broccoli and a few carrots, but there aren't many onions.
N Right, onions …
S Oh, and don't forget – your nephews are coming tomorrow! We need something for them.
N OK, lots of crisps and ice-cream. Anything else?
S I don't think so. But for goodness sake, *don't* forget the nappies. Oh, and a big bunch of flowers for me!

T 4.3

1 'Did you meet anyone nice at the party?'
  'Yes. I met someone who knows you!'
2 'Ouch! There's something in my eye!'
  'Let me look. No, I can't see anything.'
3 'Let's go somewhere hot for our holidays.'
  'Yes, but we can't go anywhere that's too expensive.'
4 'I'm so unhappy. Nobody loves me.'
  'I know someone who loves you. Me.'
5 I've lost my glasses. I've looked everywhere, but I can't find them.
6 'Did you buy anything at the shops?'
  'No, nothing. I didn't have any money.'
7 I'm bored. I want something interesting to read, or someone interesting to talk to, or somewhere interesting to go.
8 It was a great party! Everyone loved it!

T 4.4 *I bought it on eBay!*

Linda The first time I used eBay I bought a cooker! It's for the kitchen in my new house. I was amazed, because it was so easy. And it was cheap, too! I bought an expensive Italian cooker for only £100, and I went to get it yesterday. It looks fantastic in my new kitchen. I think eBay's a brilliant idea. I'm going to buy a fridge next!

Megan Oooh! Don't talk to me about eBay! It's a real problem for me – I like it too much. Parcels arrive every day, usually with shoes. I just love buying shoes on eBay. Yesterday a beautiful pair of green sandals arrived. They only cost £2. Can you believe it? My boyfriend says he gets worried every time he sees the postman – but you can't have too many shoes, can you?

Charlie I can't believe it! I'm so stupid! I bought a car on eBay, and it was a big mistake. I've bought plenty of other things on eBay, and it usually works very well. And I heard that a car sells every two minutes on eBay, and the sellers are usually very good. So I paid £1,000 for an old Volvo, and I went to get it last week. But on the way home the car stopped. A mechanic told me it was worth less than half the price I paid. Now I don't know what to do. But I'm not going to use eBay again for a while.

T 4.5

a chemist's tissues; deodorant; aspirin;
shaving foam
a café an espresso; a doughnut; a toasted sandwich;
a sparkling mineral water
a post office a parcel; envelopes; scales;
a book of stamps
a clothes shop a T-shirt; a tie; a belt; a leather jacket

T 4.6

1 A Good morning. Can I have a coffee, please?
  B Espresso?
  A Yes, please. Oh, and a doughnut, please.
  B I'm afraid there aren't any left. We've got some delicious carrot cake, and chocolate cake.
  A OK. Carrot cake, then.
  B Here you are. Is that all?
  A Yes, thanks.
2 A Hello. I wonder if you could help me? I've got a bad cold and a sore throat. Can you give me something for it?
  B Yes, of course. Are you allergic to aspirin?
  A No, I'm not.
  B OK. You can take these three times a day.
  A Thank you. Could I have some tissues as well, please?
  B Sure. Anything else?
  A No, that's all, thanks.
3 A Good morning. Can I help you?
  B I'm just looking, thanks.
  A No problem.
  A And you sir? Can I help you?
  C Yes, please. I'm looking for a jacket like this, but in black, not brown. Do you have one?
  A I'll just have a look. What size are you?
  C Medium.
  A Ah yes. You're in luck. This is the last one. Here you are.
  C That's great. Can I try it on?
  A Of course. The changing rooms are over there.
  C Mmm. I really like it.
  A It suits you.
  C OK. I'll take it.
4 A Hello. I'd like to send this parcel to France, please.
  B Put it on the scales, please. … That's £4.10.
  A Will it get there by Monday?
  B Well, it will if you send it special delivery but that's £3.85 extra.
  A Oh, OK then. And a book of first class stamps, please.
  B Certainly. That'll be £10.95 altogether.

T 4.7 and T 4.8 see p36

T 4.9

1 A A book of twelve first class stamps, please.
  B Three pounds eighty-four, please.
2 A How much is this jumper?
  B Thirty-four pounds fifty.
3 A A white loaf and three rolls, please.
  B A brown loaf and six rolls –er that'll be …
  A Er, no, I said a white loaf and three rolls
  B Sorry. That'll be one pound eighty-two.

4 A Two bottles of sparkling mineral water, please.
  B That's two euros thirty.
5 A Here's the twenty dollars I owe you.
  B Not twenty dollars. Thirty dollars.
  A Thirty dollars! I'm sure it was twenty.
  B No, thirty. Thirty dollars and 40 cents to be exact.
6 A What a fantastic house!
  B Darling! It cost two million pounds!
7 A How much was your car?
  B Ten thousand dollars.
8 A How much was the cheque for?
  B A hundred and sixty dollars.

T 4.10

1 A Hello. I'm looking for this month's edition of Vogue?
  B Over there. Middle shelf. Next to Marie Claire and Cosmopolitan.
  A Thanks. How much is it?
  B £2.60.
  A Here you are.
  B Right, that's £2.40 change.
  A Just a minute! I gave you a £10 note, not a £5 note.
  B I am sorry. That's £7.40, then.
2 A I'd like to change these dollars into sterling, please.
  B Right. How much is here?
  A $200.
  B That's £150, plus £2 commission.
  A OK, thanks. And can I cash a traveller's cheque for $100?
  B Certainly. Have you got your passport?
  A Yes, here it is.
3 A Hello. How much is it to get in?
  B £8 for an adult, £4.50 for children under 12.
  A OK. Two adults and three children, please.
  B Then it's cheaper if you have a family ticket. That's £24.50, please.
  A Thank you very much.

UNIT 5

T 5.1

Ella Well, I'd like to be a vet. I've got three pets – two rabbits and a kitten called Princess. I love looking after them, so I think I'll be a good vet. I asked my mum if I could have a puppy, but she said no. When I'm a vet, I want to have two dogs and a horse as well.

Joe I can already play the piano, but now I'm learning to play the electric guitar. I love it! I'd love to be in a rock band. I want to play lead guitar. And write all the songs. I'm thinking of asking my friends if they want to start a band.

Juliet It's an important year for me at school this year. I'm doing nine subjects. I'm going to study hard and get really good grades in all my exams, so I can go to university. But I'm still going to have fun. I'm seeing my boyfriend tonight!

Hannah I'd like to go back to work next year. I worked in a bank before I had children, but I don't want to do that any more. I hope to go back to college and train to be a primary school teacher. I've worked part-time at Ella and Joe's school for a few years now, and I really enjoy it.

David I've been in the same job for 20 years. I'm an accountant for a big company, and I visit all the company offices regularly. I'm thinking of changing my job, because I'm tired of travelling all the time. Actually, I'd like to start my own business.

Edie Last year I joined a travel club for people my age. It's marvellous! I really enjoy meeting new people and seeing new places. I'm looking forward to going on a world cruise with my friend, Margaret. I met her on the last cruise. We're going to the Caribbean. I can't wait!

T 5.2

1 A I hope to go to university.
  B What do you want to study?
2 A One of my favourite hobbies is cooking.
  B What do you like making?
3 A I get terrible headaches.
  B When did you start getting them?
4 A We're planning our summer holidays at the moment.
  B Where are you thinking of going?
5 A I'm bored.
  B What would you like to do tonight?

T 5.3 see p40

T 5.4

1 That bag looks heavy. I'll carry it for you.
2 I bought some warm boots because I'm going skiing.
3 A Tony's back from holiday.
  B Is he? I'll give him a ring.
4 A What are you doing tonight?
  B We're going to see a play at the theatre.
5 You can tell me your secret. I won't tell anyone.
6 Congratulations! I hear you're getting married.
7 A I need to post these letters.
  B I'm going shopping soon. I'll post them for you.
8 A What are we having for lunch?
  B I'm going to make a lasagne.

T 5.5

1 That bag looks heavy.
2 I bought some warm boots because …
3 'Tony's back from holiday.' 'Is he?'
4 What are you doing tonight?
5 You can tell me your secret.
6 Congratulations! I hear …
7 I need to post these letters.
8 What are we having for lunch?

T 5.6 see p41

T 5.7

1 A I heard footsteps in the middle of the night.
  B That's really frightening!
2 A The bus was full. I had to wait for the next one, so I was late for work.
  B That's so annoying!
3 A I saw Andy eating a burger! I thought he was vegetarian.
  B That's very surprising!
4 A I was lying on the beach in the sun all day yesterday.
  B How relaxing!
5 A On my holiday it rained every day.
  B That's just so depressing!
6 A I ran my first full marathon on Sunday.
  B How exhausting!

T 5.8

1 I heard footsteps in the middle of the night. I was really frightened.
2 The bus was full. I had to wait for the next one, so I was late for work. I was so annoyed!
3 I saw Andy eating a burger! I thought he was vegetarian. I was very surprised.
4 I was lying on the beach in the sun all day yesterday. I felt so relaxed!
5 On my holiday it rained every day. I was so depressed.
6 I ran my first full marathon on Sunday. I was exhausted!

T 5.9

1 A I watched a horror film on my own last night.
  B Were you frightened?
2 A I spent four hours going round a museum.
  B Oh, no! Was it boring?
  A Actually, it was really fascinating. I loved it.

3 A Did you see the way she behaved?
  B Yes, it was shocking! Don't invite her next time.
4 I had a second interview but I didn't get the job.
  I'm so disappointed.
5 The teacher was annoyed because all the students
  were late.
6 My daughter is very excited because it's her
  birthday tomorrow.
7 I don't know how this camera works! The
  instructions are really confusing.

T 5.10

1 A I feel a bit nervous. I've got an exam today.
  B Good luck! Just do your best. That's all you
    can do.
2 A I don't feel very well. I think I'm getting a cold.
  B Oh dear! Why don't you go home to bed?
3 A I'm feeling a lot better, thanks. Not quite back
    to normal, but nearly.
  B That's good. I'm so pleased to hear it.
4 A I'm so angry! I got a parking ticket this
    morning. Sixty pounds!
  B Oh no! Didn't you get one last week as well?
5 A I'm really excited! I'm going on holiday to
    Australia tomorrow!
  B Lucky you! Have a good time!
6 A I'm fed up with this weather. It's so wet and
    miserable.
  B I know. We really need some sunshine, don't we?
7 A I'm a bit worried. My grandfather's going into
    hospital for tests.
  B I'm sorry to hear that! I'm sure he'll be all right.
8 A We're really happy! We're in love!
  B That's fantastic! I'm so pleased for you both!
9 A I sometimes feel a bit lonely, actually. I don't
    think I have many friends.
  B Cheer up! You've got me. I'm always here for
    you.

T 5.11 see p45

UNIT 6

T 6.1 I = Interviewer L = Leroy

I Welcome to another edition of *Favourite Things*.
  Today in the studio we have cool R'n'B singer,
  Leroy! Welcome, Leroy. Thank you for coming to
  talk to us about your favourite things.
L Hi there.
I So, Leroy let's look at your list of favourites. Now,
  your first choice is the film star, Al Pacino. Can you
  tell us about him? Why do you like him so much?
L Well, every time I see Al Pacino in a movie I
  think he's brilliant, he's just a brilliant actor. He's
  so talented. You know he's been nominated six
  times for Oscars, –er but in fact, he's only won
  once and that was years ago, in 1993. I can't
  believe it!
I OK. And your next favourite thing is Arsenal,
  Arsenal Football Club. So you're a big football
  fan, then?
L Yeah, I am. I'm a London boy, you see and I
  support my local team, which is Arsenal. They
  are fantastic players. And always exciting to
  watch! I still go to a match whenever I can.
I And now your number three - soul music.
L Oh yeah, I'm crazy about soul music – you
  know, it's the reason I wanted a career in the
  music business. It's beautiful music but can
  sometimes be very sad. It's where modern R'n'B
  music comes from.
I Is that right? I didn't know that. Now your
  number four is a food, chicken satay. I don't
  know that. What's it like?
L It's spicy and delicious! I just love sitting in front
  of the TV with a plate full of chicken satay.
  Mmmm!

I I must try it! And finally in your list you have
  Brave New World. I saw the film. But what's the
  book like?
L It's an amazing book about the future. It's – er
  funny, sad, and shocking. It's written by Aldous
  Huxley and it's my favourite book of all time.

T 6.2

1 Q What's London like?
  A Well, it's a really exciting city! There's so much
    going on all the time.
2 Q What's the weather like?
  A It's OK, and not very cold in winter, but
    people don't come here for the sunshine!
3 Q What are the people like?
  A They're very interesting. They come from all
    over the world. London's a very cosmopolitan
    city.
4 Q What are the buildings like?
  A Fantastic! Lots of them are historical and
    famous, but there are some wonderful modern
    ones, too.
5 Q What are the restaurants like?
  A They're great! You can find food from every
    country in the world.
6 Q What's the night-life like?
  A Oh, it's amazing! There are so many clubs and
    theatres, and, of course, the music scene is
    fantastic!

T 6.3 I = Interviewer L = Leroy

I Do you travel a lot, Leroy?
L Oh yeah. I sing all over the world. Last year I was
  in Berlin, Tokyo – oh, and of course, Detroit.
I And what are they like?
L Well, they're all big, busy cities. Tokyo's the biggest
  and the busiest. It's much bigger than Berlin.
I And is it more interesting?
L Well, they're all interesting, but, in fact, for me
  the most interesting is Detroit.
I Really? Why?
L Well, in some ways perhaps it isn't as interesting
  as the other two cities – it doesn't have historical
  buildings, or beautiful old Japanese temples – but
  you see, Detroit is the birthplace of soul music
  and that's everything to me.
I Hmm, I see. So Detroit's best for music. And
  what about food? Which is the best city for food?
L Ah, the food. For me there's no question, Tokyo
  definitely has the most delicious food – I just love
  Japanese food!
I I see. Is it even better than chicken satay?
L Ah, I don't know about that!

T 6.4 **T 6.5** and **T 6.6** see p48

T 6.7

1 The Empire State building is taller than the Eiffel
  tower, but the Petronas Towers are the tallest.
2 Monaco is smaller than Andorra, but the Vatican
  City is the smallest.
3 The Atlantic Ocean is bigger than the Arctic
  Ocean but the Pacific Ocean is the biggest.
4 A human is faster than an elephant, but a horse is
  the fastest.
5 A Porsche is more expensive than a Rolls Royce,
  but a Ferrari is the most expensive.
6 A shark is more dangerous than a lion, but a
  hippopotamus is the most dangerous.

T 6.8

1 A I moved to a new flat last week.
  B Oh, really? What's it like?
  A Well, it's bigger than my old one but it isn't as
    modern, and it's further from the shops.
2 A I hear Alice and Henry broke up.
  B Yeah. Alice's got a new boyfriend.
  A Oh, really? What's he like?
  B Well, he's much nicer than Henry, and much
    more handsome. Alice's happier now than
    she's been for a long time.

3 A We've got a new teacher.
  B Oh, really? What's she like?
  A Well, I think she's the best teacher we've ever
    had. Our last teacher was good but she's even
    better and she works us much harder.
4 A Is that your new car?
  B Well, it's second-hand, but it's new to me.
  A What's it like?
  B Well, it's faster than my old car and more
    comfortable, but it's more expensive to run. I
    love it!

T 6.9

Ben The best thing for me is my dog, Jasper. He's a
black Labrador and he's great. I got him when he
was a puppy, and I was nine. So we've grown up
together. My uncle gave him to me for my ninth
birthday, so he didn't cost anything. What's he like?
Well, he's very loving. He's also a bit crazy, and great
fun to play with. He's much more energetic than me.
I'm always really tired after taking him for a walk!

Mary Ooh, there are lots of things I like that don't
cost anything, I'm sure. Let's see … sunsets. That's
one thing I love. My house is on a hill, and in the
evening when I look out of my kitchen window,
there's sometimes a beautiful sunset. It makes
washing the dishes much easier! I also love getting
phone calls and cards from my family. I suppose
they cost something, but not to me! But actually, the
best thing of all is my first grandchild. He's the most
beautiful baby boy I've ever seen!

Michael I work in the city, so the best thing for me is
being in the countryside. I don't mind what the weather
is like. Even if it's rainy and windy, it's great to be
outside. It's much quieter than the city, so there's time
to think. Actually, the countryside costs money, because
I have to drive there first! OK, so the next best thing is
going for a walk in the park near my flat after work. It's
a lovely park with lots of trees and a small lake. It's the
most relaxing way to end the day.

Laura Em, well, I think the best thing for me is
playing with my little sister, Abby. She's nearly four,
so I'm much older than her. I've also got a brother,
Dominic. He's six. But he doesn't like the games I
like, so he isn't as much fun to play with. Abby's
always waiting for me when I come home from
school. She thinks I'm the best person in the whole
world. We usually play hospitals or schools. I'm the
doctor or teacher, of course, because I'm the biggest.

Kiera Definitely the best thing for me is being with
my boyfriend, Dan. We don't have to go out or
spend money. I love just going for a walk and
chatting with him. He makes me laugh all the time.
He's the funniest person I know. And the nicest
friend. We've been together for nearly a year, and
our relationship just gets better and better. I think
I'm really lucky.

T 6.10 see p52

T 6.11

1 A Look at all these new buildings!
  B Yes. Paris is much more modern than I expected.
2 A Wasn't that film brilliant?
  B Absolutely! It was fantastic. We loved it.
3 A Your bedroom's really untidy. Again!
  B What do you mean? It doesn't look messy to me.
4 A I couldn't believe it, their son was so impolite
    to me.
  B Don't worry. He's rude to everyone.
5 A Dan doesn't earn much, but he's always so kind.
  B He is, isn't he? He's one of the most generous
    people I know.
6 A I'm bored with this exercise!
  B I know. I'm fed up with it, too!

T 6.12 and **T 6.13** see p52

T 6.14

1 A Tokyo's such an expensive city.
 B Well, it's certainly not very cheap.
2 A Paul and Sue are so mean.
 B They're not very generous, that's for sure.
3 A Their house is always so messy.
 B I know, it's not very tidy, is it?
4 A That sales assistant was so rude!
 B Mmm … she wasn't very polite, was she?
5 A Jim looks really miserable.
 B Yes, he's not very happy at the moment, is he?
6 A This exercise is so boring!
 B Mmm, it's certainly not very exciting.

T 6.15 R= Rolf J = Jonas
 W = woman in tourist office

R Excuse me. Could you help me?
W Certainly, if I can.
R We'd like to take a trip on one of those buses that show you all the sights. You know, where you can get off and back on where you want …
W Ah, yes. You want a city sightseeing tour. It stops in twenty places, and it costs twenty euros.
R How long does the tour take?
W Well, it depends whether you get off or not, but if you stay on and don't get off, about an hour and a quarter.
J Where can we buy a ticket?
W Here, or at the bus station. But you can't go on with your backpack.
J Sorry? What did you say?
W Your backpack … you know … your bag. It's too big. You have to leave it somewhere.
J Ah, OK! No, don't worry. I'll leave it at the hostel. Thanks. Another thing. I've read that there's an exhibition of modern art on at the moment. Is that right?
W Yes, that's right. It's on at the Studio until the end of next week.
R How much is it to get in?
W Twelve euros, but it's best to book a few days in advance.
R Oh, that's a shame. We wanted to go tonight. Never mind.
J Oh, and one more thing. I need to buy a present for my mother. It's her birthday soon. Is there a gift shop around here?
W There's a good one just round the corner, but it's closed for lunch at the moment. It'll be open again at 2.00.
J OK. That's great. Thanks for all your help.
R Thanks a lot.
W Pleasure. Bye-bye.

UNIT 7

T 7.1

1 Sigmund Freud invented psychoanalysis to help his patients.
2 Prince Rainier of Monaco governed the tiny principality for nearly 56 years.
3 Bella Freud has made clothes for many famous people, including Madonna.
4 John Lennon was a founder member of *The Beatles*.
5 Sophie Dahl has modelled for *Vogue* and Yves Saint Laurent.
6 Julian Lennon has been in the music business since 1984.
7 Roald Dahl wrote many children's books, including *Charlie and the Chocolate Factory* and *The BFG (The Big Friendly Giant)*.
8 Princess Caroline of Monaco has been married three times and has four children.

T 7.2

1 John Lennon started his first band when he was 15. His eldest son, Julian, has been in the music business since he was 19. He has made five albums. He didn't know his father very well.

2 Roald Dahl wrote the story *The BFG* in 1982 for his granddaughter, Sophie. It is about a little girl called Sophie. Sophie Dahl has been a model since she was 17, but she also likes writing. She has written some short stories and one novel.
3 Sigmund Freud worked in Vienna for most of his life. His great-granddaughter, Bella Freud, was born in London and has worked there since 1990. But when she was a fashion student, she lived in Rome.
4 Prince Rainier of Monaco married American film star Grace Kelly in 1956. Their daughter, Caroline, has had quite a tragic life. She divorced her first husband after only two years and both her mother and her second husband died in terrible accidents. She has been married to her third husband, Prince Ernst of Hanover, since 1999.

T 7.3

1 When did John Lennon start his first band?
 When he was 15.
2 How long has Julian Lennon been in the music business?
 Since he was 19.
3 When did Roald Dahl write The BFG?
 In 1982.
4 How many novels has Sophie Dahl written?
 Just one.
5 Where did Sigmund Freud work?
 In Vienna.
6 Where has Bella Freud worked since 1990?
 In London.
7 Who did Prince Rainier marry?
 The American film star, Grace Kelly.
8 How many times has Princess Caroline been married?
 Three times.

T 7.4 see p56

T 7.5

A Where do you live, Anna?
B In a flat in Green Street.
A How long have you lived there?
B Only for er,… three months. Yes, since June.
A And why did you move?
B Well, we wanted to live near the park.

T 7.6

1 A What do you do?
 B I work in advertising.
 A Really? How long have you done that?
 B For … just over two years.
 A And what did you do before that?
 B I worked for a small publishing company.
2 A Have you got a car?
 B Yes, we've got a Volkswagen Golf.
 A How long have you had it?
 B Since April this year.
 A Did you pay a lot for it?
 B Not really, it was £6,000.
3 A Do you know Alan Brown?
 B Yes, I do.
 A How long have you known him?
 B For a long time – about ten years.
 A Where did you meet him?
 B We met in London – at drama school.

T 7.7 The band *Goldrush*

I = Interviewer R = Robin J = Joe
H = Hamish Ga = Garo Gr = Graham

I … and that was *Goldrush* playing the song 'Wait for the wheels' from their mini-album *Ozona*. And here we have the five band members in the studio! Welcome, guys!
All Hello. Hi, there. It's good to be here.
I Now, tell us a bit about yourselves. How long have you all been together as a band?
R Well, my brother Joe and I have always had a band!
J That's right. Since we were teenagers, really.
R First, we started a band called *Whispering Bob* in

1999. Then, in … 2002, Graham and Garo joined us and we changed our name to *Goldrush*. Finally, Hamish here, joined two years ago.
I So, Robin, how did you start?
R Well, when I was at school, I started writing songs in my bedroom and recording them on a tape machine. Our first band was with our schoolfriends, wasn't it, Joe?
J Yes, but some of our first concerts were pretty bad!
R Yeah, they were!
I So in *Goldrush*, which instruments do you all play?
R We all play several instruments. I sing and play guitar and piano.
J And I play bass, violin, trumpet, keyboards, …
R In fact, anything!
H I play bass and guitar.
Ga I play guitar as well, and drums.
Gr And I play …drums … and drums! (All laugh)
I And how would you describe your style of music?
J We're a rock band.
I Who has influenced you the most?
J Firstly, Neil Young, because he's so passionate about his music.
Ga And also a band called *The Flaming Lips*, who are just amazing.
Gr Yeah, and now we've recorded and toured with *The Flaming Lips*, which is just a dream come true for us.
All Yeah.
R And recently, I've become really interested in Bob Dylan. He's written so many fantastic songs for so many years.
I You've toured the US a few times. What was that like?
Ga It was an amazing experience! So much of the history of rock music is there.
H We had a great tour playing with Mark Gardener.
I Where else have you played? Which other countries have you been too?
R We've played in Spain twice, in Barcelona and Madrid. And last year we played in concerts in Azerbaijan and Uzbekistan!
J Yeah, they certainly aren't places we ever expected to play!
Ga And in Hong Kong we played with some great friends of ours, *Six by Seven*.
I Your first album *Don't bring me down* came out in 2002. How many albums have you made since then?
Gr We've made two mini-albums. One's called *Extended Play* and we've just finished another called *Ozona*. They have six songs on each of them.
I So what's coming up in the future? What are your plans?
R Well, first, we're going back to play in America, and then we're going to Australia for the first time! We're looking forward to that.
I Well, guys, good luck with everything. (Thanks a lot) It was great talking to you. Are you going to play us out with something?
J Yes, this song is called 'There's a world'.
I Let's hear it for *Goldrush*!

T 7.8 P = Presenter A = Aston (Reporter)
 D = Davina PA = Personal assistant

P Our reporter Aston Thompson spoke to Davina Moody outside her hotel.
A Hey Davina! Is it true what we've all read in today's Hollywood Star?
D I just don't know how you guys can write this stuff about me!
A So it's all rubbish? You don't have six bodyguards?
D No, I don't. I've never had six bodyguards. Three usually – well maybe four sometimes.
A And the carpet! What about the carpet?
D Look. It was raining and I asked for an umbrella, not a carpet!
A But not a yellow umbrella, Davina? Is it true you hate anything yellow, especially roses?

D This is crazy. OK so I've never worn yellow dresses. I look sick in yellow stuff. But red roses, yellow roses, white roses? Like, who cares? Roses are roses. They're all the same to me.

A Shame you missed the premier of your movie.

D That's so not true. I did not miss it. I was just a bit late.

A Like three hours late! How's your poor finger nail?

D Well, it's still not good …

A Aw! Davina. Hey, what about the movie? Have you read what the papers are saying about *The Lady Loves To*? They all …

PA Miss Moody does not want to talk about the movie. Come on Davina. Come on Pooksie! We have a plane to catch.

D Bye, guys.

T 7.9

artist, politician, musician, accountant, decorator, photographer, receptionist, interpreter, scientist, librarian, electrician, lawyer

T 7.10   see p60

T 7.11

1 **A** Do you like cooking?
  B Yes.
2 **A** Do you like cooking?
  B Yes, I do, especially Italian food.

T 7.12 and **T 7.13**   see p61

T 7.14

1 **A** Are those new jeans you're wearing?
  B No, they aren't. I've had them for ages.
2 **A** Have you got the time, please?
  B No, I haven't. I'm sorry my watch has stopped.
3 **A** Can you play any musical instruments?
  B Yes, I can actually. I can play the violin.
4 **A** Do you like learning English?
  B Yes, I do. Most of the time I like it a lot.

T 7.15

1 **A** Is it still raining?
  B No, it isn't. It's just stopped.
2 **A** Did you see the football last night?
  B Yes, I did. It was a great game.
3 **A** Have you got change for a pound?
  B No, sorry, I haven't. I've only got a ten-pound note.
4 **A** Have you tried the new pizza place?
  B Yes, I have. I went there last weekend with Frank.
5 **A** Are you ambitious?
  B Yes, I am. I want to have my own business one day.
6 **A** Are you doing anything tonight?
  B No, I'm not. Why? What are you doing?

UNIT 8

T 8.1   I = Interviewer   T = Tristan

I What hours do you work, Tristan?

T It depends. I sometimes have to work at night but I usually work about eight to ten hours a day. It's hard to be exact.

I How often do you have to work at night?

T Well, I have to be on call two nights a week.

I And do you have to work at weekends?

T Sometimes. In this job you have to work very unsocial hours. You never know if there'll be an emergency.

I Tell me about your days.

T Well, there's always variety and that's good. In the mornings I work here in the surgery but in the afternoons I have to go out on visits – often, here in the countryside, to farms.

I What's the most difficult thing about the job?

T Well, it's the night shifts really. When I'm on call at night I don't have to stay in the surgery, I can go home but I can never relax. I can't watch TV or have a drink. And when I get back home after an emergency I find it really difficult to sleep.

I I hear the training's quite hard.

T Oh yes, I had to study for five years. I was at Liverpool University, and as part of my training I came here to do work experience and when I graduated, they offered me a job. I didn't have to look for a job.

I That was lucky.

T Yes, I know, but the other students on my course have all got good jobs now.

I Are you well-paid?

T It's not too bad! When I have my own practice it'll be better.

I And what are the secrets of being good at your job?

T Well, obviously you have to love working with animals, but also you have to be sensitive to their owners – pets are important to people and sometimes you have to give bad news. You have to stay calm in emergencies. Two nights ago I helped a sheep have triplets – three's quite unusual for a sheep. The farmer was delighted. When I save an animal's life, that's fantastic, no matter what time of night it is.

I And what are your plans for the future?

T Well, as I said, eventually I'd like to have my own practice. Anyway, nice to talk to you. I've got to go now. Bye!

I Thanks, and bye!

T 8.2   see p63

T 8.3

1 **A** My ex-boyfriend is going to my best friend's wedding. He was horrible to me. Should I go?
  B Of course you should. But look happy and wear a fantastic dress! I think you should show your ex that you're fine without him.
2 **A** There's a group of bullies at school. They're making my life miserable.
  B You must tell your parents and your head teacher about this. You shouldn't let these cowards ruin your life.
3 **A** I've fallen in love with my boss. Should I tell him?
  B No, you shouldn't. It will only cause problems at work. I don't think you should have relationships with people you work with.
4 **A** I'm 16. I chat to a boy on the Internet. He wants to meet me. Should I go?
  B I don't think you should. You have no idea what he's really like. If you do go to meet him, you must take a friend with you. This is really important.

T 8.4   Leaving home

Ian Mitchell   My daughter Evie is living in London now. She went there four months ago, and I'm really very worried about her. She says she's having a great time but I just think London's such a dangerous place for a young girl, and she's still only 18. She shouldn't live so far away from home. Her mother went with her to help her look for somewhere to live. But I didn't go. I don't like London – I don't like big cities.
Why did she have to go there? I don't understand. She says she wants to be a dancer, and she's doing a sort of course, a ballet course or something. But ballet isn't a real job, and you don't earn much money being a dancer, do you? She's a clever girl. I think she should go to university.
She's living in a flat in London – with her boyfriend, I think, and I don't like that at all! We've never met the boyfriend – Michael, I think his name is. He hasn't got a job and so Evie has to earn some extra money – she works at the weekends as a dancer in a theatre or club, I think. I just hope it's a nice place.

She phones home sometimes, but not a lot, and we phone her, but so often her mobile's turned off or she doesn't answer. When I do manage to talk to her, she just tells us that we should get a mobile so she can text us. She says we shouldn't worry. How can we not worry? We're her parents, we miss her and of course we worry, sometimes I can't sleep at night. She really must come home more often.

T 8.5   Leaving home

Evie Mitchell   I want to be a professional dancer, so I came to London four months ago to start a course at the English National Ballet School. If you want a good dance career, you have to go to a good school and you have to start young – I'm almost 19, nearly too old! I know my parents are worried about me living in London, but it isn't dangerous. You just have to be careful, that's all. It was difficult in the beginning. I didn't know anybody, and London's such a big place. But I love it now. There's lots to do and see.
I'm living in a small flat near the ballet school with Francine, another dance student. We're good friends now. And I've also got a boyfriend! His name's Marco and he's doing the same course. He still lives with his parents, quite close to our flat. His parents are really kind, and I often spend the evenings with them. I want to take Marco home to meet my parents. But the train journey is expensive. And I haven't got much money. London's really expensive, so Francine and I have to work every weekend. We teach children's dance classes at a school nearby. It's good fun, actually!
I phone my parents three times a week! My dad always sounds so worried! He shouldn't be. I try to tell him not to worry but he doesn't listen. I love my mum and dad very much, but I can't live at home for the rest of my life. They really must come to London to visit me. And I think they should get a mobile. Then I could send them text messages, and maybe they wouldn't worry so much.

T 8.6   R = Rachel Foley (Jack's mother)   A = Alex

R Good morning Alex. Nice to meet you. I have to say that this is a first! Interviewing a man for this job.

A I know it's, it's unusual.

R Well, certainly a man has never applied for it before. Tell me, have you always been a nanny?

A No, not at all. I was studying engineering in Stockholm, and I knew I could earn a lot of money as an engineer but it was boring, so I stopped and decided to look at other careers.

R OK I understand that. But why a nanny? Why did you choose this career, a career in childcare?

A Well, obviously it's because I love children, but it's much more than that. You see my mother died when I was just twelve years old and I had to help my father take care of my younger brother and sister.

R Ah, I see. So you didn't have to do a lot of training to be a nanny?

A Oh yes, I did. I had to train for a year. I had to learn how to look after children properly. Actually, I was the only boy on the course – so I really enjoyed it!

R So what kind of things did you learn?

A Well, you know, how to change nappies …

R Very important!

A How to cook healthy meals for children. How to play with them and organize their days. We worked hard and we all felt fully-qualified for the job at the end of the course.

R Well, before I offer you the job I'd like you to meet Jack and spend some time with him to see how well you two get on together.

A I'd love to.

R Well, let's go and meet him. He's adorable! Oh I forgot – do you have any questions for me?

A Just one. Do I have to wear a uniform?

R No, that's not necessary. You look just fine.

A Thank you very much.
R OK, let's …

T 8.7 see p68

T 8.8

hairdresser, countryside, text message, problem page, flight attendant, housewife, train journey, firefighter

T 8.9

1 I can't stop sneezing, and blowing my nose. I've got a cold.
2 I keep being sick, and I've got diarrhoea. I've got food poisoning.
3 It hurts when I walk. I've twisted my ankle.
4 I've got stomach-ache and I keep going to the toilet. I've got diarrhoea.
5 My glands are swollen, and it hurts when I swallow. I've got a sore throat.
6 I've got a temperature, my whole body aches, and I feel awful. I've got 'flu.

T 8.10 At the doctors

D = Doctor **M** = Manuel

D Hello. Come and sit down. What seems to be the matter?
M Well, I haven't felt very well for a few days. I've got a bit of a temperature, and I just feel terrible. I've got stomach-ache as well.
D Have you felt sick?
M I've been sick a few times.
D Mm. Let me have a look at you. Your glands aren't swollen. Have you got a sore throat?
M No, I haven't.
D Have you had diarrhoea at all?
M Yes, I have, actually.
D Have you eaten anything which might have disagreed with you?
M No, I don't think so … Oh! I went to a barbecue a few days ago and the chicken wasn't properly cooked.
D It could be that, or just something that was left out of the fridge for too long.
M I think it was the chicken. I started being ill that night.
D Well, you should have a day or two in bed, and I'll give you something that will help with the stomach-ache and diarrhoea. Drink plenty of liquids, and just take things easy for a while. I'll write you a prescription.
M Thank you. Do I have to pay you?
D No, no. Seeing me is free, but you'll have to pay for the prescription. It's £7.
M Right. Thanks very much. Goodbye.
D Bye bye.

UNIT 9

T 9.1

James Well, I speak Spanish quite well, so before I go to university, I'm going to travel round South America. I've got an old school friend in Brazil and a penfriend in Guatemala, so I have some people to visit. I also want to go and see the rainforest! I'm working in a local restaurant at the moment, but as soon as I have enough money, I'll book a flight to Rio de Janeiro. I'll spend about a month in Brazil, then go on to Guatemala, I think. I'm so looking forward to going. It'll be fantastic! When I'm travelling around, I'll phone home twice a week. If I don't keep in touch, I know my parents will worry!

T 9.2

Jessie I want to do something useful before I go to college next year, so I'm going to work in an old people's home as soon as I finish school. My job is to work with the nurses and help the people get

dressed, and I'll go for walks with them – things like that. The job starts in July and it's for at least nine months. I'll also live in the home while I'm working there. I'll work until I've saved enough money for a holiday. I'm going to Greece with some friends after the job ends. I'll need to relax. I won't be tired if I have a holiday before term starts!

T 9.3

A I'm going on safari to Africa.
B Oh dear, what will you do if you get chased by wild animals?
A It'll be OK. I'll be in a car, so I won't get chased. But I hope I'll see lots of wild animals.
B But what if it's the rainy season?
A Don't be silly! I won't go when it's the rainy season.
B Oh, but what if there are lots of insects? You hate insects.
A I'm going to take lots of insect cream. It won't be a problem.
B And the sun – it'll be so hot. What if you get sunburnt?
A I'm going to take lots of suncream too. I'll be fine.
B But it'll be so frightening. What if you get lost in the bush?
A Look, I won't be alone. I'll have a driver and a guide.
B But what if your car breaks down?
A I'm sure it won't, and if it does, the driver will mend it.
B Ooh but at night! What if you have to sleep in a tent?
A I'll be happy to sleep in a tent, under the stars. It'll be exciting.
B Rather you than me. All those wild animals and mosquitos – ugh!
A Well, I'll love it. I just know I will!

T 9.4 **M** = Mum **J** = James

M Bye, my darling. Have a good flight to Rio. Remember, we're expecting a phone call from you this evening when you get there!
J I'll ring you as soon as I arrive at Diego's house.
M Good. What time will you get there?
J Well, the flight takes 12 hours. If the plane arrives on time, I'll be there about 11.30 – Rio time, of course. If you're asleep when I ring, I'll leave a message on the answerphone.
M I won't be asleep!
J OK! OK! Don't worry, Mum. I'll be fine.
M All right. But when you travel around the country, will you remember to call us regularly? Make sure you phone twice a week.
J Of course! And I'll phone you if I run out of money!
M Cheeky! But you must look after yourself, darling. Give my best wishes to Diego's parents, and don't forget to give them this present when you get to their house.
J Don't worry. I won't. Oh, they're calling my flight! Love you, Mum. Bye!
M Love you, James. Take care!

T 9.5

1 I did the washing-up last night. It's your turn tonight.
2 Please tell the children not to make a noise. I'm trying to work.
3 I did my best but I still failed the exam.
4 I don't know if I want the chicken or the fish. I just can't make up my mind.
5 My sister's very popular. She makes friends very easily.
6 Could you do me a favour and give me a lift to the station? Thanks.
7 My grandfather made a fortune in business. He's a rich man.
8 I'm going to do a course in Spanish before I go to Spain.

T 9.6

1 Everybody smile! I want to take a photo of you all.
2 I know my bedroom's a mess, but don't get angry. I'll tidy it soon.
3 Bye-bye! See you soon. Take care of yourself.
4 Atishoo! Oh dear. I think I'm getting a cold.
5 The doctor told me to take two tablets a day until I get better.
6 I like Ingrid very much. I get on well with her.
7 It takes a long time to become really fluent in a foreign language.
8 If you don't hurry up and get ready, we'll be late for the party.

T 9.7

1 How long does it take you to get ready in the morning?
2 What time did you get to school today?
3 Do you always do your homework?
4 Do you sometimes make mistakes in English?
5 When did you last get angry?
6 Who usually does the washing-up in your family?
7 Did you take many photos on your last holiday?
8 Do you know anyone who has made a lot of money?
9 Is your English getting better?
10 Would you like to do a course in another language?

T 9.8 Going nowhere

I = Interviewer **R** = Roger **M** = Mary
A = Annabel **JC** = Jean-Claude

I Good afternoon and welcome to this week's programme *People and Places*. Now usually we interview people who have been somewhere interesting, but today we will be talking to people who prefer to stay at home! Nowadays, travel is so cheap and easy that most people have been abroad, or are planning to go in the future. So, it seems a very strange idea to many of us not to go anywhere. So why don't some people like travelling at all? We find out why. …
I Here I am in Roger and Mary's little cottage in the village of Avonford. Now, you're both retired, aren't you?
R Yes, that's right.
I So what's the problem?
M Well, the problem is that Roger won't go anywhere! Here we are with the time and the money to do things, and I can't get him out of the house!
R Now, that's not true, Mary. We go and visit our friends and grandchildren, and we go shopping.
M That's not what I mean, Roger!
I Why don't you like travelling, Roger?
R Well, I don't see the point. I have everything here. We live in a nice part of the world. I love my home. My friends are all in the village. I'm always busy, and I never get bored. Going away is just too much trouble. There are delays at the airport, flights are cancelled, it's just not worth it. When you get home you have a mountain of mail and the grass needs cutting. Anyway, you can see everything on TV these days.
M And we couldn't go abroad when we were younger, because we had four children and no money.
R That's right.
M But the craziest thing is that he has a travel secret.
I Oh, what's that?
M Well, when he was a teenager, he was a sailor!
R Yes, I was in the Navy for five years, and I sailed round the world ten times. So I saw the world 45 years ago. I don't need to see it again!

…

I I'm now with Annabel, who works in a vegetarian restaurant in Bristol. So, why don't you like travelling, Annabel?
A Well, I don't like some kinds of travelling, because I don't really like being a tourist and visiting famous tourist sights.

I Why not?

A There are usually lots of other tourists, you can't see anything, and you are destroying the place as well.

I What do you mean 'destroying the place'?

A Well, I've been to a lot of famous places, like the Acropolis in Greece, and the Pyramids in Egypt, and they have too many people walking on them.

I I see. What else don't you like about travelling?

A Travelling by plane – it's bad for the environment. I think there are too many people flying to too many places. It's destroying our planet. We should try to look after what we have, instead of trying to see it all before it disappears. But if I tell my boyfriend this, he gets cross – he just wants to us have a holiday somewhere nice and hot!

…

I I'm now speaking to Jean-Claude, a French builder from Provence. Tell me, Jean-Claude, what is it about foreign travel that puts you off?

JC It's because France can give me everything I want. Why should I go to another country to have food that isn't as good, wine that isn't as good, and a climate that isn't as good? France has everything. I go skiing in winter in the Alps to the best ski slopes in the world, and in summer when it is so hot I go to the Cote d'Azur and go swimming in the lovely Mediterranean. What could be better?

I But aren't you curious to see the rest of the world? Wouldn't you like to go to the United States, for example?

JC I love Europe for its history and tradition, its culture and beauty. I don't need to travel so far. And what would I eat in America? I would be hungry all the time! I have been to Italy once and Greece once. That was enough for me.

I And your wife?

JC My wife needs to be near her mother, so she agrees with me. We stay en France.

I So there we have it. Some like to travel, others can't be bothered. It takes all sorts to make a world! Bye-bye!

T 9.9

1 A Excuse me, is there a post office near here?
  B Yes. It's in Station Road.
2 A Excuse me, is there a library near here?
  B Yes, it's in Green Street.
3 A Excuse me, where's the school?
  B It's in Church Street.

T 9.10

You go down the hill, and walk along the path, past the pond, over the bridge, and through the gate. Then you go across the road and take the path through the wood. When you come out of the wood, you walk up the path and into the church. It takes ten minutes.

UNIT 10

T 10.1

Today, paper is used for hundreds of everyday things – books and newspapers, of course, but also money, stamps, cups, bags, and even some clothes. Long ago, before paper, people wrote on animal skins, bones and stones. Then in 2700 BC, the Egyptians started to make papyrus, which was similar to paper. But the first real paper was invented in AD 105 by a Chinese government official, Ts'ai Lun. It was made from a mixture of plants and cloth. The Chinese kept their invention secret for centuries. Finally, in the 10th century, paper was brought to Europe by the Arabs. The first European paper mill was built in Spain in 1150. Since the 18th century,

most paper has been made out of wood, because it is much stronger than cloth.
Nowadays, each person uses about 300kg of paper every year. That's a lot of paper.

T 10.2

When was paper invented?
In AD 105.
Where was the first real paper invented?
In China.
Who was it invented by?
Ts'ai Lun.
When was it brought to Europe by the Arabs?
In the 10th century.
Where was the first paper mill built?
In Spain.
How long has paper been made out of wood?
Since the 18th century.
How much paper is used by each person every year?
About 300kg.

T 10.3

1 Paper is only used to make newspapers and books.
  No, it isn't. It's used to make hundreds of everyday things.
2 All clothes are made out of paper.
  No, they aren't. Only some are made out of paper.
3 Before paper, people wrote on trees.
  No, they didn't. They wrote on animal skins, bones and stones.
4 Paper was invented by a Chinese scientist.
  No, it wasn't. It was invented by a Chinese government official.
5 The Chinese gave their invention to the world immediately.
  No, they didn't. They kept it secret for centuries.
6 They made paper out of wood.
  No, they didn't. They made it out of a mixture of plants and cloth.
7 The first paper mill in Europe was built in France.
  No, it wasn't. It was built in Spain.
8 Paper has been made out of cloth since the 18th century.
  No, it hasn't. It's been made out of wood.

T 10.4

1 Do you always wear a watch?
  Yes, all the time. Don't you?
2 Are you good at telling jokes?
  No, I'm hopeless. I can never remember the ending.
3 What was the last present you gave? Who to?
  Mmmm. I think it was when I gave some flowers to my mum for Mother's Day.
4 What was the last phone call you made? Who to? Why?
  Just before I came into class. I called a friend to ask if she's doing anything tonight.
5 Do you keep a diary?
  Yes, but I don't write very personal things in it, in case someone finds it.
6 Have you, or a friend, ever made a complaint in a restaurant?
  No, but my dad often complains. I find it embarrassing, but he says it's important to do it.
7 Have you ever been homesick? Did you miss your family or your friends?
  Oh, yes, when I went on an exchange to Germany when I was 16, I missed everybody.
8 What is the best advice you've ever been given?
  If you can't say anything nice, don't say anything at all.

T 10.5 Things that really annoy me

A I can't stand it when you phone someone like British Telecom, and you get a machine, not a person, and you hear 'Please choose from these options. For sales, press 1. To report a fault, press 2. To pay a bill, press 3.'

B I know. And the problem is, you don't want any of those. What you want is something completely different! So what do you press?

A And then when you do finally make a choice, you get another menu!

B And then another, and then another.

A Then you have to hold, and you get music forever!

B Until finally you hear 'Your call is very important to us, but all our operators are busy at the moment. Please call back later.' And then you're cut off!

A It drives me mad! You never actually talk to a person.

B But it's machines I can't stand.

A What do you mean? Computers and things?

B No. All machines. I can't use our dishwasher – it has too many buttons. I can't use our washing machine. What temperature do I want? What program do I want? Do I want economy? Do I use powder or one of those little bags full of liquid?

A I know what you mean. I have no idea how to use the radio in my car. I can't even find the on/off button. It has a CD player and a cassette player, but I have no idea where they are. I tried to choose a computer in a shop the other day, but I had to walk out because I didn't understand a word that the shop assistant said.

B I use my son's computer, and I can get it to work some of the time, which is a miracle. But what drives me mad is when I'm trying to print something and the computer says 'The printer cannot be found', and I'm saying 'But it's there, right next to you, you idiot. What do you mean you can't find it?'

A Another thing is the way things get out of date so quickly. I tried to buy a new battery for my camera the other day, and I was told 'Sorry sir, but these batteries aren't made any more.' So I said 'But I only bought this camera last year!' And the assistant, this boy who looked about fourteen, said 'Sorry, sir, this camera's just about ready for a museum.' What a cheek! Kids these days have no respect.

B The thing I can't stand is choice. You don't get one of anything, you get hundreds. Have you tried choosing shampoo in a supermarket? Do you want shampoo for dry hair? For greasy hair? Normal hair? Long hair? Short hair? Blond hair? Frequent use? Do you want it with fruit? With herbs? With oil? With a smell or without a smell? I can't decide! I just close my eyes and choose one.

A Now you've really got me started. Do you know how much it costs to …?

T 10.6 and T 10.7 see p85

T 10.8 Telephoning

1 P = Pete   J = John
  P Hello?
  J Is that Pete? It's John.
  P Hi, John. How are you?
  J Good, thanks. And you?
  P Yeah, fine, thanks.
  J Pete, I'm trying to get …
  P Hello? Hello?
  J … Sorry. We were cut off. Listen, I'm calling because Jed can't make it on Thursday.
  P Oh yeah?
  J Yeah, so are you free on Friday instead?
  P I'm not sure. Can I get back to you later?
  J Sure. I'm going out now, so give me a ring on my mobile. You've got my number.
  P Yes, it's here on my mobile!
  J Oh good! Oh, and can you give me Andy's number? I can't find it anywhere.
  P I haven't got it on me, sorry. I can give it to you when I call you back.
  J Thanks! Speak to you later, then. Bye!
  P Bye for now.

2 F = Francis, Andy's flatmate   J = John
  F Hello.
  J Hello. Is that Andy?
  F No, I'm afraid he's out at the moment. Can I take a message?

J   Yes, please. Can you say that John phoned, and I'll try again later? Do you know what time he'll be back?
F   In about an hour, I think.
J   Thanks. Goodbye.
F   Goodbye.

3   R = Receptionist   DG = Darshan Gandhi
    S = Secretary   A = Annette Baker
R   Good morning. Wells International. Gemma speaking. How can I help you?
DG   Hello, could I speak to Annette Baker, please?
R   The line's busy. Would you like to hold?
DG   Yes, please.
R   It's ringing for you now.
DG   Thank you.
S   Hello. Ms Baker's office. Dawn speaking.
DG   Hello. Can I speak to Annette Baker, please?
S   Who's speaking, please?
DG   This is Darshan Gandhi.
S   I'll just see if she's at her desk, Mr Gandhi. … Yes, I'll put you through.
A   Hello. Annette Baker here. How can I help you, Mr … erm … Gandhi?
DG   Hello. Well, I saw your advertisement in the Guardian newspaper, and I wondered if you could give me a little more information about …

4   D = Dawn (secretary)   S = Simon
D   Hello. Annette Baker's office.
S   Could I speak to Dawn Edwards, please?
D   Speaking.
S   Hey, Dawn, this is Simon!
D   Simon? Simon! How are you? I haven't heard from you in ages!
S   I know. I'm sorry, I've been away. I called your mum and she gave me your work number. Listen, do you fancy meeting up at the weekend?
D   Of course!
S   Great! I'll give you a call on Friday, then.
D   Yes, do that.
S   OK. Speak to you soon. Bye for now.
D   Bye, Simon!

UNIT 11

T 11.1

1 I found a wallet in the street.
    If I were you, I'd take it to the nearest police station.
2 I don't like my sister's boyfriend.
    If I were you, I wouldn't say anything.
3 I've had a row with my mother.
    If I were you, I'd buy her some flowers.
4 I never have enough money.
    If I were you, I'd stop buying so many CDs.
5 My neighbours make a lot of noise.
    If I were you, I'd move.
6 I really need to do more exercise.
    If I were you, I'd cycle to work.

T 11.2

Nisa Isaacs I live with my parents in a shanty town outside the city. My parents collect old newspapers and junk to sell. They don't make much money, so we're poor. But I'm going to change all that. I love school. I'm studying very hard, because I'm taking my high school exams next year. Then I'm going to get a job in an office in town. But that isn't my main ambition. I really want to go to university. So I'm going to work for a while to save some money. I'm hoping to be an architect, then I can build my parents a proper house.

Viktor Panov I'm studying for my Certificate of Education, but I'm not sure what I want to study afterwards. I love doing art at school, so I might go to art college. That would be fun. I might become a designer. But I also enjoy Russian language and

literature, so I might study that at university. I'll have to get good exam results to do that. I'd also like to try living in another country. I've got family in Germany, so I might live there for a while. Perhaps I could study art and design in Berlin. That would be great!

T 11.3

1 A What's for supper?
   B We're having lamb. It's in the oven.
2 A What time are we eating?
   B Don't worry. It'll be ready before your TV programme.
3 A Who's eating with us?
   B I've invited Jerry, but he might be late. It depends on the traffic.
4 I'm going into town tomorrow. I'm having lunch with Jo at 1.00.
5 A Are you going to have a winter holiday this year?
   B I might. I haven't decided yet.

T 11.4

1 A What sort of car are you going to buy?
   B Well, I'd like to buy a Mercedes or a BMW. But of course, they would be too expensive, so I might get a Fiat or a Toyota. One thing's for sure, it'll be second-hand.
2 A Where are you going on holiday this year?
   B As usual Tom and I can't agree, so we might go to Scotland, or maybe Spain. You know us, we always book at the last minute anyway!
3 A What are we having to eat tonight?
   B Well, it might be steak or it might be just a takeaway pizza. Probably the pizza – I feel too tired to cook.
4 A Who are you going to the dance with?
   B Well, I might ask Tony, but then there's also Richard. He's a great dancer, so I might ask him.
5 A What would you do if you won the lottery?
   B In my dreams! But what would I do? Well, I might just give it all away to a dogs' home. No, actually, I think I might travel the world.

T 11.5   At a crossroads in life

Andy I've had some bad news about my job. I'm going to be made redundant in three months' time. It's such a shock! I've worked for the same computer company for 12 years. But I need to think what to do next.
Actually, I've always dreamed of emigrating to Australia. So I might try that! I have a friend in Melbourne, and I'm sure he would help me to find a job there. But if I went to Australia, my parents would be so sad. And they wouldn't be able to visit me very much. It's so expensive. So I would have to find a really good job, so that I could come home a lot, or pay for them to visit me. That might not be easy.
Another thing I might do is start my own business, using my redundancy money. What if I started a computer servicing company? People are always having problems with their computers. If I did that, I'd have to work really hard in the beginning. It wouldn't be easy, but I would enjoy it, I think.

Lucy I'm so surprised! My boyfriend's just asked me to marry him! It was terrible, because I couldn't give him an answer immediately. You see, I really love my boyfriend, and I think I want to marry him sometime, but not yet.
He wants us to get married next June. That's only nine months away. I think it might be better to wait. If we got married in June, we'd have to save all our money for the wedding and a house. But I don't want to do that. I want us to enjoy ourselves while we're young. I want to go away and travel. I'd like to learn how to ride a horse and how to scuba-dive. Oh, there's lots of things I want to do. If we waited a bit, we could do all those things.
If I got married now, I might feel trapped. That would be terrible. But what if I told him I didn't want to marry him yet? Would he understand? He might not, and I don't want to lose him. I do want to

marry him. I just want to put the wedding off for a while. That's all.

Maureen Well, my husband died three months ago, and I've got to decide what to do next. He was ill for a long time, so it wasn't a shock. But we were married for 41 years, and I can't imagine life without him. I don't think I want to live in this house anymore. Anyway, it's so big for just one person. So I might sell it and move to a flat. I'd feel safer if I lived in a flat, because there would be other people around. I think it might be difficult living on my own. Or my daughter says I can live with her and her family. So I might do that, but I'm not sure. I love my daughter and my grandchildren very much. But if I lived with them, I wouldn't feel independent anymore. And I'm still young – I'm only 68! I'm healthy with plenty of friends. There's lots I can still do with my life, I'm sure. I just need to keep busy.

T 11.6

Andy Well, I am now the proud owner of a new business called 'Computer Solutions'. It has been difficult, but everything's going well at the moment. In fact, my first customer was a lovely girl called Annabel, and she's now my girlfriend! And guess where she's from – that's right! – Australia! We're going there at Christmas to visit her family.

Lucy I'm not married, but yes, I'm still with Steve. He was really upset with me at first, when I told him I didn't want to get married yet. But we talked and talked about it, and he finally agreed that we should wait. We're saving a little money every month for our future wedding. But we are also saving to go on holiday! We're going to Mexico next month. I can't wait!

Maureen I still miss Tony every day, but life's getting a bit easier. I sold the house, and I've moved into a little flat in a retirement home. It's not too far from my daughter's house, so I see her and my grandchildren a lot. It's very nice here, and I've made some new friends. I have a special friend here called Jeff. He's on his own, too, so we do lots of things together.

T 11.7

1 I'm looking for my glasses. Have you seen them anywhere?
2 I like these jeans. Can I try them on?
3 You shouldn't drop litter on the floor! Pick it up!
4 Don't throw away the newspaper. I haven't read it yet.
5 If you don't feel well, go and lie down.
6 'Do you like my dress?' 'Let me see. Turn round. Yes. Very nice.'
7 Why are all these lights on? Turn them off .

T 11.8

1 Can I look up this word in your dictionary?
2 I've run out of milk, so I can't have any cereal.
3 My boss is a great guy. I get on well with him.
4 Leave little Ela here. I'll look after her while you're out.
5 Oh no! Our car's broken down, and there isn't a garage for miles!
6 Look out! There's some broken glass on the floor.

T 11.9

1 How do you get on with your parents?
2 When did you last catch a plane? Did it take off on time?
3 Have you ever looked after a baby? Whose?
4 Do you throw away all your rubbish, or do you recycle some of it?
5 When did you last try something on in a clothes shop? Did you buy it?
6 When you see litter in the street, do you pick it up?
7 Have you ever run out of petrol? What did you do?
8 If you won a lot of money, would you give any of it away? Who to?

T 11.10 and **T 11.11** see p93

T 11.12

1 Their house is such a mess! I don't know how they live in it.
2 There were so many people at the party! There was nowhere to dance.
3 I'm so hungry! I could eat a horse.
4 Jane and Pete are such nice people! But I can't stand their kids.
5 I've spent so much money this week! I don't know where it's all gone.
6 A present! For me? You're so kind! You really didn't have to.
7 We've had such a nice time! Thank you so much for inviting us.
8 Molly's such a clever dog! She understands every word I say.

T 11.13 see p114

 UNIT 12

T 12.1 I = Interviewer   A = Al

1 I How long have you been sleeping on the streets?
 A For a year. It was very cold at first, but after a while you get used to it.
2 I Why did you come to New York?
 A I came here to look for work, and I never left.
3 I How long have you been selling *Street News*?
 A For six months. I'm outside the subway station seven days a week selling the magazine.
4 I Have you made many friends?
 A Lots. But I get fed up with people who think I drink or take drugs. My problem is I'm homeless. I want a job, but I need somewhere to live before I can get a job. So I need money to get somewhere to live, but I can't get money because I don't have a job, and I can't get a job because I haven't got anywhere to live. I'm trapped! But now I'm trying hard to make some money by selling *Street News*.
5 I How many copies do you sell a day?
 A Usually about seventy. But I've brought a hundred with me.
6 I How many copies have you sold today?
 A So far, ten. But it's still early. Here, take one!

T 12.2

1 How long have you been trying to find a job?
2 How many jobs have you had?
3 How long have you been standing here today?
4 How did you lose your business?
5 How long have you had your dog?
6 Who's your best friend?
7 Where did you meet him?
8 How long have you known each other?

T 12.3

1 How long have you been trying to find a job?
 For over a year. It's been really hard.
2 How many jobs have you had?
 About 20, maybe more. I've done everything.
3 How long have you been standing here today?
 Since 8.00 this morning, and I'm freezing.
4 How did you lose your business?
 I had a small company, but it went out of business, and then I started having health problems. But without the job, I didn't have health insurance anymore, so things got worse.
5 How long have you had your dog?
 I've had him for about two months, that's all.
6 Who's your best friend?
 A guy named Bob, who's also from Pennsylvania, like me.

7 Where did you meet him?
 I met him here in New York.
8 How long have you known each other?
 Almost a year. I met him right after I came to New York.

T 12.4

1 A Goodbye, everyone! I'm going on holiday tomorrow.
 B Where are you going?
 A Australia. I'm taking my family to visit their cousins in Sydney.
 B Lucky you! When you come back, bring me a T-shirt!
2 A Listen, class! Please finish your work before you go home. And tomorrow, don't forget to bring in your money for the school trip. We're going to the Natural History Museum.
 B Oh, Miss Jones! Can't you take us somewhere more exciting?
3 A Daniel, you were very late last night. What time did you come home?
 B It was before midnight, Mum, honest. Mick brought me home in his car.
4 A I've been decorating my new flat. You must come and visit me on Saturday. And bring Emma and Jake with you. I'll cook you a meal.
 B Great! We'll bring some champagne to toast your new home!
5 (In London)
 A I'll miss you when I go back home to Spain. You must come and visit me at Christmas.
 B I'd love to! I want you to take this photo with you. It will remind you of the day we went to Oxford together.
 A OK. And when you visit, bring me some more English books to read!
6 (In France)
 A I'm going to London tomorrow, so tonight my best friend is coming round to my house to say goodbye. She's bringing a present she wants me to take to her sister in London.
 B Well, have a good trip!

T 12.5 See p100

T 12.6

1 A Excuse me! Can I get past?
 B Pardon?
 A Can I get past, please?
 B I'm sorry. I didn't hear you. Yes, of course.
 A Thanks a lot.
2 A I hear you're getting married soon. Congratulations!
 B That's right, next July. July 21st. Can you come to the wedding?
 A Oh, what a pity! That's when we're going away on holiday.
 C Never mind. We'll send you some wedding cake.
 A That's very kind.
3 A Good luck in your exam!
 B Same to you. I hope we both pass.
 A Did you go out last night?
 B No, of course not. I went to bed early. What about you?
 A Me, too. See you later after the exam. Let's go for a drink.
 B Good idea.
4 A Here's my train!
 B Don't worry. It doesn't leave for another five minutes.
 A Well, I'd better get on, anyway, and find my seat. It was lovely staying with you. Thank you for having me.
 C You're welcome. It was a pleasure.
 A Goodbye, then. See you again soon, I hope.
 B&C Bye! Safe journey!

T 12.7

1 Excuse me! You're sitting in my seat.
2 Have a great weekend!
3 Excuse me, do you know the way …?
4 Thanks for all your help.
5 I can't come to your leaving party.
6 Bye! I'll give you a ring when I arrive home.
7 Anna was so rude to everyone last Christmas. Are you going to invite her again?
8 I've got my driving test tomorrow.
9 I passed my driving test!
10 We're really glad you came to stay with us.

Grammar Reference

 UNIT 1

1.1 Tenses ▶ Ex. 1

This unit has examples of the Present Simple and Present Continuous, the Past Simple, and two future forms: *going to* and the Present Continuous for the future. All these are covered again in later units.

Present tenses   Unit 2
Past tenses   Unit 3
Future forms   Units 5 and 9

The aim in this unit is to revise what you already know.

Present tenses	**Past tense**
He **lives** with his parents.	He **went** to America last year.
I'm **enjoying** the course.	I **started** learning English two years ago.

Future forms
I'm **going to work** as a doctor.
What **are** you **doing** tonight?

1.2 Auxiliary verbs ▶ Ex. 2

Present Continuous
The Present Continuous uses the auxiliary verb *to be* in the positive, questions, and negatives.

Positive	**Question**
I'm studying medicine.	**Are** you enjoying the course?
She's living at home.	

Negative
We **aren't** learning French.

Present Simple and Past Simple
The Present Simple and the Past Simple use the auxiliary verb *do* in questions and negatives. There is no auxiliary verb in the positive.

Positive	**Question**
He lives in Spain.	Where **does** she work?
We went out last night.	Who **did** you see yesterday?

Negative
I **don't** have a job.
They **didn't** watch TV.

1.3 Questions ▶ Ex. 3–4

1   *Yes/No* questions have no question word.
    Are you hot?   *Does he smoke?*

2   Questions can also begin with a question word.

what	where	which	how	who	when	why	whose

Where's the station?
Why are you laughing?
Whose is this coat?
How does she go to work?

3   *What*, *which*, and *whose* can be followed by a noun.
    What time is it?
    Which coat is yours?
    Whose book is this?

4   *Which* is generally used when there is a limited choice.
    Which is your pen? The black one or the blue one?

    This rule is not always true.
    What ⎫
    Which ⎬ newspaper do you read?

5   *How* can be followed by an adjective or an adverb.
    How big is his new car?
    How fast does it go?

    How can also be followed by *much* or *many*.
    How much is this sandwich?
    How many brothers and sisters have you got?

EXERCISES

1   Write the verbs in brackets in the correct tense.

1   The Pope _____ (live) in the Vatican.
2   Last year we _____ (visit) Paris.
3   _____ you _____ (go) out yesterday?
4   My sister _____ (speak) three languages.
5   I like the shirt you _____ (wear).
6   They _____ (not/see) the film last night.
7   _____ you _____ (know) my brother?
8   They _____ (arrive) at 11.00 pm tomorrow.
9   Vicky _____ (enjoy) meeting new people.
10 I _____ (not/like) working late at night.

2   Complete the sentences with a verb form from the box.

don't   Do   's   doesn't   'm   didn't   aren't (x2)

1   I _____ really enjoying this book.
2   _____ you always walk to work?
3   Why _____ you come to school yesterday?
4   He _____ going to study Greek art next year.
5   Jo _____ eat meat. She's a vegetarian.
6   They _____ coming by bus, they've got a car.
7   Sorry, I _____ understand.
8   We _____ working tonight. We're going out.

3   Choose the correct question word.

which   whose   who   why   where   when   what   how

1	_____ is the bank?	6	_____ do you live with?
2	_____ are you smiling?	7	_____ is yours – this one
3	_____ time is it?		or that one?
4	_____ do I open this?	8	_____ did you last see
5	_____ books are these?		Peter?

4   Write questions for these answers.

1	They're watching the news.	6	I like blues and rock 'n' roll.
	_____		_____
2	James arrived yesterday.	7	It costs 25 euros.
	_____		_____
3	She lives in Madrid.	8	No, he didn't enjoy the film.
	_____		_____
4	Joanna comes from Poland.	9	They're coming at 3 o'clock.
	_____		_____
5	Yes, I can drive.		
	_____		

UNIT 2

2.1 Present Simple ▶ Ex. 1

Form

Positive and negative

I We You They	live don't live	near here.
He She It	lives doesn't live	

Question

Where	do	I we you they	live?
	does	he she it	

Short answer

Do you like Peter?   **Yes**, I **do**.
Does he speak French?   **No**, he **doesn't**.

Use

The Present Simple is used to express:
1 a habit.
    *I **get up** at 7.30.*
    *He **smokes** too much.*
2 a fact which is always true.
    *Vegetarians **don't eat** meat.*
    *We **come** from Spain.*
3 a fact which is true for a long time.
    *I **live** in Oxford.*
    *She **works** in a bank.*

2.2 Present Continuous ▶ Ex. 2

Form

am/is/are + *-ing* (present participle)

Positive and negative

I	'm 'm not	
He She It	's isn't	working.
We You They	're aren't	

Question

What	am	I	wearing?
	is	he she it	
	are	we you they	

Short answer

Are you going?   **Yes**, I **am**./**No**, I'm **not**.
Is Anna working?   **Yes**, she **is**./**No**, she **isn't**.

Use

The Present Continuous is used to express:
1 an activity happening now.
    *They**'re playing** football in the garden.*
    *She can't talk now because she**'s washing** her hair.*
2 an activity happening around now, but perhaps not
    at the moment of speaking.
    *She**'s studying** maths at university.*
    *I**'m reading** a good book by Henry James.*
3 a planned future arrangement.
    *I**'m meeting** Jane at 10.00 tomorrow.*
    *What **are** you **doing** this evening?*

2.3 Present Simple and Continuous ▶ Ex. 3–4

1 Look at the right and wrong sentences.
    *Hans **comes** from Germany.*
    NOT   ~~Hans is coming from Germany.~~

    *It's a great party. Everyone **is having** fun.*
    NOT   ~~It's a great party. Everyone has fun.~~

2 Some verbs express a state, not an activity,
    and are usually used in the Present Simple.
    *I **like** Coke.*
    NOT   ~~I'm liking Coke.~~

    *I **know** what you mean.*
    NOT   ~~I'm knowing what you mean.~~
    Similar verbs are *think, agree, understand, love.*

2.4 *have/have got* ▶ Ex. 5

Form

Positive

I	have 've got	two sisters.

Negative

She	doesn't have hasn't got	any money.

Question

Do they have	a new car?
Have they got	

Short answer

Do you have a camera?   **Yes**, I **do**./**No**, I **don't**.
Have you got a camera?   **Yes**, I **have**./**No**, I **haven't**.

Use

1 *Have* and *have got* mean the same.
    Have got is informal. We use it more when we speak
    than when we write.
    *'**Have** you **got** a light?'*
    *England **has** a population of 60 million.*
2 When *have* expresses an activity or a habit, *have*
    (not *have got*) is used.
    *I **have** a shower every day.*
    NOT   ~~I've got a shower every day.~~

    *What time **do** you **have** lunch?*
    NOT   ~~What time have you got lunch?~~

    *We **don't have** wine with our meals.*
    NOT   ~~We haven't got wine with our meals.~~

3 In the past tense, we use *had* (with *did* and *didn't*).
    *I **had** a bicycle when I was young.*
    ***Did** you **have** a nice weekend?*
    *They **didn't have** any money.*

EXERCISES

1 Complete the sentences with the Present Simple form of the verbs in the box.

forget   not eat   go   live   play   have   finish   not speak

1 My cousin _____ in the States.
2 I _____ French or Spanish.
3 Bill often _____ people's names.
4 The exam _____ at 12.30 exactly.
5 Nadia _____ very healthy food.
6 I _____ shopping for clothes every weekend.
7 My dad _____ the guitar.
8 We _____ a karate lesson on Friday afternoon.

2 Complete the sentences with the Present Continuous form of the verbs in brackets.

1 He _____ (study) biology at college.
2 We _____ (not/go) away this summer.
3 Sue _____ (not/enjoy) the meal.
4 _____ you _____ (see) the doctor tomorrow?
5 Where _____ you _____ (go) on holiday?
6 Why _____ they _____ (laugh)?
7 Everyone _____ (have) a great time.
8 You _____ (not/listen) to me.

3 Tick (✓) the correct sentences.

1 ☐ Mario is coming from Italy.
  ☐ Mario comes from Italy.
2 ☐ We usually go by bus.
  ☐ We're usually going by bus.
3 ☐ He speaks Mandarin and Japanese.
  ☐ He's speaking Mandarin and Japanese.
4 ☐ What a great meal! Everyone enjoys it.
  ☐ What a great meal! Everyone's enjoying it.
5 ☐ I'm loving coffee ice cream.
  ☐ I love coffee ice cream.
6 ☐ What do you do tonight?
  ☐ What are you doing tonight?

4 Complete the sentences with the Present Simple or Continuous form of the verbs in brackets.

1 Alex _____ (go) to the gym three times a week.
2 I _____ (think) he's really fit.
3 We _____ (meet) Hanna at 9 o'clock tonight.
4 What _____ you _____ (do) now?
5 Amanda always _____ (look) beautiful!
6 _____ you _____ (come)? The film is starting.

5 Write two sentences, one with a form of *have* and one with a form of *have got*.

1 I / six cousins.   _____ .
                        _____ .
2 we / any milk?   _____ ?
                        _____ ?
3 He / not / a car.   _____ .
                        _____ .
4 My car / a CD player. _____ .
                        _____ .

UNIT 3

3.1 Past Simple ▶ Ex. 1–2

Form

The form of the Past Simple is the same for all persons.

Positive and negative

I He She It We You They	arrived went _____ didn't arrive didn't go	yesterday.

Question

When	did	she/you/they/etc.	arrive?

Did you go to work yesterday?   **Short answer**
Yes, I **did**./**No**, I **didn't**.

Spelling of regular verbs

1 The normal rule is to add *-ed* or *-d*.
   work**ed**   start**ed**   live**d**   love**d**
2 Some short verbs with only one syllable double the consonant.
   sto**pp**ed   pla**nn**ed
3 For verbs ending in a consonant + *-y*, change the *-y* to *-ied*.
   stud**ied**   carr**ied**

There are many common **irregular verbs**. See the list on p158.

Use

1 The Past Simple expresses a past action that is now finished.
   We **played** tennis last Sunday.
   I **worked** in London from 1994 to 1999.
   John **left** two minutes ago.
2 Notice the time expressions that are used with the Past Simple.

	last year.
	last month.
I did it	five years ago.
	yesterday morning.
	in 1985.

3.2 Past Continuous ▶ Ex. 3–4

Form

was/were + verb + *-ing* (present participle)

Positive and negative

I He She It	was wasn't	working.
We You They	were weren't	

Question

	was	I he she it	doing?
What	were	we you they	

Were you working yesterday?   **Short answer**
Yes, I **was**./**No**, I **wasn't**.

Use

1 The Past Continuous expresses a past activity that has duration.
*I had a good time while I **was living** in Paris.*
*You **were making** a lot of noise last night. **Were** you **having** a party?*

2 The activity was in progress *before*, and probably *after*, a time in the past.
*'What **were** you **doing** at 8.00 last night?' 'I **was watching** TV.'*
*When I woke up this morning, the sun **was shining**.*

3.3 Past Simple and Continuous

1 The Past Simple expresses completed past actions. The Past Continuous expresses activities in progress. Compare:
*It **rained** every day of our holiday.*
*We **went** for a swim even though it **was raining**.*

2 A Past Simple action can interrupt a Past Continuous activity in progress.
*When I **phoned** Simon he **was having** a shower.*
*I **was doing** my homework when Jane **arrived**.*

3 In stories, the Past Continuous can describe the scene. The Past Simple tells the action.
*It was a beautiful day. The sun **was shining** and the birds **were singing**, so we **decided** to go for a picnic. We **put** everything in the car …*

4 Notice how the questions refer to different time periods.
*What **were** you **doing** when you lost your passport?*
*I **was shopping**.*

*What **did** you **do** when you lost your passport?*
*I **went** to the police station.*

3.4 Prepositions in time expressions ▶ Ex. 5

at	in	on
at six o'clock at midnight at Christmas at the weekend	in 2007 in the morning/afternoon/ evening in December in summer in two weeks' time	on Saturday on Monday morning on Christmas Day on January 18
no preposition		
yesterday (evening) the day before yesterday	last night/week two weeks ago	

EXERCISES

1 Complete the sentences with the Past Simple of the verbs in brackets.

1 I _____ (stop) working at 8 pm.
2 Nick _____ (work) in a hotel last summer.
3 We _____ (not-see) our friends last week.
4 _____ they ___ (go) to Greece in July?
5 Alan _____ (leave) school in 2005.
6 When ___ you _____ (arrive)?
7 Laura _____ (fix) my computer for me last night.
8 My grandparents ____ (have) a house by the sea.
9 When ___ the programme ____ (finish)?
10 They ____ (organize) a surprise party for us.

2 Write the Past Simple sentences in the correct order.

1 lost / Jack / his job / ago / a month
_____ .
2 didn't / last / We / have / year / a holiday
_____ .
3 lunchtime / We / to the park / yesterday / a picnic / took
_____ .
4 sent / you / I / an email / but / reply / didn't
_____ .
5 go / Why / night / did / so late / you / to bed / last
_____ ?

3 Write the Past Continuous sentences in the correct order.

1 left / playing / when / they / I / were / in the garden
_____ .
2 I / when / just leaving / was / rang / the phone / home
_____ .
3 laughing / Why / you / me / at / you / were
_____ ?
4 wasn't / my computer / couldn't / I / so / working / send emails
_____ .

4 Complete the text. Use the Past Simple and Past Continuous.

It was such a terrible night! The wind (1) _____ (blow) and the trees (2) _____ (make) a lot of noise. Suddenly, I (3) _____ (hear) a big crash of thunder and it (4) _____ (start) to rain. As I (5) _____ (run) home, I (6) _____ (fall) over and got soaking wet. The rain (7) _____ (come) down so hard that it (8) _____ (be) difficult to see anything. I was very happy when I finally (9) _____ (arrive) back at my house.

5 Choose the correct preposition.

1 They started the course *on/at/in* April.
2 Let's meet *on/in/at* 8.30.
3 I went to university *in/at/on* the 1990s.
4 What would you like to do *at/in/on* the morning?
5 We always go shopping *on/in/at* the weekend.
6 Wendy bought a car *at/on/in* November.
7 Do you eat special food *at/on/in* Christmas?
8 What did he do *at/on/in* Sunday?
9 I'll give you a call *at/on/in* two weeks' time.
10 *In/On/At* New Year's Day we often go to the beach.

UNIT 4

4.1 Expressions of quantity ► Ex. 1–4

Count and uncount nouns

1 It is important to understand the difference between count and uncount nouns.

Count nouns	Uncount nouns
a cup	water
a girl	sugar
an apple	milk
an egg	music
a pound	money

We can say *three cups, two girls, ten pounds*. We can count them. We cannot say ~~two waters, three musics, one money~~. We cannot count them.

2 Count nouns can be singular or plural.
*This **cup is** full.*
*These **cups are** empty.*
Uncount nouns can only be singular.
*The **water is** cold.*
*The **weather was** terrible.*

much and many

1 We use *much* with uncount nouns in questions and negatives.
*How **much money** have you got?*
*There isn't **much milk** left.*

2 We use *many* with count nouns in questions and negatives.
*How **many people** were at the party?*
*I didn't take **many photos** on holiday.*

some and any

1 *Some* is used in positive sentences.
*I'd like **some** sugar.*

2 *Any* is used in questions and negatives.
*Is there **any** sugar in this tea?*
*Have you got **any** brothers and sisters?*
*We don't have **any** washing-up liquid.*
*I didn't buy **any** apples.*

3 We use *some* in questions that are requests or offers.
*Can I have **some** cake?*
*Would you like **some** tea?*

4 The rules are the same for the compounds *someone, anything, anybody, somewhere*, etc.
*I've got **something** for you.*
*Hello? Is **anybody** there?*
*There isn't **anywhere** to go in my town.*

a few and a little

1 We use *a few* with count nouns.
*There are **a few cigarettes** left, but not many.*

2 We use *a little* with uncount nouns.
*Can you give me **a little help**?*

a lot/lots of

1 We use *a lot/lots of* with both count and uncount nouns.
*There's **a lot of butter**.*
*I've got **lots of friends**.*

2 *A lot/lots of* can be used in questions and negatives.
*Are there **lots of tourists** in your country?*
*There isn't **a lot of butter**, but there's enough.*

4.2 Articles – *a* and *the* ► Ex. 5

1 The indefinite article *a* or *an* is used with singular, countable nouns to refer to a thing or an idea for the first time.
*We have **a cat** and **a dog**.*
*There's **a supermarket** in Adam Street.*

2 The definite article *the* is used with singular and plural, countable and uncountable nouns when both the speaker and the listener know the thing or idea already.
*We have a cat and a dog. **The cat** is old, but **the dog** is just a puppy.*
*I'm going to **the supermarket**. Do you want anything?* (We both know which supermarket.)

Indefinite article

The indefinite article is used:
1 with professions.
*I'm **a teacher**.*
*She's **an architect**.*

2 with some expressions of quantity.
a pair of   a little   a couple of   a few

3 in exclamations with *what* + a count noun.
What a lovely day!
What a pity!
What clever children!

Definite article

The definite article is used:
1 before seas, rivers, hotels, pubs, theatres, museums, and newspapers.
the Atlantic   the British Museum
The Times   the Ritz

2 if there is only one of something.
the sun   the Queen   the Government

3 with superlative adjectives.
*He's **the richest man** in the world.*
*Jane's **the oldest** in the class.*

No article

There is no article:
1 before plural and uncountable nouns when talking about things in general.
I like potatoes.
Milk is good for you.

2 before countries, towns, streets, languages, magazines, meals, airports, stations, and mountains.
I had lunch with Paul.
I bought Cosmopolitan at Paddington Station.

3 before some places and with some forms of transport.

at home	in/to bed	by car
at/to school/university	by bus	by plane
at/to work	by train	on foot

She goes to work by bus.
I was at home yesterday evening.

4 in exclamations with *what* + an uncount noun.
***What** beautiful **weather**!*
***What** loud **music**!*

Note

In the phrase *go home*, there is no article and no preposition.
*I **went home** early.*   NOT   ~~I went to home early.~~

EXERCISES

1 Write C (count) or U (uncount).

1 butter ___   5 banana ___
2 time ___   6 sugar ___
3 advice ___   7 child ___
4 girl ___   8 weather ___

2 Write how much, how many, much or many.

1 _____ time have we got left?
2 There isn't _____ milk.
3 _____ hours do you work every day?
4 There weren't _____ people at the party.
5 _____ children has Sue got?

3 Choose the correct option.

1 Just *a few/a little* milk in my coffee, please.
2 There's *lots of/a few* sugar in the cupboard.
3 Let's play *a few/a little* more songs.
4 I don't know *anything/something* about it.
5 There isn't *a lot of/many* time, but we'll get there.
6 Luke's got *something/anything* to tell you.
7 There is *a few/a lot of* traffic in Athens.
8 Is *nobody/anybody* in the house?

4 Use a word from the box to complete the conversations.

| something   anything   everything   someone/somebody
| anywhere   no-one/nobody   anyone/anybody (x2)
| somewhere   nothing   nowhere

1 **A** I think I can hear _____ walking on the stairs!
  B Hello, is there _____ there?
  A I can't see _____ .
  B O.K. There's obviously _____ there.

2 **A** Let's go _____ nice this weekend.
  B Good. We didn't go _____ last weekend.

3 **A** What's the matter?
  B Oh, I'm going to a party on Saturday and I can't find _____ to wear!
  A Don't worry. I've got _____ you can borrow.

4 **A** Where did you go on holiday?
  B _____ I just stayed at home.

5 **A** What did you buy at the shops?
  B _____ . _____ was too expensive.

5 Correct these sentences using a, an or the.

1 I'm going to ᵗʰᵉ⌄shops. Would you like anything?
2 My brother's architect in big company in London.
3 Tokyo is capital city of Japan.
4 I bought pair of sunglasses on Oxford Street.
5 I live in small village in mountains in Switzerland.
6 What beautiful new coat you're wearing!
7 I'm reading interesting book at the moment.
8 The life is wonderful when the sun is shining.

UNIT 5

5.1 Verb patterns ▶ Ex. 1

Here are four verb patterns. There is a list of **verb patterns** on inside back cover.

1 Verb + *to* + infinitive
  They **want to buy** a new car.
  I'd **like to go** abroad.
2 Verb + *-ing*
  We **love going** to parties.
  I **enjoy travelling** abroad.
3 Verb + *-ing* or + *to* + infinitive with no change in meaning
  It **started to rain/raining**.
  I **continued to work/working** in the library.
4 Verb + preposition + *-ing*
  We**'re thinking of moving** house.
  I**'m looking forward to having** more free time.

like doing and *would like to do*

1 *Like* + *doing* and *love* + *doing* express a general enjoyment.
  I **like working** as a teacher. = I am a teacher and I enjoy it.
  I **love dancing**. = This is one of my hobbies.
2 *Would like to do* and *would love to do* express a preference now or at a specific time.
  I**'d like to be** a teacher. = When I grow up, I want to be a teacher.
  Thanks. I**'d love to dance**. = At a party. I'm pleased you asked me.
3 Notice the short answers.
  Would you like to dance?   **Yes, I'd love to./No, thanks.**

5.2 Future forms ▶ Ex. 2

will

Form

will + infinitive without *to*
Will is a modal auxiliary verb. There is an introduction to **modal auxiliary verbs** on p136. The forms of *will* are the same for all persons.

Positive and negative

I He She It We You They	'll (will) won't	come. help you. invite Tom.

Question
*What time **will** you **be** back?*

Use

Will is used:
1 to express a future intention made *at the moment of speaking*.
  'It's Jane's birthday.' 'Is it? **I'll buy** her some flowers.'
  I'll give you my phone number.
  'Do you want the blue or the red pen?' 'I**'ll take** the red one.'
2 to express an offer.
  I'll carry your suitcase.   We**'ll do** the washing-up.

Other uses of *will* are covered in Unit 9.

going to

Form

am/is/are + going + to + infinitive

Positive and negative

I	'm 'm not	
He She It	's isn't	going to leave.
We You They	're aren't	

Question

What's he going to do?
When are you going to leave?

	Short answer
Are they going to get married?	**Yes, they are./No, they aren't.**

Use

Going to is used:
1 to express a future decision, intention, or plan made *before* the moment of speaking.
 I'm going to study hard.
 What are you going to do after college?
2 when we can see or feel now that something is certain to happen in the future.
 Look at these clouds! It's going to rain.
 Watch out! That box is going to fall.

will or going to? ▶ Ex. 3–4

Compare the use of *will* and *going to* in these sentences:
I'm going to make a chicken casserole for dinner.
(I decided this morning and bought everything for it.)
What shall I cook for dinner? Er ... I know! I'll make a chicken casserole!
(I decided at the moment of speaking.)

Present Continuous ▶ Ex. 5

The Present Continuous for the future is used:
1 to express a planned future arrangement.
 'What are you doing on Saturday?'
 'We're having a party. Can you come?'
2 with the verbs *go* and *come*.
 My parents are coming for dinner.
 We're going to the cinema. Do you want to come?

EXERCISES

1 Complete the sentences with the infinitive or the -*ing* form of the verbs in brackets.

1 They want _____ (go) for a walk.
2 She loves _____ (dance).
3 I'd like _____ (see) you very soon.
4 We're thinking of _____ (change) our car.
5 I'm looking forward to _____ (hear) from you soon.

2 Write sentences to respond to these statements. Use *will*.

1 This bag's heavy.
 I'll carry it for you.
2 I need a cup of coffee.
 _____
3 Do you want a cheese sandwich or a ham sandwich?
 _____
4 I haven't got your email address.
 _____
5 I'm tired and I haven't done the washing-up.
 _____

3 Choose the correct form.

1 *I'll be/I'm going to be* an astronaut when I grow up.
2 'The phone's ringing!' 'OK, *I'll answer/I'm answering* it.'
3 *I'm seeing/I'll see* the dentist tomorrow at 10.00.
4 I've decided *I'm going to get/I'll get* a new job.
5 Helen's pregnant. *She's going to have/She'll have* a baby.
6 Look at the mess! *I'll help/I'm going to help you* clear it up.
7 Oh dear, I think *I'll sneeze/I'm going to sneeze*.
8 I'm not sure which one to buy. OK, *I'll take/I'm going to take* the blue one.

4 Write the sentences and questions in the correct order.

1 I'm / on business / New York / going / to
 _____ .
2 How long / are / stay / with / to / Suzy / going / you / ?
 _____ ?
3 You / be / are / to / going / very surprised
 _____ .
4 holiday / this / going / a / have / isn't / She / to / year
 _____ .
5 I / rain / it's / to / going / think
 _____ .

5 Complete the sentences using the verb in brackets and a future form.

1 I _____ (have) a party on Friday. Would you like to come?
2 I've decided that I need a new car. I _____ (buy) a Ford Mondeo.
3 If you have a problem, ask the teacher. She _____ (help) you.
4 It _____ (be) a lovely day. Would you like to go to the park?
5 We _____ (go) to Scotland for our holidays this year.

UNIT 6

6.1 What ... like? ► Ex. 1

Form

1 Look at the questions and answers.
   A **What's** your teacher **like**?
   B She's very nice – kind and patient.

   A **What are** his parents **like**?
   B They're strict and a bit frightening.

   A **What was** your holiday in Turkey **like**?
   B Great, thanks. Good weather, good food.

   A **What were** the people **like**?
   B Fabulous. Friendly and welcoming.

   Note
   We don't use like in the answer.
   She's very nice.   NOT ~~She's like very nice.~~

2 In the question What ... like?, like is a preposition.
   'What's Jim **like**?'
   'He's intelligent and kind, and he's got lovely blue eyes.'

   In these sentences, like is a verb:
   'What does Jim **like**?'
   'He **likes** motorbikes and playing tennis.'

Use

1 What ... like? means 'Describe somebody or something. Tell me about them. I don't know anything about them.'
   What's Megan's new boy friend **like**?

2 How's your mother? asks about health. It doesn't ask for a description.
   'How's your mother?' 'She's very well, thank you.'

6.2 Comparative and superlative adjectives ► Ex. 2–4

Form

1 Look at the chart.

		Comparative	Superlative
Short adjectives	cheap small *big	cheaper smaller bigger	cheapest smallest biggest
Adjectives that end in -y	funny early heavy	funnier earlier heavier	funniest earliest heaviest
Adjectives with two syllables or more	careful boring expensive interesting	more careful more boring more expensive more interesting	most careful most boring most expensive most interesting
Irregular adjectives	far good bad	further better worse	furthest best worst

* For short adjectives with one vowel + one consonant, double the consonant: hot/hotter/hottest; fat/fatter/fattest.

2 Than is often used after a comparative adjective.
   I'm **younger than** Barbara.
   Barbara's **more intelligent than** Sarah.

   Much can come before the comparative to give emphasis.
   She's **much nicer than** her sister.
   Is Tokyo **much more modern than** London?

3 The is used before superlative adjectives.
   He's **the funniest** boy in the class.
   Which is **the tallest** building in the world?

Use

1 Comparatives compare one thing, person, or action with another.
   She's **taller** than me.
   London's **more expensive** than Rome.

2 Superlatives compare somebody or something with the whole group.
   She's the **tallest** in the class.
   It's the **most expensive** hotel in the world.

3 As ... as shows that something is the same or equal.
   Jim's **as tall as** Peter.
   I'm **as worried as** you are.

4 Not as/so ... as shows that something isn't the same or equal.
   She **isn't as tall as** her mother.
   My car **wasn't so expensive as** yours.

EXERCISES

1 **Match the questions and answers.**

1 What's Phil like? 2 What does Phil like? 3 How's Phil?	a Very well, thanks. b Oh, the usual things – good food and nice people. c He's tall, funny and very kind.

2 **Write the comparative and superlative of each adjective.**

1 easy   easier   easiest
2 expensive   _____   _____
3 far   _____   _____
4 sad   _____   _____
5 interesting _____   _____
6 big   _____   _____
7 good   _____   _____
8 funny   _____   _____

3 **Complete the sentences with the comparative or superlative form of the adjective in brackets.**

1 This restaurant is _____ (cheap) than the other one in this street. The food is really good. I think it's the _____ (delicious) food in town.

2 Who is the _____ (popular) actor in your country?

3 Michael is a good player, but John is a _____ (good) player than him. But Peter is the _____ (talented) player in the team.

4 Could you tell me the _____ (quick) way to get to London from here?

5 Eva is generous, but Laura is even _____ (generous) than her.

6 I've never been _____ (happy). This is the _____ (happy) day of my life.

4 **Complete the sentences. Use as ... as and a word from the box.**

long difficult exciting much fast hot quiet high spicy

1 I don't think a hippopotamus can run _____ a lion.
2 Today is warm, but it's not _____ yesterday.
3 I'm early. The journey didn't take _____ I expected.
4 The children are asleep, so I'll be _____ I can.
5 I got an A. The exam wasn't _____ I expected.
6 The Alps aren't _____ the Himalayas.
7 My curry isn't _____ yours.
8 I didn't expect the film to be _____ it was!

UNIT 7

7.1 Present Perfect ▶ Ex. 1–3

Form

have/has + *-ed* (past participle)
The past participle of regular verbs ends in *-ed*. There are many common **irregular past participles**. See the list on p158.

Positive and negative

I We/You/They	've (have) haven't	lived abroad.
He/She/It	's (has) hasn't	

Question

Have	I we/you/they	been to the United States?
Has	he/she/it	

Short answer
Have you been to Egypt?　　**Yes**, I **have**./**No**, I **haven't**.

Use

1　The Present Perfect looks back from the present into the past, and expresses what has happened before now. The action happened at an indefinite time in the past.
I've met a lot of famous people. (before now)
She has won awards. (in her life)
She's written twenty books. (up to now)

The action can continue to the present, and probably into the future.
She's lived here for twenty years. (she still lives here)

2　The Present Perfect expresses an experience as part of someone's life.
I've travelled a lot in Africa.
They've lived all over the world.

Ever and *never* are common with this use.
Have you ever been in a car crash?
My mother has never flown in a plane.

3　The Present Perfect expresses an action or state which began in the past and continues to the present.
I've known Alice for six years.
How long have you worked as a teacher?

The time expressions *for* and *since* are common with this use. We use *for* with a period of time, and *since* with a point in time.
We've lived here for two years. (a period of time)
I've had a tattoo since I was a teenager. (a point in time)

Note
In many languages, this use is expressed by a present tense. But in English, we say:
Peter has been a teacher for ten years.
NOT　*Peter is a teacher for ten years.*

4　The Present Perfect expresses a past action with results in the present. It is often a recent past action.
I've lost my wallet. (I haven't got it now.)
The taxi's arrived. (It's outside the door now.)
Has the postman been? (Are there any letters for me?)

The adverbs *just*, *already*, and *yet* are common with this use. *Yet* is used in questions and negatives.
She's just had some good news.
I've already had breakfast.
Has the postman been yet?
It's 11.00 and she hasn't got up yet.

7.2 Present Perfect and Past Simple ▶ Ex. 4–5

1　Compare the Past Simple and Present Perfect.

> **Past Simple**
> 1　The Past Simple refers to an action that happened at a definite time in the past.
> *He died in 1882.*
> *She got married when she was 22.*
>
> The action is finished.
> *I lived in Paris for a year* (but not now).
>
> 2　Time expressions
>
> | I did it | in 1999.
last week.
two months ago.
on March 22.
for two years. |
> |---|---|

> **Present Perfect**
> 1　The Present Perfect refers to an action that happened at an indefinite time in the past.
> *She has written short stories.*
> *He's made five albums.*
> *I've never been to America.*
>
> The action can continue to the present.
> *She's lived there for twenty years* (and she still does.)
>
> 2　Time expressions
>
> | I've worked here | for twenty years.
since 2002.
since I left school. |
> |---|---|
>
> *We've never been to America.*

2　Compare the right and wrong sentences.
I broke my leg last year.
NOT　~~I've broken my leg last year.~~

He has worked as a musician all his life.
NOT　~~He works as a musician all his life.~~

When did you go to Greece?
NOT　~~When have you been to Greece?~~

How long have you had your car?
NOT　~~How long do you have your car?~~

EXERCISES

1　Make sentences in the Present Perfect.

1　You / do / homework?
　Have you done your homework?

2　You / see / Sarah?
　_____

3　You / make / decision / yet?
　_____

4　How long / know / Jamie?
　_____

5　She / be / Sweden / twice.
　_____

6　Their plane / just / land.
　_____

7　Where / you / be?
　_____

8　What / do / your hair?
　_____

2 Write Present Perfect questions for these answers.

1 _____ ?
No, I've never been to Brazil. But I'd like to go.

2 _____ ?
Yes, I saw an elephant when I was on holiday in Thailand.

3 _____ ?
No, but I'd love to win some money one day!

3 Use the Present Perfect and the words in brackets to describe these situations.

1 He's carrying a suitcase. (He / be / on / holiday)
   He's been on holiday.
   _____

2 His plate is empty. (He / eat / everything)
   _____

3 She can't find her bag. (She / lose / bag)
   _____

4 Her leg is in plaster. (She / broke / leg)
   _____

5 The final score is 3–1 to our team. (Our / team / win / match)
   _____

6 I haven't got any more money. (I / spend / all / my / money)
   _____

4 Find and correct a mistake in each sentence.

1 I am here since last week.
2 Kevin had his new job for nine months. He loves it.
3 I lived here for ten years but I'm going to move soon.
4 Bridgit knows Philip for a year and a half.
5 We have been to China in 2005.
6 How long do you have your dog?
7 They have known each other since three days.
8 She's had a sore throat for this morning.
9 Jane was a vet for thirty years and she still enjoys it.
10 How long do you live in this city?

5 Choose the best answer.

1 *Did you ever hear/Have you ever heard* of an actor called Sylvia Halliwell?
2 *I never went/I've never been* to Zimbabwe.
3 *He never met/He's never met* his father. He died before he was born.
4 *Did you talk/Have you talked* to Maggie yesterday?
5 *I've never heard/I never heard* this music before.
6 *Have you seen/Did you see* the news last night?
7 *I never won/I've never won* a competition in my life.
8 *Did you ever dream/Have you ever dreamt* that you could fly?

UNIT 8

8.1 *have to* ▶ Ex. 1

Form

has/have + to + infinitive

Positive and negative

I We/You/They	have don't have	to	work hard.
He/She/It	has doesn't have		

Question

*Do you **have to** work hard?*
*Does he **have to** get up early?*

*Do you **have to** wear a uniform?*

Short answer
*Yes, I **do**./No, I **don't**.*

Note

The past tense of *have to* is *had to*, with *did* and *didn't* in the question and the negative.
*I **had to** get up early this morning.*
*Why **did** you **have to** work last weekend?*
*They liked the hotel because they **didn't have to** do any cooking.*

Use

1 *Have to* expresses strong obligation. The obligation comes from 'outside' – perhaps a law, a rule at school or work, or someone in authority.
   *You **have to** have a driving licence if you want to drive a car.* (That's the law.)
   *I **have to** start work at 8.00.* (My company says I must.)
   *The doctor says I **have to** do more exercise.*

2 *Don't/doesn't have to* expresses absence of obligation (it isn't necessary).
   *You **don't have to** do the washing-up. I've got a dishwasher.*
   *She **doesn't have to** work on Monday. It's her day off.*

Note

Have got to expresses an obligation on one particular occasion.
*I'm going to bed. **I've got to get up** early tomorrow.*
*She**'s got to work** hard. Her exams start next week.*

To express obligation as a habit, we use *have to*, not *have got to.*
*I **have to write** two essays a week.*
*Do you **have to wear** a uniform?*

8.2 Introduction to modal auxiliary verbs ▶ Ex. 2–4

These are modal auxiliary verbs.

can   could   must   shall   should   will   would

1 They go with another verb and add meaning.
   *She **can drive**.*
   *I **must get** my hair cut.*
2 There is no *-s* in the third person singular:
   *He **can dance** very well.*
   *It **will rain** tomorrow.*
3 There is no *do/does* in the question.
   ***Can** she **sing**?*
   ***Shall** we **go**?*
4 There is no *don't/doesn't* in the negative.
   *I **won't have** a cup of tea, thank you.*
   *I **can't speak** French.*
5 Most modal verbs refer to the present and future. Only *can* has a past tense form, *could*.
   *I **could swim** when I was three.*

8.3 should ▶ Ex. 3–4

Form

should + infinitive
The forms of should are the same for all persons.

Positive and negative

I He/She We/You/They	should shouldn't	do more exercise. tell lies.

Question

Should I see a doctor?
Do you think I **should** see a doctor?

Use

1 Should is used to express what the speaker thinks is right or the best thing to do. It expresses mild obligation, or advice.
   I **should** do more work. (This is my opinion.)
   You **should** do more work. (I'm telling you what I think.)
   Do you think we **should** stop? (I'm asking for your opinion.)
2 Shouldn't expresses negative advice.
   You **shouldn't** sit so close to the TV. It's bad for your eyes.
3 Should expresses the opinion of the speaker, and it is often introduced by I think or I don't think.
   I think politicians **should** listen more.
   I don't think people **should** get married until they're 21.

8.4 must

Form

must + infinitive
The forms of must are the same for all persons.

Positive and negative

I He/She We/You/They	must mustn't	try harder. steal.

Question

Questions with must are possible, but have to is more common.
What time do I **have to** start?

Use

1 Must expresses strong obligation. Generally, this obligation comes from 'inside' the speaker.
   I **must** get my hair cut. (I think this is necessary.)
2 Because must expresses the authority of the speaker, you should be careful of using You must … . It sounds bossy!
   You **must** help me. (I am giving you an order.)
   Could you help me? is much better.
3 You must … can express a strong suggestion.
   You must see the Monet exhibition. It's wonderful.
   You must give me a call when you're next in town.

EXERCISES

1 Rewrite the sentences. Use a form of *have to*.

1 It's necessary for the children to wear a uniform.
   The children _____ a uniform.
2 I can stay in bed until late tomorrow.
   I _____ get up early tomorrow.
3 Why was it necessary for you to go to the office?
   Why _____ the office?
4 Must you leave so soon?
   _____ so soon?
5 I needed to make a phone call.
   I _____ a phone call.
6 It wasn't necessary for us to work on Sunday.
   We _____ on Sunday.

2 Correct the sentences.

1 Do you can drive a car?
2 I'm afraid we must to go now.
3 She cans sing very well.
4 She musts go to the dentist this afternoon.
5 You don't should drink and drive.
6 It won't raining tomorrow.
7 Could you to help me?
8 I don't would like to be a policeman.

3 Rewrite the sentences using a modal verb from the box.

can can't could must mustn't 'll should shouldn't

1 I'd like the salt, please.
   _____ you pass me the salt, please?
2 I don't think it's a good idea for you to stay.
   You _____ stay.
3 It is certain to rain this afternoon.
   It _____ rain this afternoon.
4 Do you know how to drive?
   _____ you drive?
5 Do not leave luggage here. It isn't allowed.
   You _____ leave luggage here.
6 It's very important that you stop smoking.
   You _____ stop smoking.
7 Janet doesn't know how to play an instrument.
   Janet _____ play an instrument.
8 I think it would be a good idea to apologize.
   You _____ apologize.

4 Choose the correct option.

1 You *should / have to* show your passport at the airport.
2 *I don't think you should / You mustn't* read that book. It isn't very good.
3 If you want to lean English, you *must / should* get an English pen friend.
4 I think we *should / must* take some flowers when we go to Sue's for dinner.
5 We *mustn't / don't have to* forget Robert's birthday tomorrow.
6 I *must / should* pay my taxes soon. I don't want to go to prison.
7 She's very rich, so she *doesn't have to / mustn't* work.
8 You *mustn't / shouldn't* smoke in here. It isn't allowed.

UNIT 9

9.1 Time clauses ▶ Ex. 1–2

1 Look at this sentence.
I'll give her a call when I get home.
It consists of two clauses: a main clause *I'll give her a call*, and a secondary clause *when I get home*.

2 These conjunctions of time introduce secondary clauses.

when while as soon as after before until

They refer to future time, but we use a present tense.

When I get home, I'll …	NOT	~~When I'll get~~ …
While we're away, …	NOT	~~While we'll be away~~ …
As soon as I hear from you, …	NOT	~~As soon as I'll hear~~ …
Wait here **until I get** back.	NOT	… ~~until I'll get back.~~

9.2 *will*

Form

For the forms of *will*, see p132.

Use

1 *Will* expresses a decision or intention made at the moment of speaking.
Give me your case. I'll carry it for you.

2 It also expresses a future fact. The speaker thinks 'This action is sure to happen in the future'.
Manchester will win the cup.
Tomorrow's weather will be warm and sunny.
This use is like a neutral future tense. The speaker is predicting the future, without expressing an intention, plan, or personal judgement.

9.3 First conditional ▶ Ex. 3–4

Form

If + Present Simple, *will* + infinitive without *to*

Positive and negative

If I work hard, I'll (will) pass my exams.
If we don't hurry up, we'll (will) be late.

Question

What will you do if you don't go to university?

Note

1 We do not usually use *will* in the condition (*if*) clause.
If it rains …   NOT   ~~If it will rain~~ …

2 The condition clause *if* … can come at the beginning of the sentence or at the end.
If I work hard, I'll pass my exams.
I'll pass my exams if I work hard.

Use

The first conditional is used to express a possible condition and a probable result in the future. English uses a present tense in the condition (*if*) clause, but a future form in the result clause.
If my cheque comes, I'll buy us all a meal.
You'll get wet if you don't take an umbrella.

Note

If expresses a possibility that something will happen; *when* expresses what the speaker sees as certain to happen.
If I find your book, I'll send it to you.
When I get home, I'll have a bath.

EXERCISES

1 Choose the correct sentence in each pair.

1 A I'll get a newspaper when I go to the shops.
  B I get a newspaper when I will go to the shops.

2 A She's going to wait until he'll come.
  B She's going to wait until he comes.

3 A As soon as you turn left, you'll see the church.
  B As soon as you'll turn left, you'll see the church.

4 A Pietro's going to meet us before he sees Janet.
  B Pietro's going to meet us before he'll see Janet.

2 Choose the correct answer. Sometimes two answers are possible.

1 We were really surprised _____ he arrived unexpectedly.
  a) if   b) when   c) as soon as

2 I'm really hungry! Let's go for dinner _____ the film finishes.
  a) before   b) as soon as   c) when

3 Wait _____ you've had lunch!
  a) until   b) after   c) when

4 I'm very busy, but I'll go shopping _____ I have time.
  a) until   b) when   c) if

5 I'll have a shower _____ I go to bed.
  a) before   b) after   c) while

6 Oh no! I forgot to feed the cat! I'll do it _____ we get home.
  a) after   b) as soon as   c) when

7 We'll go skiing this weekend _____ it snows enough this week.
  a) when   b) after   c) if

8 We're staying in a guesthouse _____ our new house is built.
  a) until   b) when   c) before

3 Complete the sentences with the correct form of the verb in brackets.

1 If it's sunny, we _____ (go) to the beach.
2 What _____ you _____ (do) if you fail the exam?
3 If we _____ (not/leave) soon, we'll be late.
4 You _____ (get) wet if you go out. It's raining!
5 If Sonya _____ (lie) to me once more, I'll be furious!

4 Complete the first conditional questions.

1 Perhaps it'll rain.
  What __will you do__ if it rains?
2 It's possible David will lose his job.
  What _____ if he loses his job?
3 It's possible there won't be any tickets.
  What will I do if _____ any tickets?
4 Perhaps Alice will miss her flight.
  What _____ if she misses her flight?
5 It's possible that your taxi will be late.
  What _____ if the taxi is late?
6 Perhaps Alan won't reply to your email.
  What will you do if _____ to your email?

UNIT 10

10.1 The passive ▶ Ex. 1–4

Form

am/is/are was/were has/have been will	+ -ed (past participle)

The past participle of regular verbs ends in *-ed*. There are many common **irregular past participles**. See the list on p158.

Present
English **is spoken** all over the world.
Nikon cameras **are made** in Japan.
Coffee **isn't grown** in England.
Are cars **made** in your country?

Past
My car **was stolen** last night.
The animals **were frightened** by a loud noise.
He **wasn't injured** in the accident.
How **was** the window **broken**?

Present Perfect
I've been robbed!
X-ray machines **have been used** for many things.
They **haven't been invited** to the party.
Has my car **been repaired**?

will
10,000 cars **will be produced** next year.
The cars **won't be sold** in the UK.
Will the children **be sent** to a new school?

	Short answer
Are cars made in your country?	**Yes**, they **are**./**No**, they **aren't**.
Has my car been repaired?	**Yes**, it **has**./**No**, it **hasn't**.

Note
The passive infinitive (*to be* + *-ed*) is used after modal auxiliary verbs and other verbs which are followed by an infinitive.
Driving should **be banned** in city centres.
The house is going **to be knocked down**.

Use

1 The rules for tense usage in the passive are the same as in the active.
Present Simple expresses habit:
My car **is serviced** regularly.

Past Simple expresses a finished action in the past:
America **was discovered** by Christopher Columbus.

Present Perfect expresses an action which began in the past and continues to the present:
Diet Coke **has been made** since 1982.

2 The object of an active verb becomes the subject of a passive verb. Notice the use of *by* in the passive sentence.

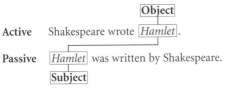

3 The passive is not just another way of expressing the same sentence in the active. We choose the active or the passive depending on what we are more interested in.
Hamlet **was written** in 1600. (We are more interested in *Hamlet*.)
Shakespeare **wrote** comedies, histories, and tragedies. (We are more interested in Shakespeare.)

Note
1 The subject of an active sentence is not mentioned in the passive sentence if it is not really important.

Active	*They built this house in 1937.*
Passive	*This house was built in 1937.*
	NOT ~~*This house was built in 1937 by them.*~~

Active	*People speak German in parts of Italy.*
Passive	*German is spoken in parts of Italy.*
	NOT ~~*German is spoken in parts of Italy by people.*~~

2 Some verbs, for example, *give, send, show*, have two objects, a person and a thing.
She gave **me** *a* **book** *for my birthday.*

In the passive, we often make the person the subject, not the thing.
I *was given a book for my birthday.*
She *was sent the information by post.*
You'll be shown where to sit.

EXERCISES

1 Rewrite the active sentences in the passive.

1 Someone sells tickets at the box office.

_____

2 People built Stonehenge thousands of years ago.

_____

3 Someone has serviced my car.

_____

4 They opened three new hospitals last year.

_____

2 Complete the sentences with the correct passive form of the verbs in the box.

> discover   make   invent   build   paint
> write   give   steal   invite   employ

1 Around £50,000 _____ from a bank in Oslo last night.

2 The first train _____ by George Stevenson in the mid 19th century.

3 In China, red envelopes full of money _____ to children at New Year.

4 X-rays _____ accidentally _____ by Wilhelm Konrad Roentgen in 1896.

5 Hundreds of new homes _____ since March.

6 Next year 3 million mobile phones _____ in Finland.

7 Do you think we _____ to Helen's wedding?

8 Many people in Scotland _____ in the whisky industry.

9 _Romeo and Juliet_ _____ by William Shakespeare.

10 _La Giocanda_ _____ by Picasso.

3 Rewrite these sentences using a form of the passive.

1 People will eat six million hamburgers this year.
Six million hamburgers will be eaten this year.

2 They cancelled the football match because of heavy rain.

_____

3 A man told us not to walk on the grass.

_____

4 How do people use chopsticks?

_____

5 Someone cleans the kitchen every morning.

_____

6 The police arrested the escaped prisoner late last night.

_____

7 How did scientists discover DNA?

_____

4 Find and correct two sentences that are wrong.

1 The money was stole from the shop.
2 Dinner is usually served at 6 o'clock.
3 A new bridge will be built next year.
4 Spanish spoken in Latin America.
5 These cars are made in Germany.

11.1 Second conditional ▶ Ex. 1–2

Form

_If_ + Past Simple, _would_ + infinitive
Would is a modal auxiliary verb (see p136).
The forms of _would_ are the same for all persons.

Positive and negative
_If_ I had more money, **I'd** (would) buy a CD player.
_If_ she knew the answer, she'**d** (would) tell us.
_If_ we didn't have to, we **wouldn't** work so hard.

Question
What **would** you do **if** you had a year off?

	Short answer
Would you travel round the world?	**Yes**, I **would**./**No**, I **wouldn't**.

Note
1 The condition clause can come at the beginning or the end of the sentence.
If I had more time, I'd help.
I'd help **if** I had more time.
2 _Were_ can be used instead of _was_ in the condition clause.
If I **were** you, I'd go to bed.
If he **were** here, he'd know what to do.

Use

The second conditional is used to express an unreal or improbable condition and its result. The past forms are used to show this is different from reality.
The condition is unreal because it is different from the facts that we know. We can always say 'But … '.
If I **were** Prime Minister, I'**d increase** tax for rich people. (But I'm not Prime Minister.)
If they **lived** in a big house, they'**d have** a party. (But they live in a small house.)
What **would** you **do if** you **saw** a ghost? (But I don't think that you will see a ghost.)

11.2 _might_ ▶ Ex. 3

Form

might + infinitive
Might is a modal auxiliary verb (see p136).
The forms of _might_ are the same for all persons.

Positive and negative

I He/She We/You/They	might might not	go to the party. be late. rain tomorrow. go out for a meal tonight.

Question
The inverted question _Might you … ?_ is unusual. It is more common to ask a question with _Do you think … + will … ?_

Do you think	you'll get here on time? it'll rain? they'll come to our party?

	Short answer
Do you think he'll come?	He **might**.
Do you think it'll rain?	It **might**.

Use

1 *Might* is used to express a future possibility. It contrasts with *will*, which, in the speaker's opinion, expresses a future certainty.
   *England **will** win the match.*
   (I am sure they will.)
   *England **might** win the match.*
   (It's possible, but I don't know.)

2 Notice that, in the negative, these sentences express the same idea of possibility.
   *It **might not** rain this afternoon.*
   *I **don't think it'll** rain this afternoon.*

11.3 *so, such (a), so many, so much* ▶ Ex. 4

Form

so + adjective / adverb
*I was **so scared**!*
*He always drives **so fast**.*

such a + adjective + singular noun
*She's **such a nice person**.*

such + adjective + plural/uncountable noun
*The Smiths are **such friendly neighbours**.*

so many + plural nouns
*Some children have **so many toys**!*

so much + uncountable nouns
*Footballers earn **so much money** these days.*

Use

So and *such* are used more in spoken than written English. They are used for emphasizing an adjective, an adverb, or a noun. They are often written with an exclamation mark (!).

*He works **so hard**!* is stronger than *He works **very** hard.*

EXERCISES

1 Choose the correct answer.

1 If we *didn't/don't* have to work, we'd travel round the world.
2 If you *took/take* more exercise, you'd be fitter.
3 *I'd help/I'll help* you if I had more time.
4 If I *am/were* you, I'd forget all about it.
5 If I *win/won* the lottery, I'd give all the money to charity.

2 Match the two halves of each sentence.

1 He'd move to Spain
2 If she got the job,
3 If the weather was nicer,
4 I'd drive to work
5 I'd take an aspirin,

a she'd be very happy.
b if I were you.
c if I had a car.
d we'd have a barbecue.
e if he spoke Spanish.

3 Complete the conversations with *might/might not* or *will/won't*.

1 **A** Are you going to watch the football tonight?
   B Yes I am. Who do you think _____ win?
   A Well, I'm not sure. Barcelona are the better team, but Porto are playing well at the moment, so they _____ win tonight.
   B If no one wins, they _____ have to play again next week.

2 **A** Are you going to Mark's party this Saturday?
   B I'm not sure. I'm tired, so I _____ go. I _____ just watch a DVD and relax instead.
   A Oh, go on, I _____ go if you go. It _____ be fun.
   B OK then, I _____ pick you up at 8.00.

3 **A** Hi Nora. I'm sorry, but we _____ be able to get to the cinema by 6.45. Our car has broken down.
   B That's OK. Do you think you _____ be able to get here by 9.00? There's another showing of the film then.
   A Well, Max thinks he _____ be able to fix it. If not, we _____ get the bus. See you there at 9.00.

4 Complete the sentences with *so, such, so much* or *so many*.

1 It was _____ a nice day that we decided to have a picnic.
2 That book was _____ interesting I couldn't put it down.
3 I've got _____ work to do. I won't finish it by this evening.
4 You've worked _____ hard all week. You deserve a break.
5 It was _____ a great party that no one wanted to leave!
6 There were _____ people in town it took ages to do the shopping.
7 That's _____ a fantastic dress. You look _____ smart.
8 I'm looking forward to my holiday _____ .
9 Some people have _____ money they don't know what to do with it!
10 That film was _____ bad! I've never seen _____ an awful film.

UNIT 12

12.1 Present Perfect Continuous ▶ Ex. 1–4

Form

has/have + been + -ing (present participle)

Positive and negative

I We You They	've (have) haven't	been working.
He She It	's (has) hasn't	

Question

*How long **have** you **been working**?*
*How long **has** he **been learning** English?*

	Short answer
Have you been running?	*Yes, I **have**./No, I **haven't**.*

Use

The Present Perfect Continuous is used:

1 to express an activity which began in the past and continues to the present.
   *We've **been waiting** here for hours!*
   *It's **been raining** for days.*
2 to refer to an activity with a result in the present.
   *I'm hot because I've **been running**.*
   *I haven't got any money because I've **been shopping**.*

Note

1 Sometimes there is little or no difference in meaning between the Present Perfect Simple and Continuous.
   *How long **have** you **worked** here?*
   *How long **have** you **been working** here?*
2 Some verbs have the idea of a long time – *wait, work, learn, live, play*. They are more often found in the Present Perfect Continuous.
   *I've **been playing** tennis since I was a boy.*
   Some verbs have the idea of a short time – *find, start, buy, die, lose, break, stop*. It is unusual to find them in the Present Perfect Continuous.
   *I've **bought** a new dress.*
   *My cat **has died**.*
   *My radio's **broken**.*
3 Verbs that express a state – *like, love, know, have* (for possession) – are not found in the Present Perfect Continuous.
   *We've **known** each other for a few weeks.*
   NOT   ~~We've been knowing each other for a few weeks.~~
4 The Present Perfect Simple looks at the completed action. This is why the Present Perfect Simple is used if the sentence gives a number or a quantity.
   *I've **written** three letters today.*
   NOT   ~~I've been writing three letters today.~~

EXERCISES

1 Choose the best answer.

1 At last! *I've understood / been understanding* the question.
2 The athletes are tired. They've *trained / been training* all day.
3 So, what have you *done / been doing* recently? Anything fun?
4 My friend has *been buying / bought* a new computer.
5 Have you *swum / been swimming*? Your hair looks wet.
6 Great news! Joanna has *been having / had* a baby boy!
7 I've never *believed / been believing* in horoscopes.
8 Oh, there you are! I've *looked / been looking* for you everywhere!

2 Make sentences using the Present Perfect Continuous.

1 **A** You're a really good singer!
   B I / practise / a lot / recently
   _____ .

2 **A** You look really tired.
   B We / work / hard / this week.
   _____ .

3 **A** Your English is good!
   B Thanks. I / learn it / eight years.
   _____ .

4 **A** Have I got blue paint in my hair?
   B Yes. What / you / paint?
   _____ ?

5 **A** You both look really brown!
   B We / sunbathe / at / beach.
   _____ .

3 Complete the sentences with the Present Perfect or Present Perfect Continuous form of the verb in backets.

1 **A** What (1) _____ (do) to your arm?
   B I (2) _____ (play) tennis a lot this week, and I (3) _____ (hurt) my elbow.

2 **A** Your house looks fantastic! You (1) _____ (decorate) it beautifully.
   B Yes, but it's hard work. I (2) _____ (paint) the bedroom all afternoon and I (3) _____ (only paint) three walls.
   A Never mind. It will look great when you (4) _____ (finish) it.

3 **A** Hi Jack. I (1) _____ (not / see) you for ages. What (2) _____ (you /do) recently?
   B I (3) _____ (travel).
   A That's fantastic! Where (4) _____ (you / be)?
   B I (5) _____ (be) to Asia. Have (6) _____ (you / ever / go) there?
   A No, I haven't, but I (7) _____ (want) to go for a long time.

4 **A** Hi. (1) _____ (have) a good day?
   B Yes. I (2) _____ (shop). But I (3) _____ (spend) a lot of money!
   A Show me what you (4) _____ (buy).
   B Well, I'm afraid I (5) _____ (not buy) anything for you! I (6) _____ (try) to find you a birthday present for ages, but I (7) _____ (find) anything yet.

Pairwork activities Student A

UNIT 1 *p8*

PRACTICE
Exchanging information

Ask and answer questions to complete the information about Mary Steiner.

> Where does Mary Steiner live?
>> In Santa Barbara, California.
>> How many children does she have?
> She has twin sons.

Dr Mary Steiner lives in ... (*Where?*). She's married and has twin sons. Her husband's name is ... (*What ... name?*) and he's a surgeon. They met ... (*When?*). Both her sons went to Harvard University and studied ... (*What?*), and now they both work for Miramax film studios in California.

Mary started working as a radio agony aunt ... (*When?*), and does five programmes a week. Every day more than 60,000 people try to phone her. They have ... problems – all sorts! (*What sort?*) The programme lasts an hour, and at the end Mary feels ... (*How?*).

At the moment she's writing a book about marriage, because ... (*Why ... a book about marriage?*). Her own parents divorced when she was five.

She's going to retire ... (*When?*). She wants to spend more time travelling.

UNIT 3 *p25*

PRACTICE
Exchanging information

Ask and answer questions to complete the information about Hugo Fenton-Jones.

Teenager goes on spending spree with father's credit card

> What did Hugo steal?
>> He stole his father's credit card.
>> Where was his father working?
> He was working in the garden.

BIG SPENDER: Hugo Fenton-Jones

Teenager Hugo Fenton-Jones stole ... (*What?*) while his father was working in the garden. He then went to ... (*Where?*) and stayed in the Ritz Hotel. His room was £... a night (*How much?*). While he was shopping in the Champs-Élysées, he bought ... (*What?*).

He phoned two English friends because he wanted them to come to Paris. They were eating breakfast ... (*Where?*) when Hugo's father, James, phoned. His credit card company wanted to know why he was spending so much money. They thought James was staying in the Ritz.

Hugo went ... (*Where?*), where his father was waiting for him. 'He isn't speaking to me at the moment,' said Hugo yesterday. 'He's a bit angry with me.'

PRACTICE

Exchanging information

Name and age	Chantal, 35	Mario and Rita, 69
Town and country		Siena, Italy
Family		1 married daughter, 1 grandson
Occupation		retired bank manager, housewife
Free time/holiday		opera, visit their daughter in the USA
Present activity		preparing to go to the USA

Where does Chantal come from?

Marseilles, in France.

 UNIT 4 *p32*

PRACTICE

Find the differences

Ask and answer questions to find the differences between your picture, and your partner's.

Ask about these things.

towels	toilet paper
soap	shaving foam
nappies	make-up
toothbrushes	deodorant
toothpaste	perfume/aftershave
shampoo	hairbrushes

How much ... is there?
many ... are there?

Have they got any ... ?

Is
Are there any ...?

(Yes,) lots/a lot
a few/a little

(No,) There isn't any
aren't

What are you doing tonight?

You study in the mornings. You need to arrange a time to meet when you and your partner are free. Look at your diary and talk with your partner to find a time when you are both free.

> What are you doing on Monday afternoon?

> I'm playing tennis with Andy. Are you doing anything on Tuesday evening?

	morning	afternoon	evening
Monday	study		meet Frank 8.00
Tuesday	study	visit Auntie Pat	
Wednesday	study		go to cinema with Jane
Thursday	study		cook meal for mum and dad
Friday	study	have driving lesson	

PRACTICE

Exchanging information

Ask and answer questions to complete the information about Stelios Haji-Ioannou.

> Where was Stelios born?

> In Greece.

> When was he born?

> In 1967.

Stelios Haji-Ioannou
The creator of EasyJet airlines and the 'easy' brand

Stelios was born _____ (*Where?*) in 1967. He was educated in _____ (*Where?*), and then studied economics at the London School of Economics. When he was only 17, he drove a _____ (*What sort of car ...?*).

He started his first business, a shipping company, when he was 25. He sold it in _____ (*When?*) for $1.3 billion. He now has a fortune worth at least £400 million.

Stelios is best-known for creating EasyJet, which he has been running since _____ (*How long?*). EasyJet is Europe's largest low-cost airline. It has over 100 jets, which fly to more than forty destinations. In its lifetime, EasyJet has carried over _____ passengers (*How many?*).

Over the years, Stelios has started several businesses – Internet cafés, travel, leisure, and personal finance.

Stelios supports various educational schemes. He has been helping students by _____ (*How?*) since 2005. He has so far given the college _____ (*How much?*).

Since 2004, he has been working with 100 employees in Camden, north London. He also works in Athens. He travels for about four months a year, because _____ (*Why?*). His motto is 'The cheaper you can make something, the more people there are who can afford it.'

Pairwork activities Student B

 UNIT 1 *p8*

PRACTICE
Exchanging information

Ask and answer questions to complete the information about Mary Steiner.

> Where does Mary Steiner live?
>
> In Santa Barbara, California.
>
> How many children does she have?
>
> She has twin sons.

Dr Mary Steiner lives in Santa Barbara, California. She's married and has ... (*How many children?*). Her husband's name is Dan and he's a ... (*What ...do?*). They met when they were both at college. Both her sons went to ... University (*Which university?*) and studied law, and now they both work for ... (*Who ... for?*).

Mary started working as a radio agony aunt thirty years ago, and does ... programmes a week (*How many?*). Every day more than 60,000 people try to phone her. They have money problems, relationship problems, work problems – all sorts! The programme lasts ... (*How long?*), and at the end Mary feels really tired.

At the moment she's writing ... (*What?*) because she's worried about the number of divorces. Her own parents divorced when she was ... (*How old ... parents divorced?*)

She's going to retire next year. She wants to ... (*What ... do?*).

 UNIT 3 *p25*

PRACTICE
Exchanging information

Ask and answer questions to complete the information about Hugo Fenton-Jones.

Teenager goes on spending spree with father's credit card

> What did Hugo steal?
>
> He stole his father's credit card.
>
> Where was his father working?
>
> He was working in the garden.

BIG SPENDER: Hugo Fenton-Jones

Teenager Hugo Fenton-Jones stole his father's credit card while his father was working ... (*Where?*). He then went to Paris and stayed in the ... Hotel (*Which hotel?*). His room was £500 a night. While he was shopping in the ... (*Where?*), he bought clothes, jewellery, and perfume.

He phoned two English friends because ... (*Why?*). They were eating breakfast in the Ritz when Hugo's father, James, phoned. His credit card company wanted to know ... (*What?*). They thought James was staying in the Ritz.

Hugo went home to London, where ... was waiting for him (*Who?*). 'He isn't speaking to me at the moment,' said Hugo yesterday. 'He's a bit angry with me.'

PRACTICE
Exchanging information

Name and age	Chantal, 35	Mario and Rita, 69
Town and country	Marseilles, France	
Family	single, one brother	
Occupation	fashion buyer	
Free time/holiday	goes to the gym, holiday home in Biarritz	
Present activity	buying clothes in Milan	

Where do Mario and Rita come from?

Siena, in Italy.

UNIT 4 *p32*

PRACTICE
Find the differences

Ask and answer questions to find the differences between your picture, and your partner's.

Ask about these things.

towels	toilet paper
soap	shaving foam
nappies	make-up
toothbrushes	deodorant
toothpaste	perfume/aftershave
shampoo	hairbrushes

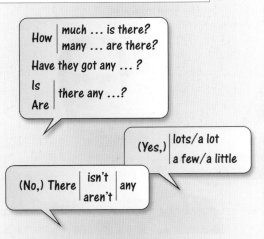

How | much ... is there?
    | many ... are there?

Have they got any ... ?

Is | there any ...?
Are |

(Yes,) | lots/a lot
       | a few/a little

(No,) There | isn't | any
            | aren't |

What are you doing tonight?

You study in the mornings. You need to arrange a time to meet when you and your partner are free. Look at your diary and talk with your partner to find a time when you are both free.

> **What are you doing on Monday afternoon?**

> **I'm playing tennis with Andy. Are you doing anything on Tuesday evening?**

	morning	afternoon	evening
Monday	study	play tennis with Andy	
Tuesday	study		watch the football at Mike's house
Wednesday	study	visit James in hospital	
Thursday	study		
Friday	study		

PRACTICE

Exchanging information

Ask and answer questions to complete the information about Stelios Haji-Ioannou.

> **Where was Stelios born?**

> **In Greece.**

> **When was he born?**

> **In 1967.**

Stelios Haji-Ioannou
The creator of EasyJet airlines and the 'easy' brand

Stelios was born in Greece in _____ (*When?*). He was educated in Athens, and then studied _____ at the London School of Economics (*What?*). When he was only 17, he drove a Porsche.

He started his first business, a shipping company, when he was _____ (*How old ... when...?*). He sold it in 2005 for _____ (*How much ... for?*). He now has a fortune worth at least £400 million.

Stelios is best-known for creating EasyJet, which he has been running since 1995. EasyJet is Europe's largest low-cost airline. It has over _____ jets (*How many?*), which fly to more than forty destinations. In its lifetime, EasyJet has carried over 150 million passengers.

Over the years, Stelios has started several businesses – _____ (*What sort of ...?*).

Stelios supports various educational schemes. He has been helping students by giving them money to study at the London School of Economics _____ (*How long?*). He has so far given the college over £2m.

Since 2004, he has been working with 100 employees in _____ (*Where?*). He also works in Athens. He travels for about four months a year, because he is looking for new business ideas. His motto is '_____' (*What?*).

Extra materials

STORY SUMMARY

Francisco Scaramanga is an assassin or 'hit man' who charges $1 million a job. He is called 'the man with the golden gun' because of the golden gun he carries and the gold bullets he uses. He has already killed one British spy, 002, so when James Bond receives a gold bullet with 007 engraved on it, he knows he is next on Scaramanga's list. 'M', James Bond's boss, says James cannot do any more work as a secret agent until Scaramanga is caught and killed. The gold bullet was made in China so James leaves for Hong Kong where he meets a fellow secret agent, Mary Goodnight. Unfortunately, Scaramanga follows Mary to Bond's hotel, and after a fight captures her and takes her to his secret island. James escapes and flies after them to the island. There, he not only saves Mary and shoots Scaramanga, but also finds the missing 'Solar Agitator' which Scaramanga was planning to use to rule the world. James and Mary sail away together on a slow boat back to China.

WRITING A STORY

Aunt Camilla's Portrait

My Aunt Camilla is quite old and very rich indeed. One day she was looking in the mirror when she suddenly decided that she wanted a portrait of herself. Immediately, she booked an appointment with the world-famous portrait painter, Rolf Unwin.

Twice a week she went to his studio. Rolf worked extremely hard and painted her portrait very carefully and secretly. He didn't want my aunt to see the picture until it was completely finished.

Finally, after three months the portrait was ready. My aunt was very excited and hurried to the studio to see it. The portrait was excellent and it looked exactly like my aunt. Unfortunately, she was absolutely furious and refused to pay Rolf. She ordered him to paint it again.

This time my aunt didn't visit the studio at all. After another three months, the portrait was ready and my aunt went to see it. The face was that of a beautiful, young girl, (in fact it was Rolf's girlfriend, Cassandra). It didn't look like my aunt at all, but of course, she absolutely loved it. She paid Rolf very generously indeed, so he and Cassandra had enough money to get married and they all lived happily ever after.

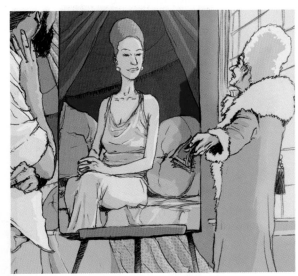

WRITING A STORY

The French Burglar

One beautiful, clear summer's evening last June, a burglar broke into a big house in Paris. First he went into the living room and quietly put some of the valuable things in the room into his bag.

Next he went into the kitchen to look for more things to steal. He opened the fridge and saw some delicious French cheese. Cheese was his favourite food!

He was feeling hungry, so he took a large piece of cheese and some lovely fresh bread, and sat down at the kitchen table to eat. Then he remembered that there were two bottles of champagne in the fridge.

He went back to the fridge and quickly drank one of the bottles of champagne. It was excellent, so he opened the other bottle and drank that too.

After that he went upstairs to look for more things in the bedrooms, but suddenly he felt really tired, so he decided to lie down on one of the nice, soft beds and have a little rest.

Unfortunately, he fell asleep immediately, and the next morning when he woke up, there were two smiling policeman standing at the side of the bed!

The voice within
Christina Aguilera

Young girl don't cry
I'll be right here when your world starts to fall
Young girl it's alright
Your tears will dry, you'll soon be free to fly

When you're safe inside your room you tend to _____ | *dream / think*
Of a place where nothing's harder than it seems
No one ever wants or _____ to explain | *bothers / tries*
Of the _____ life can bring and what it means | *pain / heartache*

Chorus
When there's no one else, look inside yourself
Like your oldest friend just trust the voice within
Then you'll find the strength that will guide your way
If you will learn to begin to trust the voice within

Young girl don't _____ | *leave / hide*
You'll never change if you just _____ away | *run / walk*
Young girl just hold _____ | *on / tight*
Soon you're going to see a brighter _____ | *day / dawn*

Chorus

Life is a _____ | *journey / train*
It can take you anywhere you _____ to go | *want / choose*
As long as you're learning
You'll find all you'll ever _____ to know | *need / have*
(be strong)
You'll make it
(hold on)
You'll make it
Just don't go _____ yourself | *forsaking / losing*
(no one can tell you what you _____ do) | *can / can't*
No one can _____ you, you know that I'm talking to you | *hurt / stop*

Chorus

Young girl don't cry
I'll be right here when your world starts to fall

Discussion – Dilemmas

Work in small groups and discuss what you would do in these situations and why.

1 You have the choice between a very well paid, but boring job, or a job you would love, but which doesn't pay much money. Which would you choose?

2 Someone who your family really doesn't like has asked you to get married. You understand your family's worries, but you are in love. Would you marry him/her?

3 Your best friend wants you to lie to his wife/her husband. You have to say that he/she was with you yesterday. Would you do it?

4 You see your neighbour's daughter steal something from a shop. You like her and your neighbour. What would you do?

UNIT 7 *p57*

Roleplay

Use the prompts for your role to help prepare for the interview.

Band members

Work with the other members of your band. Talk together to prepare your information.

- the name of the band
- what kind of music the band plays
- who plays what instruments
- how long you have been together
- who has influenced your music
- the albums you have made
- the places you have visited

Journalists

Work together with other journalists to think of some questions to ask. You can use these ideas, but you can ask anything you want!

- Name of band?
- Kind of music?
- Instruments?
- How long / together?
- How / musical career / begin?
- Who / influenced? How?
- Albums / made?
- Places / visited?
- When / tour next?
- Enjoy touring?
- New album?

When you are ready, have the interview.

Article 2

Faster than her father

Snow girl wins in Arctic

The teenage daughter of the well known polar explorer, David Hempleman-Adams, was celebrating yesterday. She's just become the youngest person to complete a route to the North Pole on foot.

'It was amazing.'

Alicia Hempleman-Adams said, 'We were walking up waterfalls and mountains, and across frozen lakes. It was amazing.'

Alicia has survived temperatures of -45°C and strong winds to finish the 200-mile walk in 10 days, two days quicker than planned. She has also finished the journey faster than her father did it!

How does she feel at the end of her Arctic adventure? 'It's a really good feeling. I'm glad we completed it. It's more of an achievement.'

'I'm extremely proud.'

But how does her father feel about her achievement?

Mr Hempleman-Adams said, 'I'm extremely proud, of course. I always wanted her to enjoy it. It has certainly given her a new maturity. I'm very proud – and a bit annoyed! She took a day less than I did – of course, she had much better skis than I had!'

Alicia is flying back to Britain today, as she is going back to school on Monday. She says she doesn't want to be an explorer, though. She would prefer to do something 'more arty' in the future!

Word list

Here is a list of most of
the new words in the units of
New Headway Pre-Intermediate
Student's Book.

adj = adjective
adv = adverb
conj = conjunction
coll = colloquial
n = noun
opp = opposite

pl = plural
prep = preposition
pron = pronoun
pp = past participle
v = verb
US = American English

UNIT 1

advice *n* /əd'vais/
agony aunt *n* /'ægəni ˌɑːnt/
art gallery *n* /'ɑːt ˌgæləri/
adventure *n* /əd'ventʃə(r)/
bar *n* /bɑː(r)/
blind date *n* /ˌblaind 'deit/
brave *adj* /breiv/
can *v, n* /kæn, kən, kæn/
casual *adj* /'kæʒʊəl/
Cheers! /tʃɪəz/
chewing gum *n* /'tʃuːɪŋ ˌgʌm/
club *n* /klʌb/
comfortable *adj* /'kʌmftəbl/
conference *n* /'kɒnfərəns/
couple *n* /'kʌpl/
course *n* /kɔːs/
date *n* /deit/
designer *n* /di'zainə(r)/
diary *n* /'daɪəri/
discover *v* /di'skʌvə(r)/
diving *n* /'daɪvɪŋ/
Don't mention it.
   /ˌdəʊnt 'menʃn ˌit/
downtown (US) *n* /'daʊntaʊn/
end *n* /end/
environmental *adj*
   /inˌvaɪrən'mentl/
essay *n* /'esei/
everyday *adj* /'evridei/
exchange *v* /iks'tʃeindʒ/
Excuse me! /iks'kjuːz ˌmiː/
factory *n* /'fæktəri/
foreign *adj* /'fɒrən/
funny *adj* /'fʌni/
go clubbing *v* /ˌgəʊ 'klʌbiŋ/
good fun *adj* /ˌgʊd 'fʌn/
good looking *adj* /ˌgʊd 'lʊkiŋ/
graduate *v* /'grædjʊeit/
grow up *v* /ˌgrəʊ 'ʌp/
guilty *adj* /'gilti/
hairbrush *n* /'heəbrʌʃ/
hard (= difficult) *adj* /hɑːd/
Have a good weekend /ˌhæv ə
   ˌgʊd 'wiːk'end/
information *n* /ˌinfə'meiʃn/
It doesn't matter /it ˌdʌznt
   'mætə(r)/
kid (child) *n* /kid/
kind *n, adj* /kaind/
last *v* /lɑːst/
last *adj* /lɑːst/
lawyer *n* /'lɔːjə(r)/
leave *v* /liːv/
mean *v, adj* /miːn/
medicine *n* /'medsn/ or /'medisn/
midnight *n* /'midnait/
mouse mat *n* /'maʊs ˌmæt/

Never mind /'nevə ˌmaind/
No problem /ˌnəʊ 'prɒbləm/
object *n* /'ɒbdʒikt/
outgoing *adj* /ˌaʊt'gəʊiŋ/
pencil sharpener *n*
   /'pensl ˌʃɑːpnə(r)/
Pleased to meet you
   /ˌpliːzd tə 'miːt ˌjuː/
poor *adj* /pʊə(r)/ or /pɔː(r)/
problem *n* /'prɒbləm/
relationship *n* /ri'leiʃnʃip/
retired *adj* /ri'taɪəd/
ring *v, n* /riŋ/
rubber *n* /'rʌbə(r)/
ruler *n* /'ruːlə(r)/
scissors *n* /'sizəz/
See you later. /ˌsiː ˌjuː 'leitə(r)/
separate *adj* /'seprət/
share *v* /ʃeə(r)/
single *adj* /'siŋgl/
snowboard *v* /'snəʊbɔːd/
sometimes *adv* /'sʌmtaimz/
star sign *n* /'stɑː ˌsain/
store *n* /stɔː(r)/
successful *adj* /sək'sesfl/
sunglasses *n* /'sʌnglɑːsiz/
surfing *n* /'sɜːfiŋ/
theatre *n* /'θɪətə(r)/
tissues *n* /'tiʃuːz/
twin *n* /twin/
vegetarian *adj* /ˌvedʒə'teəriən/
wallet *n* /'wɒlit/
wonderful *adj* /'wʌndəfl/

UNIT 2

abroad *adv* /ə'brɔːd/
accent *n* /'æksənt/
accident *n* /'æksidənt/
act the part *coll* /ˌækt ðə 'pɑːt/
almost *adv* /'ɔːlməʊst/
always *adv* /'ɔːlweiz/
at least *adv* /ət 'liːst/
at the moment (= now)
   /ət ðə 'məʊmənt/
awful *adj* /'ɔːfl/
bedtime *n* /'bedtaim/
boss *n* /bɒs/
bring *v* /briŋ/
celeb (celebrity) *n*
   /sə'leb (sə'lebrəti)/
clear up *v* /ˌklɪər 'ʌp/
coast *n* /kəʊst/
communication *n*
   /kəˌmjuːni'keiʃn/
competition *n* /ˌkɒmpə'tiʃn/
contact lenses *n pl*
   /'kɒntækt ˌlenziz/
conversation *n* /ˌkɒnvə'seiʃn/
disadvantage *n* /ˌdisəd'vɑːntidʒ/
distance *n* /'distəns/
divide *v* /di'vaid/
divorced *adj* /di'vɔːst/
do overtime *v* /ˌduː 'əʊvətaim/
dormitory *n* /'dɔːmətri/
employ *v* /im'plɔi/
essential *adj* /i'senʃl/
European *adj* /ˌjʊərə'piːən/
exchange *v* /iks'tʃeindʒ/
exhausting *adj* /ig'zɔːstiŋ/
factory *n* /'fæktəri/
farmhouse *n* /'fɑːmhaʊs/
First things first! /ˌfɜːst ˌθiŋz
   'fɜːst/
flat *adj* /flæt/
glamorous *adj* /'glæmərəs/
Guess what! /ˌges 'wɒt/
guest *n* /gest/
hairdresser *n* /'heədresə(r)/
a handfull /ə 'hændfʊl/
have something in common (= to
   share interests or experiences)
   /ˌhæv ˌsʌmθiŋ in 'kɒmən/
hundred *n* /'hʌndrəd/
hurt *v* /hɜːt/
impossible *adj* /im'pɒsəbl/
interested *adj* /'intrəstid/
just *adv* /dʒʌst/
keep (us) busy *v* /ˌkiːp (əs) 'bizi/
landscape *n* /'lændskeip/
lifestyle *n* /'laifstail/
lonely *adj* /'ləʊnli/
loft *n* /lɒft/

lucky *adj* /'lʌki/
make-up *n* /'meik ʌp/
manicure *n* /'mænikjʊə(r)/
mess *n* /mes/
miss *v* /mis/
monthly *adv* /'mʌnθli/
nail (= on your finger) *n* /neil/
national park *n* /ˌnæʃnəl 'pɑːk/
never *adv* /'nevə(r)/
occupation *n* /ˌɒkjə'peiʃn/
often *adv* /'ɒfn, 'ɒftən/
pearl *n* /pɜːl/
politician *n* /ˌpɒlə'tiʃn/
poster *n* /'pəʊstə(r)/
practise *v* /'præktis/
prefer *v* /pri'fɜː(r)/
private *adj* /'praivət/
province *n* /'prɒvins/
racing *n* /'reisiŋ/
rent *v* /rent/
robot *n* /'rəʊbɒt/
rooftop *adj* /'ruːftɒp/
routine *n* /ruː'tiːn/
sale *n* /seil/
send *v* /send/
sip *v* /sip/
situated *pp* /'sitʃueitid/
skills *n pl* /skilz/
social life *n* /'səʊʃl ˌlaif/
society *n* /sə'saiəti/
sometimes *adv* /'sʌmtaimz/
strange *adj* /streindʒ/
surprise *n* /sə'praiz/
technology *n* /tek'nɒlədʒi/
test *v* /test/
text *v* /tekst/
That's really kind of you.
   /ˌðæts ˌriːəli 'kaind əv ˌjuː/
tiring *adj* /'taɪəriŋ/
transatlantic *adj* /ˌtrænzət'læntik/
trendy *adj* /'trendi/
twins *n* /twinz/
uniform *n* /'juːnifɔːm/
useful *adj* /'juːsfl/
usually *adv* /'juːʒʊəli/
view *n* /vjuː/
view of *n* /'vjuː əv/
voice *n* /vɔis/
wage *n* /weidʒ/
wear (your hair) up *v*
   /ˌweə (jɔː 'heər) 'ʌp/
wonderful *adj* /'wʌndəfl/
worst *adj* /wɜːst/

UNIT 3

air-conditioning n /'eə kən,dɪʃnɪŋ/
aloud adv /ə'laʊd/
amazed adj /ə'meɪzd/
angrily adv /'æŋgrəli/
angry (with sb) adj /'æŋgri (wɪð ...)/
apartment n /ə'pɑːtmənt/
apologize v /ə'pɒlədʒaɪz/
appointment n /ə'pɔɪntmənt/
assassin n /ə'sæsɪn/
bang v /bæŋ/
big spender /,bɪg 'spendə(r)/
bowl n /bəʊl/
break into v /'breɪk ,ɪntuː, ,ɪntə/
breathe v /briːð/
bullet n /'bʊlɪt/
burglar n /'bɜːglə(r)/
cage n /keɪdʒ/
canal n /kə'næl/
capture v /'kæptʃə(r)/
carefully adv /'keəfəli/
connection n /kə'nekʃn/
copy n /'kɒpi/
credit card n /'kredɪt ,kɑːd/
crept (past tense of creep) v /krept/
crime n /kraɪm/
curse v /kɜːs/
curtain n /'kɜːtn/
date n /deɪt/
destroy v /dɪ'strɔɪ/
documentary n /,dɒkjə'mentri/
downstairs adv /,daʊn'steəz/
dream (about sth) v /'driːm (ə,baʊt ...)/
engrave v /ɪn'greɪv/
exactly adv /ɪg'zæktli/
feel ill v /'fiːl 'ɪl/
felt (past tense of feel) v /felt/
figure n /'fɪgə(r)/
fill v /fɪl/
fortunately adv /'fɔːtʃənətli/
ghost n /gəʊst/
golden adj /'gəʊldən/
gradually adv /'grædʒʊəli/
guiltily adv /'gɪltɪli/
gunman n /'gʌnmən/
happily ever after /,hæpili ,evər 'ɑːftə(r)/
haunt v /hɔːnt/
heavily adv /'hevəli/
hide v /haɪd/
hit man n /'hɪt ,mæn/
HQ (= headquarters) n /,eɪtʃ 'kjuː/
hungry adj /'hʌŋgri/
immediate adv /ɪ'miːdiət/
invitation n /,ɪnvɪ'teɪʃn/
joke n /dʒəʊk/
knock on the door v /,nɒk ɒn ðə 'dɔː(r)/
laugh v /lɑːf/
lazily adv /'leɪzɪli/
lead v /liːd/
let out v /,let 'aʊt/
lock v /lɒk/
lorry n /'lɒri/

lose v /luːz/
lovingly adv /'lʌvɪŋli/
marks (get good marks in an exam) n /mɑːks
mend v /mend/
message n /'mesɪdʒ/
midnight n /'mɪdnaɪt/
missing adj /'mɪsɪŋ/
movement n /'muːvmənt/
museum n /mju:'ziːəm/
mystery n /'mɪstri/
nervously adv /'nɜːvəsli/
noise n /nɔɪz/
original adj /ə'rɪdʒənl/
outside adv /aʊt'saɪd/
passport n /'pɑːspɔːt/
peacefully adv /'piːsfəli/
perhaps adv /pə'hæps/
pick up (the phone) v /,pɪk ʌp (ðə 'fəʊn)/
poem n /'pəʊɪm/
point (straight at sth/sb) v /,pɔɪnt ('streɪt ət ...)/
poker n /'pəʊkə(r)/
portrait n /'pɔːtreɪt/
printer n /'prɪntə(r)/
prison n /'prɪzn/
pull v /pʊl/
quietly adv /'kwaɪətli/
refuse (say no) v /rɪ'fjuːz/
relief n /rɪ'liːf/
reporters n pl /rɪ'pɔːtəz/
run out of v /,rʌn 'aʊt əv/
sadly adv /'sædli/
secret agent n /,siːkrət 'eɪdʒənt/
security guard n /sɪ'kjʊərəti ,gɑːd/
shine v /ʃaɪn/
shoot v /ʃuːt/
softly adv /'sɒftli/
spending spree n /'spendɪŋ ,spriː/
staff n /stɑːf/
stand up v /,stænd 'ʌp/
steal v /stiːl/
still adv /stɪl/
straight adv /streɪt/
suddenly adv /'sʌdnli/
supper n /'sʌpə(r)/
switch off v /,swɪtʃ 'ɒf/
teenager n /'tiːneɪdʒə(r)/
terrorist n /'terərɪst/
thief n /θiːf/
throw v /θrəʊ/
thump (of the heart) v /θʌmp/
title n /'taɪtl/
together adv /tə'geðə(r)/
tragically adv /'trædʒɪkli/
translation n /træns'leɪʃn/
turn on v /,tɜːn 'ɒn/
twins n pl /twɪnz/
unfortunately adv /ʌn'fɔːtʃənətli/
unlock v /ʌn'lɒk/
urgently adv /'ɜːdʒəntli/
went off (a gun = fired) v /,went 'ɒf/
whisper v /'wɪspə(r)/
with feeling adv /,wɪð 'fiːlɪŋ/
worry v /'wʌri/
worth adj /wɜːθ/

UNIT 4

adult n /'ædʌlt/
allergic adj /ə'lɜːdʒɪk/
amazing adj /ə'meɪzɪŋ/
ancient adj /'eɪnʃnt/
antique n /æn'tiːk/
anybody pron /'enibɒdi/
anyone pron /'eniwʌn/
anything pron /'eniθɪŋ/
aromatic adj /,ærə'mætɪk/
aspirin n /'æsprɪn/
backpack n /'bækpæk/
baker's (shop) n /'beɪkəz (,ʃɒp)/
bargain (for sth) v /'bɑːgɪn (fə ...)/
be packed with /bɪ 'pækt wɪð/
belt n /belt/
book (of) n /,bʊk (əv)/
bored adj /bɔːd/
brands n /brændz/
bridge n /brɪdʒ/
bunch (of) n /,bʌntʃ (əv)/
businesses n pl /'bɪznəsɪz/
busy adj /'bɪzi/
canal n /kə'næl/
carpet n /'kɑːpɪt/
cash (a cheque) v /,kæʃ (ə 'tʃek)/
cashier n /kæ'ʃɪə(r)/
cent (U.S currency) n /sent/
certainly adv /'sɜːtnli/
change n /tʃeɪndʒ/
changing room n /'tʃeɪndʒɪŋ ruːm/
chemist's n /'kemɪsts/
choose v /tʃuːz/
clever idea n /,klevər aɪ'dɪə/
cloth n /klɒθ/
clothing n /'kləʊðɪŋ/
collect v /kə'lekt/
colourful adj /'kʌləfl/
commission n /kə'mɪʃn/
contrast n /'kɒntrɑːst/
cooker n /'kʊkə(r)/
cost n /kɒst/
count (money) v /,kaʊnt ('mʌni)/
covered (with sth) adj /'kʌvd (wɪð ...)/
create v /kri'eɪt/
currency n /'kʌrənsi/
customer n /'kʌstəmə(r)/
delicious adj /dɪ'lɪʃəs/
deodorant n /di'əʊdərənt/
desert n /'dezət/
dollar (U.S currency) n /'dɒlə(r)/
doughnut n /'dəʊnʌt/
dozen n /ə ,dʌzn 'egz/
endless adj /'endləs/
euro (European currency) n /'jʊərəʊ/
everything pron /'evriθɪŋ/
exactly adv /ɪg'zæktli/
exchange rate n /ɪk'stʃeɪndʒ ,reɪt/
fascinating adj /'fæsɪneɪtɪŋ/
film set n /'fɪlm ,set/
fine (= good quality) adj /faɪn/
float v /fləʊt/

for goodness sake! /fə ,gʊdnəs 'seɪk/
for sale /fə 'seɪl/
forget v /fə'get/
furniture n /'fɜːnɪtʃə(r)/
glasses n pl /'glɑːsɪz/
global adj /'gləʊbl/
greengrocer's n /'griːngrəʊsəz/
grocer's (shop) n /'grəʊsəz (,ʃɒp)/
grown (grown locally) pp /grəʊn (,grəʊn 'ləʊkəli)/
half /hɑːf/
herb n /hɜːb/
hobby n /'hɒbi/
huge adj /hjuːdʒ/
international adj /,ɪntə'næʃnəl/
invented pp /ɪn'ventɪd/
jewellery n /'dʒuːəlri/
kilo (of) n /'kiːləʊ (əv)/
Let's see /,lets 'siː/
litre (of) n /'liːtər (əv)/
loaf (of) n /'ləʊf (əv)/
luxurious adj /lʌg'ʒʊəriəs/
market n /'mɑːkɪt/
mechanic n /mə'kænɪk/
nappy n /'næpi/
narrow adj /'nærəʊ/
newsagent's n /'njuːzeɪdʒənts/
noisy adj /'nɔɪzi/
packet (of) n /,pækɪt əv/
parcel n /'pɑːsl/
pavement n /'peɪvmənt/
peaceful adj /'piːsfl/
pick from v /'pɪk frəm/
picnic n /'pɪknɪk/
pints n /paɪnts/
pound (pounds sterling = British currency) n /paʊndz/
product n /'prɒdʌkt/
quantity n /'kwɒntɪti/
roll n /rəʊl/
rug n /rʌg/
scales n pl /skeɪlz/
scientist n /'saɪəntɪst/
seller n /'selə(r)/
shaving foam n /'ʃeɪvɪŋ fəʊm/
shopping list n /'ʃɒpɪŋ ,lɪst/
silver n /'sɪlvə(r)/
size n /saɪz/
soaps n pl /'səʊps/
sore throat /,sɔː 'θrəʊt/
spectacular adj /spek'tækjələ(r)/
spice n /spaɪs/
spoonful n /'spuːnfl/
stalls n pl /stɔːlz/
sterling (= British currency) n /'stɜːlɪŋ/
strange adj /streɪndʒ/
survey (conduct a survey) n /'sɜːveɪ (kən,dʌkt ə 'sɜːveɪ)/
tissue n /'tɪʃuː/
traditional adj /trə'dɪʃənl/
traveller's cheque n /'trævələz ,tʃek/
village n /'vɪlɪdʒ/
website n /'websaɪt/
wooden adj /'wʊdn/

UNIT 5

affect *v* /əˈfekt/
alcohol *n* /ˈælkəhɒl/
ambition *n* /æmˈbɪʃn/
annoyed *adj* /əˈnɔɪd/
annoying *adj* /əˈnɔɪɪŋ/
applicable *adj* /əˈplɪkəbl/
argue (with sb) *v* /ˈɑːgjuː
   (wɪð ...)/
army *n* /ˈɑːmi/
arrange *v* /əˈreɪndʒ/
average *adj* /ˈævərɪdʒ/
be pleased for sb /bɪ ˈpliːzd fə/
be responsible *v* /biː rɪˈspɒnsəbl/
behaviour *n* /bɪˈheɪvjə(r)/
blame *v* /bleɪm/
body piercing *n* /ˈbɒdi ˌpɪəsɪŋ/
boots *n* pl /buːts/
bored *adj* /bɔːd/
boring *adj* /ˈbɔːrɪŋ/
brat *n* /bræt/
bullying *n* /ˈbʊliɪŋ/
camp *n* /kæmp/
cheating *n* /ˈtʃiːtɪŋ/
Cheer up! /tʃɪər ˈʌp/
chorus *n* /ˈkɔːrəs/
confused *adj* /kənˈfjuːzd/
confusing *adj* /kənˈfjuːzɪŋ/
cried (past tense of cry) *v* /kraɪd/
cruise *n* /kruːz/
delete *v* /dɪˈliːt/
depressed *adj* /dɪˈprest/
depressing *adj* /dɪˈpresɪŋ/
desperate *adj* /ˈdespərət/
disappointed *adj* /ˌdɪsəˈpɔɪntɪd/
disappointing *adj* /ˌdɪsəˈpɔɪntɪŋ/
discuss *v* /dɪsˈkʌs/
divorced *adj* /dɪˈvɔːst/
end up *v* /ˌend ˈʌp/
exam *n* /ɪgˈzæm/
excited *adj* /ɪkˈsaɪtɪd/
exciting *adj* /ɪkˈsaɪtɪŋ/
exhausting *adj* /ɪgˈzɔːstɪŋ/
experience *n* /ɪkˈspɪəriəns/
fascinated *adj* /ˈfæsɪneɪtɪd/
fascinating *adj* /ˈfæsɪneɪtɪŋ/
fault *n* /fɔːlt/
fed up with /ˌfed ˈʌp wɪð/
feel depressed *adj* /ˌfiːl dɪˈprest/
feel sorry for *v* /ˌfiːl ˈsɒri fɔː(r),
   fə(r)/
fighting *n* /ˈfaɪtɪŋ/
footsteps *n* pl /ˈfʊtsteps/
frightened *adj* /ˈfraɪtnd/
frightening *adj* /ˈfraɪtnɪŋ/
get married *v* /ˌget ˈmærɪd/
give sb a ring (= call sb on the
   phone) *coll* /ˌgɪv ... ə ˈrɪŋ/
give up (= stop doing sth) *v*
   /ˌgɪv ˈʌp/
grade *n* /greɪd/
have a drug problem *n*
   /ˌhæv ə ˈdrʌg ˌprɒbləm/
headache *n* /ˈhedeɪk/
heartache *n* /ˈhɑːteɪk/
heavy *adj* /ˈhevi/

hike *n* /haɪk/
hope *n* /həʊp/
horrible (to sb) *adj*
   /ˈhɒrəbl (tə ...)/
hurt *adj* /hɜːt/
incredible *adj* /ɪnˈkredəbl/
innocence *n* /ˈɪnəsəns/
instruction *n* /ɪnˈstrʌkʃn/
intelligent *adj* /ɪnˈtelɪdʒənt/
invite *v* /ɪnˈvaɪt/
lend *v* /lend/
lie *n* /laɪ/
look forward to (doing sth)
   /ˈlʊkɪŋ ˌfɔːwəd tə .../
marathon *n* /ˈmærəθən/
marital status *n* /ˈmærɪtl ˌsteɪtəs/
nurse *n* /nɜːs/
occupation *n* /ˌɒkjʊˈpeɪʃn/
orders (follow orders) *n* pl
   /ˈɔːdəz (ˌfɒləʊ ˈɔːdəz)/
out of control /ˌaʊt əv kənˈtrəʊl/
permanent *adj* /ˈpɜːmənənt/
physical activity *n* /ˌfɪzɪkl
   ækˈtɪvəti/
piercings *n* pl /ˈpɪəsɪŋz/
plan (to do sth) *v* /ˌplæn
   (tə ˈduː ...)/
play truant (= not go to school) *v*
   /ˌpleɪ ˈtruːənt/
post (letters / parcels) *v* /pəʊst/
postcode *n* /ˈpəʊstkəʊd/
problem *n* /ˈprɒbləm/
promise *v* /ˈprɒmɪs/
primary school *n* /ˈpraɪməri
   ˌskuːl/
prison *n* /ˈprɪzn/
psychologist *n* /saɪˈkɒlədʒɪst/
rebel (against sb or sth) *v*
   /rɪˈbel əˌgenst .../
relaxing *adj* /rɪˈlæksɪŋ/
remarried *adj* /ˌriːˈmærɪd/
save money /ˌseɪv ˈmʌni/
secret *n* /ˈsiːkrət/
self-control *n* /ˌself kənˈtrəʊl/
seriously *adv* /ˈsɪəriəsli/
shocked *adj* /ʃɒkt/
shocking *adj* /ˈʃɒkɪŋ/
signature *n* /ˈsɪgnətʃə(r)/
situation *n* /ˌsɪtjʊˈeɪʃn/
spy story *n* /ˈspaɪ ˌstɔːri/
stand your ground /ˌstænd jɔː
   ˈgraʊnd/
steal *v* /stiːl/
sunshine *n* /ˈsʌnʃaɪn/
surprised *adj* /səˈpraɪzd/
surprising *adj* /səˈpraɪzɪŋ/
swearing *n* /ˈsweərɪŋ/
take drugs *v* /ˌteɪk ˈdrʌgz/
tell (a secret/lie) *v* /ˌtel (ə
   ˈsiːkrət, ˈlaɪ)/
therapy *n* /ˈθerəpi/
tired of *adj* /ˈtaɪəd əv/
tough *adj* /tʌf/
train *v* /treɪn/
troubled *adj* /ˈtrʌbld/
trust *n, v* /trʌst/
vet *n* /vet/

UNIT 6

absolutely *adv* /ˈæbsəluːtli/
according to *prep* /əˈkɔːdɪŋ tə/
advantage *n* /ədˈvɑːntɪdʒ/
afford *v* /əˈfɔːd/
amazing *adj* /əˈmeɪzɪŋ/
angry *adj* /ˈæŋgri/
back to normal /ˌbæk tə ˈnɔːml/
backpack *n* /ˈbækpæk/
be accepted *v* /ˌbiː əkˈseptɪd/
birthplace *n* /ˈbɜːθpleɪs/
bit (= small piece) *n* /bɪt/
book (a room) *v* /ˌbʊk (ə ˈruːm)/
booking fee *n* /ˈbʊkɪŋ ˌfiː/
break up *v* /ˌbreɪk ˈʌp/
brilliant *adj* /ˈbrɪliənt/
building *n* /ˈbɪldɪŋ/
character *n* /ˈkærəktə(r)/
check in /ˈtʃek ɪn, ˌtʃek ˈɪn/
client *n* /ˈklaɪənt/
comedy *n* /ˈkɒmədi/
community *n* /kəˈmjuːnəti/
contemporary *adj*
   /kənˈtempərəri/
cosmopolitan *adj*
   /ˌkɒzməˈpɒlɪtən/
diverse *adj* /daɪˈvɜːs/
dorm (dormitory) *n* /dɔːm/
earn *v* /ɜːn/
expiry date *n* /ɪkˈspaɪəri ˌdeɪt/
facility *n* /fəˈsɪləti/
fashionable *adj* /ˈfæʃnəbl/
fed up *adj* /ˌfed ˈʌp/
fluency *n* /ˈfluːənsi/
foreigner *n* /ˈfɒrənə(r)/
friendliest *adj* /ˈfrendliəst/
friendship *n* /ˈfrendʃɪp/
gender *n* /ˈdʒendə(r)/
general knowledge *n*
   /ˌdʒenrəl ˈnɒlɪdʒ/
generous *adj* /ˈdʒenərəs/
get better /ˌget ˈbetə(r)/
get on well *v* /ˌget ɒn ˈwel/
Good luck! /ˌgʊd ˈlʌk/
guide *n* /gaɪd/
halves (pl of half) *n* /hɑːvz/
hippopotamus *n* /ˌhɪpəˈpɒtəməs/
historical *adj* /hɪˈstɒrɪkl/
homeland *n* /ˈhəʊmlænd/
host *v* /həʊst/
hostel *n* /ˈhɒstəl/
human *n* /ˈhjuːmən/
I'm sorry to hear that /ˌaɪm ˈsɒri
   tə ˈhɪər ˌðæt, ðət .../
immigrant *n* /ˈɪmɪgrənt/
impolite *adj* /ˌɪmpəˈlaɪt/
in particular /ˌɪn pəˈtɪkjələ(r)/
in the beginning /ˌɪn ðə bɪˈgɪnɪŋ/
independence *n* /ˌɪndɪˈpendəns/
industrial *adj* /ɪnˈdʌstriəl/
interest *n* /ˈɪntrəst/
jazz *n* /dʒæz/
leaflet *n* /ˈliːflət/
lonely *adj* /ˈləʊnli/
mean *adj* /miːn/
mentioned *pp* /ˈmenʃnd/
messy *adj* /ˈmesi/

miserable *adj* /ˈmɪzrəbl/
modern *adj* /ˈmɒdn/
music scene *n* /ˈmjuːzɪk ˌsiːn/
nationality *n* /ˌnæʃəˈnæləti/
neighbour *n* /ˈneɪbə(r)/
Oh dear! /ˌəʊ ˈdɪə(r)/
online *adv* /ɒnˈlaɪn/
owner *n* /ˈəʊnə(r)/
passion *n* /ˈpæʃn/
pleasure *n* /ˈpleʒə(r)/
polite *adj* /pəˈlaɪt/
population *n* /ˌpɒpjʊˈleɪʃn/
principle *n* /ˈprɪnsəpl/
quiz *n* /kwɪz/
rap *n* /ræp/
receptionist *n* /rɪˈsepʃənɪst/
romance *n* /rəʊˈmæns/
rude *adj* /ruːd/
run *v* /rʌn/
science fiction *n* /ˌsaɪəns ˈfɪkʃn/
sculpture *n* /ˈskʌlptʃə(r)/
second-hand *adj* /ˌsekənd ˈhænd/
separate *adj* /ˈseprət/
a shame /ə ˈʃeɪm/
shark *n* /ʃɑːk/
shocking *adj* /ˈʃɒkɪŋ/
sights *n* pl /saɪts/
sightseeing *n* /ˈsaɪtsiːɪŋ/
sightseeing tour *n* /ˈsaɪtsiːɪŋ
   ˌtʊə(r)/
spicy *adj* /ˈspaɪsi/
stare *v* /steə(r)/
stick together (= stay together)
   v, coll /ˌstɪk təˈgeðə(r)/
sunset *n* /ˈsʌnset/
talented *adj* /ˈtæləntɪd/
temple *n* /ˈtempl/
terms and conditions *n* pl /ˌtɜːmz
   ən kənˈdɪʃnz/
terrible *adj* /ˈterəbl/
test *n* /test/
That's fantastic! /ˌðæts fænˈtæstɪk/
thief *n* /θiːf/
thriller *n* /ˈθrɪlə(r)/
tour *n* /tʊə(r)/
trip *n* /trɪp/
untidy *adj* /ʌnˈtaɪdi/
vibrant *adj* /ˈvaɪbrənt/
vitality *n* /vaɪˈtæləti/
worried *adj* /ˈwʌrɪd/

accident n /ˈæksɪdənt/
account n /əˈkaʊnt/
accountant n /əˈkaʊntənt/
advertise v /ˈædvətaɪz/
advertisement n /ədˈvɜːtɪsmənt/
album n /ˈælbəm/
alive adj /əˈlaɪv/
ambitious adj /æmˈbɪʃəs/
art n /ɑːt/
artist n /ˈɑːtɪst/
attend v /əˈtend/
bad-tempered adj /ˌbæd ˈtempəd/
band n /bænd/
bass n /beɪs/
bodyguard n /ˈbɒdigɑːd/
calm adj /kɑːm/
camping n /ˈkæmpɪŋ/
career n /kəˈrɪə(r)/
chaffeur n /ˈʃəʊfə(r)/
chef n /ʃef/
corridor n /ˈkɒrɪdɔː(r)/
courage n /ˈkʌrɪdʒ/
danger n /ˈdeɪndʒə(r)/
decide v /dɪˈsaɪd/
decision n /dɪˈsɪʒn/
decorate v /ˈdekəreɪt/
decorator n /ˈdekəreɪtə(r)/
dietician n /ˌdaɪəˈtɪʃn/
difference n /ˈdɪfrəns/
disaster n /dɪˈzɑːstə(r)/
disastrous adj /dɪˈzɑːstrəs/
drama queen n /ˈdrɑːmə ˌkwiːn/
drum n /drʌm/
easy-going adj /ˌiːzi ˈgəʊɪŋ/
electric adj /ɪˈlektrɪk/
electrician n /ɪˌlekˈtrɪʃn/
employ v /ɪmˈplɔɪ/
employer n /ɪmˈplɔɪə(r)/
employment n /ɪmˈplɔɪmənt/
entourage n /ˈɒntərɑːʒ/
explain v /ɪkˈspleɪn/
explanation n /ˌekspləˈneɪʃn/
fame n /feɪm/
famous adj /ˈfeɪməs/
film premiere n /ˈfɪlm ˌpremɪeə(r)/
fire (from a job) v /ˌfaɪə/
flopped (= been unsuccessful) pp /flɒpt/
founder member n /ˈfaʊndə ˌmembə(r)/
friendly adj /ˈfrendli/
governed pp /ˈgʌvnd/
great granddaughter n /ˌgreɪt ˈgrændɔːtə(r)/
guitar n /gɪˈtɑː(r)/
have a break (= have a rest) /ˌhæv ə ˈbreɪk/
havoc (play havoc with sth) n /ˈhævək/
heir n /eə(r)/
hire v /ˈhaɪə(r)/
imagination n /ɪˌmædʒɪˈneɪʃn/
including prep /ɪnˈkluːdɪŋ/
industry n /ˈɪndəstri/
influenced (by sb/sth) pp /ˈɪnflʊənst (ˌbaɪ ...)/

interpret v /ɪnˈtɜːprɪt/
interpreter n /ɪnˈtɜːprɪtə(r)/
invent v /ɪnˈvent/
invitation n /ˌɪnvɪˈteɪʃn/
journalist n /ˈdʒɜːnəlɪst/
keyboard n /ˈkiːbɔːd/
kind adj /kaɪnd/
kindness n /ˈkaɪndnəs/
law n /lɔː/
librarian n /laɪˈbreəriən/
library n /ˈlaɪbrəri/
lighting n /ˈlaɪtɪŋ/
manicurist n /ˈmænɪkjʊərɪst/
member n /ˈmembə(r)/
misfortunes n pl /mɪsˈfɔːtʃuːnz/
model v /ˈmɒdl/
moody adj /ˈmuːdi/
movie (= film) n US /ˈmuːvi/
music business n /ˈmjuːzɪk ˌbɪznəs/
musical instrument n /ˌmjuːzɪkl ˈɪnstrəmənt/
musician n /mjuːˈzɪʃn/
nervous breakdown n /ˌnɜːvəs ˈbreɪkdaʊn/
noisy adj /ˈnɔɪzi/
novel n /ˈnɒvl/
organization n /ˌɔːgənaɪˈzeɪʃn/
organize v /ˈɔːgənaɪz/
PA (personal assistant) n /ˌpiː ˈeɪ, (ˌpɜːsənl əˈsɪstənt/)
paparazzi n pl /ˌpæpəˈrætsi/
patient adj /ˈpeɪʃnt/
patient n /ˈpeɪʃnt/
perform v /pəˈfɔːm/
performance n /pəˈfɔːməns/
personal trainer n /ˌpɜːsənl ˈtreɪnə(r)/
photographer n /fəˈtɒgrəfə(r)/
piano n /piˈænəʊ/
politician n /ˌpɒləˈtɪʃn/
politics n pl /ˈpɒlətɪks/
principality n /ˌprɪnsɪˈpæləti/
private jet n /ˌpraɪvət ˈdʒet/
psychoanalysis n /ˌsaɪkəʊəˈnæləsɪs/
reception n /rɪˈsepʃn/
refer to v /rɪˈfɜː, tə/
related adj /rɪˈleɪtɪd/
sack n /sæk/
saxophone n /ˈsæksəfəʊn/
science n /ˈsaɪəns/
selfish adj /ˈselfɪʃ/
series n /ˈsɪəriːz/
sidewalk (= pavement) n US /ˈsaɪdwɔːk/
spoilt adj /spɔɪlt/
staff n /stɑːf/
temperamental adj /ˌtemprəˈmentl/
ten pound note n /ˌten ˌpaʊnd ˈnəʊt/
thoughtful adj /ˈθɔːtfl/
tragedy n /ˈtrædʒədi/
tragic adj /ˈtrædʒɪk/
trumpet n /ˈtrʌmpɪt/
unkind adj /ʌnˈkaɪnd/
upset adj /ʌpˈset/

ability n /əˈbɪləti/
ache v /eɪk/
agency n /ˈeɪdʒənsi/
ankle n /ˈæŋkl/
apologize v /əˈpɒlədʒaɪz/
apply v /əˈplaɪ/
application n /ˌæplɪˈkeɪʃn/
architect n /ˈɑːkɪtekt/
assistance n /əˈsɪstəns/
be on call /bi ˌɒn ˈkɔːl/
behave v /bɪˈheɪv/
bill n /bɪl/
blow your nose /ˌbləʊ jɔː ˈnəʊz/
builder n /ˈbɪldə(r)/
bully n /ˈbʊli/
career n /kəˈrɪə(r)/
chat v /tʃæt/
childcare n /ˈtʃaɪldkeə(r)/
country n /ˈkʌntri/
coward n /ˈkaʊəd/
definition n /ˌdefɪˈnɪʃn/
detective n /dɪˈtektɪv/
development n /dɪˈveləpmənt/
diarrhoea n /ˌdaɪəˈrɪə/
enclosed adj /ɪnˈkləʊzd/
engineering n /ˌendʒɪˈnɪərɪŋ/
enquire v /ɪnˈkwaɪə(r)/
equal opportunities n /ˌiːkwəl ˌɒpəˈtjuːnətiz/
ex-boyfriend n /ˌeks ˈbɔɪfrend/
fall in love /ˌfɔːl ɪn ˈlʌv/
farmer n /ˈfɑːmə(r)/
feed v /fiːd/
fire fighter n /ˈfaɪə ˌfaɪtə(r)/
food poisoning n /ˈfuːd ˌpɔɪzənɪŋ/
gardener n /ˈgɑːdnə(r)/
gender n /ˈdʒendə(r)/
gender gap n /ˈdʒendə ˌgæp/
glands n pl /glændz/
hairdresser n /ˈheədresə(r)/
ignore v /ɪgˈnɔː(r)/
inform v /ɪnˈfɔːm/
interview n, v /ˈɪntəvjuː/
liquid n /ˈlɪkwɪd/
mechanic n /məˈkænɪk/
message n /ˈmesɪdʒ/
nanny n /ˈnæni/
nappy n /ˈnæpi/
necessary adj /ˈnesəsəri/
night shift n /ˈnaɪt ˌʃɪft/
non-traditional adj /ˌnɒn trəˈdɪʃnl/
obligation n /ˌɒblɪˈgeɪʃn/
opinion n /əˈpɪnjən/
optician n /ɒpˈtɪʃn/
painter n /ˈpeɪntə(r)/
plumber n /ˈplʌmə(r)/
possession n /pəˈzeʃn/
prejudice n /ˈpredʒʊdɪs/
prescribe v /prɪˈskraɪb/
prescription n /prɪˈskrɪpʃn/
profession n /prəˈfeʃn/
psychology n /saɪˈkɒlədʒi/
racism n /ˈreɪsɪzm/

reassure v /ˌriːəˈʃʊə(r)/
regret (to inform you) v /rɪˈgret (tuː ɪnˌfɔːm juː)/
ruin v /ˈruːɪn/
satisfaction n /ˌsætɪsˈfækʃn/
seat belt n /ˈsiːtbelt/
sexism n /ˈseksɪzm/
signature n /ˈsɪgnətʃə(r)/
sneeze v /sniːz/
soldier n /ˈsəʊldʒə(r)/
sore throat /ˌsɔː ˈθrəʊt/
stay calm /ˌsteɪ ˈkɑːm/
stomach-ache n /ˈstʌmək ˌeɪk/
strangely adv /ˈstreɪndʒli/
surgery n /ˈsɜːdʒəri/
swallow v /ˈswɒləʊ/
swollen pp /ˈswəʊlən/
symptom n /ˈsɪmptəm/
take care of v /ˌteɪk ˈkeər əv/
taxi-driver n /ˈtæksi ˌdraɪvə(r)/
temperature /ˈtemprətʃə(r)/
tough adj /tʌf/
traditionally adv /trəˈdɪʃənəli/
twist v /twɪst/
unsocial adj /ˌʌnˈsəʊʃl/
workplace n /ˈwɜːkpleɪs/

UNIT 9

addict n /'ædɪkt/
answerphone n /'ɑ:nsəfəʊn/
army n /'ɑ:mi/
as soon as /əz 'su:n əz/
atmosphere n /'ætməsfɪə(r)/
awful adj /'ɔ:fl/
be bothered /bɪ 'bɒðəd/
be determined to do something /bɪ
    dɪ,tɜ:mɪnd tə 'du:/
be in control (of a situation) /,bi:
    ɪn kən,trəʊl/
brochure n /'brəʊʃə(r)/
buffet car (on a train) n /'bʌfeɪ
    ,kɑ:(r)/
carefree adj /'keəfri:/
consultant n /kən'sʌltənt/
crowded adj /'kraʊdɪd/
debt n /det/
delayed adj /dɪ'leɪd/
desire n /dɪ'zaɪə(r)/
destination n /,destɪ'neɪʃn/
distance n /'dɪstəns/
door to door /,dɔ: tə 'dɔ:/
earn v /ɜ:n/
environment n /ɪn'vaɪrənmənt/
escape v /ɪ'skeɪp/
favour n /'feɪvə(r)/
firework n /'faɪəwɜ:k/
fluent adj /'flu:ənt/
flight n /flaɪt/
fortune (= a lot of money) n
    /'fɔ:tʃu:n/
freedom n /'fri:dəm/
gap year n /'gæp jɪə(r)/
gate n /geɪt/
chase v /tʃeɪs/
get on well (with sb) v /,get ɒn
    'wel (wɪð ...)/
harmed by (= damaged by) pp
    /'hɑ:md ,baɪ/
I can't see the point coll
    /aɪ ,kɑ:nt ,si: ðə 'pɔɪnt/
I can't be bothered coll
    /aɪ ,kɑ:nt bɪ 'bɒðəd/
insect n /'ɪnsekt/
It's your turn. coll /ɪts 'jɔ: ,tɜ:n/
join v /dʒɔɪn/
mess n /mes/
message n /'mesɪdʒ/
money worries /'mʌni ,wʌriz/
normal adj /'nɔ:ml/
navy n /'neɪvi/
old people's home n
    /,əʊld 'pi:plz ,həʊm/
path n /pɑ:θ/
plan n /plæn/
pollute v /pə'lu:t/
pond n /pɒnd/
pros and cons /,prəʊz ən 'kɒnz/
put sb off sth (= stop sb liking
    sth) v /,pʊt ... 'ɒf .../
readjust v /,ri:ə'dʒʌst/
refer to v /rɪ'fɜ: tu:/
retired adj /rɪ'taɪəd/
routine n /ru:'ti:n/
ruin v /'ru:ɪn/

run away v /,rʌn ə'weɪ/
sailor n /'seɪlə(r)/
salary n /'sæləri/
save v /seɪv/
settle v /'setl/
snack n /snæk/
stressful adj /'stresfl/
sunburnt adj /'sʌnbɜ:nt/
tablet n /'tæblət/
Take care! /,teɪk 'keə(r)/
the bush (= African/Australian
    countryside) n /ðə 'bʊʃ/
traffic jam n /'træfɪk ,dʒæm/
travel brochure n /'trævl
    ,brəʊʃə(r)/
unwillingness n /ʌn'wɪlɪŋnəs/
wild adj /waɪld/
without doubt /wɪ,ðaʊt 'daʊt/
wood n /wʊd/

UNIT 10

accurate adj /'ækjərət/
annoy v /ə'nɔɪ/
automated adj /'ɔ:təmeɪtɪd/
awarded pp /ə'wɔ:dɪd/
be broke (= have no money) v coll
    /,bɪ 'brəʊk/
be related to (sb) v /,bɪ rɪ'leɪtɪd
    tə .../
body n /'bɒdi/
bone n /bəʊn/
borrow v /'bɒrəʊ/
briefcase n /'bri:fkeɪs/
cell n /sel/
century n /'sentʃəri/
certain adj /'sɜ:tn/
chemical adj /'kemɪkl/
chemist n /'kemɪst/
climb v /klaɪm/
cloth n /klɒθ/
commit (a crime) v /kə'mɪt/
company n /'kʌmpəni/
complain v /kəm'pleɪn/
complaint n /kəm'pleɪnt/
contain v /kən'teɪn/
criminal n /'krɪmɪnl/
cure n /kjʊə(r)/
cut open v /,kʌt 'əʊpən/
develop n /dɪ'veləp/
dialogue n /'daɪəlɒg/
discovered pp /dɪ'skʌvəd/
discovery n /dɪ'skʌvəri/
disease n /dɪ'zi:z/
DNA n /,di: en 'eɪ/
domestic adj /də'mestɪk/
dream v /dri:m/
dream of v /'dri:m əv/
electricity n /ɪ,lek'trɪsəti/
experiment v /ɪk'sperɪmənt/
fault n /fɔ:lt/
government official n
    /,gʌvənmənt ə'fɪʃl/
graveyard n /'greɪvjɑ:d/
gun n /gʌn/
guilty adj /'gɪlti/
heartbroken adj /'hɑ:tbrəʊkən/
helicopter n /'helɪkɒptə(r)/
homesick adj /'həʊmsɪk/
hopeless adj /'həʊpləs/
human adj /'hju:mən/
illegal adj /ɪ'li:gl/
imaging n /'ɪmədʒɪŋ/
immediately adv /ɪ'mi:diətli/
invention n /ɪn'venʃn/
item n /'aɪtəm/
keep a secret v /,ki:p ə 'si:krət/
lie n /laɪ/
lift n /lɪft/
litter n /'lɪtə(r)/
luggage n /'lʌgɪdʒ/
machine n /mə'ʃi:n/
make a complaint v
    /,meɪk ə kəm'pleɪnt/
match v /mætʃ/
memory n /'meməri/
miracle n /'mɪrəkl/
monster n /'mɒnstə(r)/

novel (= book) n /'nɒvl/
operation n /,ɒpə'reɪʃn/
paper mill n /'peɪpə ,mɪl/
papyrus n /pə'paɪrəs/
passenger n /'pæsɪndʒə(r)/
penicillin n /,penə'sɪlɪn/
pick v /pɪk/
plastic n /'plæstɪk/
plot n /plɒt/
poet n /'pəʊɪt/
popularity n /,pɒpjə'lærəti/
prepare v /prɪ'peə(r)/
press v /pres/
produce v /prə'dju:s/
project n /'prɒdʒekt/
published pp /'pʌblɪʃt/
radium n /'reɪdiəm/
rarely adv /'reəli/
recently adv /'ri:səntli/
result n /rɪ'zʌlt/
science fiction /,saɪəns 'fɪkʃn/
search engine n /'sɜ:tʃ ,endʒɪn/
structure n /'strʌktʃə(r)/
successful adj /sək'sesfl/
suspect n /'sʌspekt/
technology n /tek'nɒlədʒi/
the atom n /ði 'ætəm/
the truth n /ðə 'tru:θ/
translated pp /træns'leɪtɪd/
unique adj /ju:'ni:k/
weblink n /'weblɪŋk/
weight n /weɪt/
work of art n /,wɜ:k əv 'ɑ:t/
worldwide adj /'wɜ:ldwaɪd/
X-ray n /'eks ,reɪ/

UNIT 11

accept *v* /ək'sept/
active *adj* /'æktɪv/
afterwards *adv* /'ɑːftəwədz/
agree *v* /ə'griː/
ambition *n* /æm'bɪʃn/
ambitious *adj* /æm'bɪʃəs/
ash *n* /æʃ/
at the last minute /ət ðə ˌlɑːst 'mɪnɪt/
ban *v* /bæn/
be made redundant /bi ˌmeɪd rɪ'dʌndənt/
billion *n* /'bɪljən/
can't stand /ˌkɑːnt 'stænd/
blocked *pp* /blɒkt/
break down *v* /ˌbreɪk 'daʊn/
carry on *v* /ˌkæri 'ɒn/
certain *adj* /'sɜːtn/
chatter *v* /'tʃætə(r)/
cloud *n* /klaʊd/
contaminated *adj* /kən'tæmɪneɪtɪd/
control *v* /kən'trəʊl/
crazy *adj* /'kreɪzi/
crops *n pl* /krɒps/
crossroads *n pl* /'krɒsrəʊdz/
currently *adv* /'kʌrəntli/
decision *n* /dɪ'sɪʒn/
do well (= be successful) *v* /ˌduː 'wel/
dream of something /'driːm əv ˌ.../
earth *n* /ɜːθ/
education *n* /ˌedʒʊ'keɪʃn/
erupt *v* /ɪ'rʌpt/
eventually *adv* /ɪ'ventʃʊəli/
excitedly *adv* /ɪk'saɪtɪdli/
expression *n* /ɪk'spreʃn/
extinct *adj* /ɪk'stɪŋkt/
fail *v* /feɪl/
famine *n* /'fæmɪn/
floor *n* /flɔː(r)/
freeze *v* /friːz/
frightening *adj* /'fraɪtnɪŋ/
geyser *n* /'giːzə(r)/
give away *v* /ˌgɪv ə'weɪ/
global *adj* /'gləʊbl/
greenhouse *n* /'griːnhaʊs/
have a row (= argument) *v* /ˌhæv ə 'raʊ/
heating *n* /'hiːtɪŋ/
housing *n* /'haʊzɪŋ/
huge *adj* /hjuːdʒ/
impressed *adj* /ɪm'prest/
junk *n* /dʒʌŋk/
landscape (design) *n* /'lændskeɪp ('lændskeɪp dɪˌzaɪn)/
leader *n* /'liːdə(r)/
lie down *v* /ˌlaɪ 'daʊn/
literature *n* /'lɪtrətʃə(r)/
look for *v* /'lʊk fɔː(r), fə(r)/
Look out! /ˌlʊk 'aʊt/
look up *v* /ˌlʊk 'ʌp/
ordinary *adj* /'ɔːdnri/
oven *n* /'ʌvn/
pick up *v* /ˌpɪk 'ʌp/

plant *n* /plɑːnt/
possibility *n* /ˌpɒsə'bɪləti/
put off *v* /ˌpʊt 'ɒf/
recycle *v* /ˌriː'saɪkl/
rock *n* /rɒk/
row *n* /raʊ, rəʊ/
run (a company) *v* /ˌrʌn (ə 'kʌmpəni)/
run out of *v* /ˌrʌn 'aʊt əv/
second-hand *adj* /ˌsekənd 'hænd/
shanty town *n* /'ʃænti ˌtaʊn/
shock *n* /ʃɒk/
shoot up *v* /ˌʃuːt 'ʌp/
so /səʊ/
stranger *n* /'streɪndʒə(r)/
such /sʌtʃ/
sunlight *n* /'sʌnlaɪt/
take off *v* /ˌteɪk 'ɒf/
a talk *n* /ə 'tɔːk/
throw away *v* /ˌθrəʊ ə'weɪ/
try on *v* /ˌtraɪ 'ɒn/
turn around *v* /ˌtɜːn ə'raʊnd/
turn off *v* /ˌtɜːn 'ɒf/
unlikely *adv* /ʌn'laɪkli/
volcano *n* /vɒl'keɪnəʊ/

UNIT 12

autobiography *n* /ˌɔːtəbaɪ'ɒgrəfi/
break (a record) *v* /ˌbreɪk ə 'rekɔːd/
brief *adj* /briːf/
brought *pp* /brɔːt/
challenge *n* /'tʃælɪndʒ/
climb *v* /klaɪm/
Congratulations! /kənˌgrætʃʊ'leɪʃnz/
continent *n* /'kɒntɪnənt/
copies (pl of copy) *n* /'kɒpɪz/
cover *v* /'kʌvə(r)/
crowded *adj* /'kraʊdɪd/
daughter *n* /'dɔːtə(r)/
decorate (a house) *v* /'dekəreɪt (ə 'haʊs)/
delighted *adj* /dɪ'laɪtɪd/
delivery *n* /dɪ'lɪvəri/
dig *v* /dɪg/
dirty *adj* /'dɜːti/
disguise *v* /dɪs'gaɪz/
explorer *n* /ɪk'splɔːrə(r)/
explore *v* /ɪk'splɔː(r)/
fed up *adj, coll* /ˌfed 'ʌp/
flat *n* /flæt/
follow *v* /'fɒləʊ/
footsteps *n pl* /'fʊtsteps/
fresh air *n* /ˌfreʃ 'eə(r)/
frozen *adj* /'frəʊzn/
get used to sth *v* /ˌget 'juːst tə .../
hard *adj* /hɑːd/
Have a good trip! *coll* /ˌhæv ə ˌgʊd 'trɪp/
hero *n* /'hɪərəʊ/
hide *v* /haɪd/
homeless *adj* /'həʊmləs/
honest *adj* /'ɒnɪst/
hurt *v* /hɜːt/
in somebody's footsteps /ɪn ˌ...z 'fʊtsteps/
income *n* /'ɪnkʌm/
journey *n* /'dʒɜːni/
let *v* /let/
mend *v* /mend/
Oh, what a pity! *coll* /ˌəʊ ˌwɒt ə 'pɪti/
outdoor *adj* /'aʊtdɔː(r)/
Pardon? /'pɑːdn/
peak (of a mountain) *n* /piːk/
physical education *n* /ˌfɪzɪkl ˌedʒʊ'keɪʃn/
pretty (= quite) *adv coll* /'prɪti/
present *v* /prɪ'zent/
reason *n* /'riːzn/
record books *n* /'rekɔːd ˌbʊks/
remind *v* /rɪ'maɪnd/
seat /siːt/
silly *adj* /'sɪli/
stay calm *v* /ˌsteɪ 'kɑːm/
subway station (= underground station) *n US* /'sʌbweɪ ˌsteɪʃn/
succeed *v* /sək'siːd/
successful *adj* /sək'sesfl/
swear (= I promise) *v* /sweə(r)/
sympathetic *adj* /ˌsɪmpə'θetɪk/
take drugs *v* /ˌteɪk 'drʌgz/

take it easy /ˌteɪk ɪt 'iːzi/
the North Pole *n* /ðə ˌnɔːθ 'pəʊl/
toast *v* /təʊst/
trip *n* /trɪp/
well-prepared *adj* /ˌwel prɪ'peəd/

Irregular verbs

Base form	Past Simple	Past participle
be	was/were	been
become	became	become
begin	began	begun
break	broke	broken
bring	brought	brought
build	built	built
buy	bought	bought
can	could	been able
catch	caught	caught
choose	chose	chosen
come	came	come
cost	cost	cost
cut	cut	cut
do	did	done
drink	drank	drunk
drive	drove	driven
eat	ate	eaten
fall	fell	fallen
feel	felt	felt
fight	fought	fought
find	found	found
fly	flew	flown
forget	forgot	forgotten
get	got	got
give	gave	given
go	went	gone/been
grow	grew	grown
have	had	had
hear	heard	heard
hit	hit	hit
keep	kept	kept
know	knew	known
learn	learnt/learned	learnt/learned
leave	left	left
lose	lost	lost
make	made	made
meet	met	met
pay	paid	paid
put	put	put
read /riːd/	read /red/	read /red/
ride	rode	ridden
run	ran	run
say	said	said
see	saw	seen
sell	sold	sold
send	sent	sent
shut	shut	shut
sing	sang	sung
sit	sat	sat
sleep	slept	slept
speak	spoke	spoken
spend	spent	spent
stand	stood	stood
steal	stole	stolen
swim	swam	swum
take	took	taken
tell	told	told
think	thought	thought
understand	understood	understood
wake	woke	woken
wear	wore	worn
win	won	won
write	wrote	written

Verb patterns

Verb + -ing

like love enjoy hate finish stop	swimming cooking

Verb + to + infinitive

choose decide forget promise need help hope try want would like would love	to go to work

Verb + -ing or to + infinitive

begin start	raining/to rain

Modal auxiliary verbs

can could shall will would	go arrive

Phonetic symbols

Consonants

1	/p/	as in	**pen** /pen/
2	/b/	as in	**big** /bɪg/
3	/t/	as in	**tea** /tiː/
4	/d/	as in	**do** /duː/
5	/k/	as in	**cat** /kæt/
6	/g/	as in	**go** /gəʊ/
7	/f/	as in	**four** /fɔː/
8	/v/	as in	**very** /'veri/
9	/s/	as in	**son** /sʌn/
10	/z/	as in	**zoo** /zuː/
11	/l/	as in	**live** /lɪv/
12	/m/	as in	**my** /maɪ/
13	/n/	as in	**near** /nɪə/
14	/h/	as in	**happy** /'hæpi/
15	/r/	as in	**red** /red/
16	/j/	as in	**yes** /jes/
17	/w/	as in	**want** /wɒnt/
18	/θ/	as in	**thanks** /θæŋks/
19	/ð/	as in	**the** /ðə/
20	/ʃ/	as in	**she** /ʃiː/
21	/ʒ/	as in	**television** /'telɪvɪʒn/
22	/tʃ/	as in	**child** /tʃaɪld/
23	/dʒ/	as in	**German** /'dʒɜːmən/
24	/ŋ/	as in	**English** /'ɪŋglɪʃ/

Vowels

25	/iː/	as in	**see** /siː/
26	/ɪ/	as in	**his** /hɪz/
27	/i/	as in	**twenty** /'twenti/
28	/e/	as in	**ten** /ten/
29	/æ/	as in	**stamp** /stæmp/
30	/ɑː/	as in	**father** /'fɑːðə/
31	/ɒ/	as in	**hot** /hɒt/
32	/ɔː/	as in	**morning** /'mɔːnɪŋ/
33	/ʊ/	as in	**football** /'fʊtbɔːl/
34	/uː/	as in	**you** /juː/
35	/ʌ/	as in	**sun** /sʌn/
36	/ɜː/	as in	**learn** /lɜːn/
37	/ə/	as in	**letter** /'letə/

Diphthongs (two vowels together)

38	/eɪ/	as in	**name** /neɪm/
39	/əʊ/	as in	**no** /nəʊ/
40	/aɪ/	as in	**my** /maɪ/
41	/aʊ/	as in	**how** /haʊ/
42	/ɔɪ/	as in	**boy** /bɔɪ/
43	/ɪə/	as in	**hear** /hɪə/
44	/eə/	as in	**where** /weə/
45	/ʊə/	as in	**tour** /tʊə/

OXFORD
UNIVERSITY PRESS

Great Clarendon Street, Oxford OX2 6DP

Oxford University Press is a department of the University of Oxford.
It furthers the University's objective of excellence in research, scholarship,
and education by publishing worldwide in

Oxford New York

Auckland Cape Town Dar es Salaam Hong Kong Karachi
Kuala Lumpur Madrid Melbourne Mexico City Nairobi
New Delhi Shanghai Taipei Toronto

With offices in

Argentina Austria Brazil Chile Czech Republic France Greece
Guatemala Hungary Italy Japan Poland Portugal Singapore
South Korea Switzerland Thailand Turkey Ukraine Vietnam

OXFORD and OXFORD ENGLISH are registered trade marks of
Oxford University Press in the UK and in certain other countries

ISBN: 978 0 19 471585 0

Printed in China

ACKNOWLEDGEMENTS

*The authors and publisher are grateful to those who have given permission to reproduce the
following extracts and adaptations of copyright material:* pp 18–19 'Tales of Two Cities' by
Damian Barr, *The Times Magazine*, 22 January 2005. Reproduced by permission of NI
Syndication. p 27 Extract adapted from the original text of *The Man with the Golden
Gun* by Ian Fleming. *The Man with the Golden Gun* copyright © Glidrose Productions
Ltd, 1965. Reproduced with the permission of Ian Fleming Publications Ltd. pp 41 &
150 *The Voice Within* Words & Music by Christina Aguilera & Glen Ballard © Copyright
2002 Xtina Music/Aerostation Corporation/ MCA Music Publishing Incorporated,
USA. BMG Music Publishing Limited (50%)/Universal/MCA Music Limited (50%). All
Rights Reserved. International Copyright Secured. pp 50–51 'The world in one city'
by Leo Benedictus, *The Guardian*, 21 January 2005 © Guardian Newspapers Limited
2005. pp 98–99 'Frozen footsteps' from www.weeklyreader.com. Reproduced by
permission of WRC Consumer & Custom Publishing. p 100 *If You Come Back* Written
by Lee Brennan/Ian Hope/Jimmie Ruffin/Nicole Formescu, used by kind permission
from Windswept Music (London) Ltd, Nicole Formescu Aiyana Songs Ltd.

*The publishers would like to thank the following for their kind permission to reproduce
photographs:* AKG – Images p 33 (painting); Alamy Images pp 7 (Delph, Lancashire/
Fotofacade), 9 (friends/Photo Network), 13 (airport/Stock Image), 13 (elderly men/
Photo Network), 14 (dog sled/Photo Network), 15 (Asian computer class/Julio
Etchart), 15 (Asian toy factory/Julio Etchart), 18 (Manchester/Paul Thompson
Images), 18 (New York/Jeff Greenberg), 20 (man/Pixoi), 20 (older woman/Josephine),
33 (airplane/Digistock), 33 (Ebay web page/Richard Levine), 33 (old radio/V&A
Images), 33 (car/Stan Rohrer), 35 (carpet seller/Mark Eveleigh), 35 (Isle Sur La
Sorgue/Dale Crook), 37 (hundred dollars/Westend61), 42 (teen goth/Janine Wiedel
Photo library), 46 (chicken satay/Ingram Publishing), 52 (The Sanderson Hotel/
Arcaid), 52 (The Sanderson Hotel/Arcaid), 52 (The Sanderson Hotel/Arcaid), 45 (girl
with glasses/Photofusion picture Library); 54 (John Lennon/Popperfoto), 64 (traffic
lights/James Dawson/Image Farm Inc), 67 (plumber/SuperStock), 70 (Peten Tikal
Mayan ruins/PCL), 71 (young woman/Janine Wiedel Photolibrary), 76 (elderly
couple/Photo Network), 83 (forensics/Ian Miles-Flashpoint Pictures), 85 (male on
mobile/Eureka), 89 (Lucy/Mark Lewis), 107 (students); Anthony Blake Photolibrary
p 46 (chicken satay); Art Directors and Trip Photo Library p 33 (shoes/Helene
Rogers); Bryan and Cherry Alexander Photography p 99 (ice floes); Bubbles Photo
Library p 42 (teenage boy/Jennie Woodcock); Cartoon Bank p 28 (once upon a
time/Henry Martin), 60 (i'm not really in the mood either/Charles Barsotti), 93
(you're so organized/Robert Weber); CartoonStock Ltd pp 28 (better check with

your mother first/Mike Baldwin), 52 (it's a beautiful ring/Mike Baldwin), 56 (more
pictures of your kids/Mike Baldwin), 73 (this goes out to dad/Steve Way), 81
(complaints/Mike Baldwin), 97 (bring me whatever they drop on the floor/Mike
Baldwin); Corbis pp 13 (relaxing/Tom & Dee Ann McCarthy), 19 (Nuremberg/Jon
Hicks), 20 (Nighthawks by Edward Hopper/Francis G.Mayer), 20 (hairdresser/Nelson
Jeans), 20 (male/Michael Prince), 29 (commuters/Michael Prince), 33, (rings/George
Schuseter/Zefa), 34 (Thailand/ML Sinibaldi), 35 (floating market/Richard Hamilton
Smith), 40 (male friends/Randy Faris), 46 (Arsenal/Reuters), 45 (woman yelling/Peter
Dazeley/Zefa), 45 (angry man/Peter Dazeley/Zefa), 45 (golfer/George Shelley), 45
(sick man/Turbo/Zefa); 54 (Roald Dahl/Hulton-Deutsch Collection), 54 (Sophie
Dahl/Gregory Pace), 54 (Sigmund Freud/ Bettmann), 61 (teen friends/Randy Faris),
69 (female doctor/JLP), 71 (cheetah/Joe McDonald), 79 (early x-ray/Bettmann), 82
(DNA/ Digital Art), 82 (red haired boy/Norbert Schaefer), 82 (karyotype & DNA/
Digital Art), 82 (Larry Page & Sergey Brin/Kim Kulish), 83 (Google sign/Clay McLachlan/
Reuters), 83 (Google webpage/Stephen Hird/Reuters), 88 (teen on mobile/Darama),
89 (businessman/Artiga Photo), 90 (Old Faithful Geyser/Cooperphoto), 90 (lava
flow/Roger Ressmeyer), 93 (children/Randy Faris), 103 (young boys/Norbert Schaefer),
106 (New York/Alan Schein), 109 (Princess Caroline of Monaco/Stephane Cardinale/
People Avenue), 109 (Princess Stephanie of Monaco/Reuters), 115 (David Hempleman-
Adams/Rick Wilking/Reuters); Empics Ltd pp 22 (Battersea Dogs Home/Ian
Nicholson), 22 (Red the lurcher/Ian Nicholson), 24 (Stephane Breitwieser/Christian
Lutz), 24 (searching for paintings in canal); 26 (Daniel Craig/Stefan Rousseau/PA), 63
(press photographer/Yui Mok), 98 (Alicia & David Hempleman-Adams/), 98 (Alicia
Hempleman-Adams/Johnny Green); Gavin Smith Photography pp 18 (Claire Turner),
19 (Joss Langford); Getty Images pp 7 (couple/Nick Dolding/Taxi), 6 (student/David
Young-Wolff/Photographer's Choice), 10 (woman/Ricky John Molloy/Taxi), 16 (teen
boy/ Livia Corona/Taxi), 16 (businesswoman/Danielle Levitt/Stone+), 17 (teen boys/
Olivier Ribardiere/Taxi), 19 (Cambridge/Ary Diesendruck/Stone), 29 (busy street/Jeff
Spielman/Iconica), 32 (shoes, Richard Boll), 33 (stamps/Suzanne & Nick Geary/Stone),
(34 (Marrakesh/Rohan/Stone), 37 (currency/Peter Scholey/Photographer's Choice),
49 (baby/David Sacks/The Image Bank), 49 (dog/Nicolas Russell), 49 (young man/Terry
Husebye/Photographer's Choice), 49 (sunset/Raymond Gehman/National Geographic),
54 (Julian Lennon/Time Life Pictures), 54 (Princess Caroline of Monaco/Pascal Le
Segretain), 63 (soldier/Sean Murphy/Stone+), 65 (woman on roof/AB/Photonica), 76
(Annabel/Dareell Lecorre),78 (x-ray/Hulton Archive), 78 (Wilhelm Roentgen/ Hulton
Archive), 80 (papyrus/Bridgeman Art Library), 89 (crossroads/Ryan McVay/Stone), 91
(volcano eruption/Photonica), 108 (Tyneside/Hulton Archive), 108 (Angel of the
North/Antony Edwards/The Image Bank); Kids Can Press p 86 (*If the World were a
Village* by David J.Smith, illustrated by Shelagh Armstrong); Kobal Collection pp 26
(*You Only Live Twice* poster/DANJAQ/EON/UA), 26 (*Licence to Kill* poster), 26 (*Goldeneye*
poster/EON/DANJAQ/UIP), 26 (*Octopussy* poster), 44 (*Dracula*, Bela Lugosi/Universal),
46 (Al Pacino/Columbia), 113 (*Frankenstein*/Universal); iStockphoto p 45 (worried
girl/Don Bayley), 53 (mugshot/Eva Serrabassa); Lonely Planet Images pp 6 (Zagreb/
Guy Moberly), 34 (market stall/Diana Mayfield); OUP pp 13 (teacher & student/
BananaStock), 42 (teen boy/Photodisc); Panos Pictures p 88 (Nigerian student/
Giacomo Pirozzi); Paul Hancock pp 32 (Oxford), 49 (park); Photo RMN p 24 Bulloz/p
24 (Berger Endormi/Francois Boucher (1703–1770) Chartres Musee des Beaux-Arts;
(Rene-Gabriel Ojeda/Madeleine d'Ecosse/Corneill de Lyon (1500–1575) Blois Chateau
London Aerial Photography p 50 (London); Photolibrary.com p 14 (snowy houses/
Panstock Plc Catalogue); Pictures Colour Library Ltd pp 47 (London/ Geraint Tellem),
47 (Berlin/Brian Lawrence Images Ltd); 47 (Japan/Pay Lam); PunchStock pp 9 (three
men/ Photodisc), 9 (teen friends/Brand X Pictures), 9 (female friends/IT Stock), 10
(blonde woman/BananaStock), 10 (man with backpack/BananaStock), 13 (business
meeting/Stockbyte), 14 (mature couple with skis/Digital Vision), 16 (elderly couple/
MedioImages), 29 (clock/Design Pics), 33 (red shirt/Stockdisc), 33 (football/Photodisc),
40 (couple/ image100), 40 (handing over cash/Image Source), 43 (Monument Valley/
Comstock), 46 (cheerful man/ Stockdisc), 47 (Detroit/Photodisc), 48 (shark/
Thinkstock), 49 (little girl/Photodisc), 62 (casual man/BananaStock), 63 (mechanic/
Goodshoot), 63 (chef/ Comstock), 63 (dentist/Design Pics), 63 (optician/Image
Source), 63 (hairstylist/Image Source), 84 (elderly men/Photodisc), 85 (business
call/image100), 89 (mature woman/BananaStock), 93 (scared woman/Stockbyte),
100 (man by pool/Goodshoot), 102 (two friends/Corbis), 103 (family/Corbis), 111
(couple/Corbis), 114 (class/Brand X Pictures); Redferns p 57 (Goldrush); Rex Features
pp 26 (Casino Royale/C.Sony Pics/Everett), 41a (Christina Aguilera/Reuters), 43 (Brat
Camp/ABC/Everett), 52 (The Sanderson Hotel exterior/Ray Tang), 45 (boy with
schoolbag/Image Source), 54 (Bella Freud/Richard Young), 54 (Prince Rainier/Stills
Press Agency), 96 (Stelios Haji Ioannou/Stuart Clarke); Sony Ericsson p 9 (phone);
Superstock p 76 (Michel Guerard/Jean-Marc Charles/age fotostock); Truck Records p
57 (band in rehearsal); View p 108 (Millennium Bridge/Nick Guttridge).

Illustrations by: Stuart Briers p 10; Emma Brownjohn/New Division p 97; Stephen
Conlin p 77; Paul Dickinson p 27/28; Mark Duffin pp 37, 50 (map), 53, 90, 98, 147,
150; Andy Hammond pp 69, 84, 96, 92; Leo Hartas p 105; Darren Hopes/Debut Art
pp 25, 48; Ian Kellas p 52 (tramps); Bill McConkey/Debut Art p 28; Oxford Designers
and Illustrators p 52 (soup); Matt Vincent/Anna Goodson Management p 104.

Commissioned photography by: Gareth Boden pp 7, 8, 21, 25, 30, 31, 32, 38/39, 58/59,
67/8, 70 (James), 72, 74/5; Mark Mason pp 12, 37, 46 (cd/bookcover), 53 (cd), 80; Mark
Bryan p 70 (home); Trevor Hart-Davis/Getty Assignments p 40.

Thanks to: BAA Stansted Public Affair Department, BBC Radio Oxford, Lloyds
Pharmacy Kidlington, Meltz Oxford, Le Manoir aux Quat'Saisons. Make up for
page 58/59 by Elinor Rowley (Estee Lauder, Debenhams, Oxford 01865 255041 or
07870696247) and hair styling by Kelly Bambrick, Roland of Switzerland
01865 244302